MICROCOMPUTER OPERATING SYSTEMS

Mark Dahmke

BYTE BOOKS
Subsidiary of McGraw-Hill
70 Main St., Peterborough, N.H. 03458

Library of Congress Cataloging in Publication Data

Dahmke, Mark.
    Microcomputer operating systems.

    Bibliography: p.
    Includes index.
    1. Operating systems (Computers)
2. Microcomputers.   I. Title.
QA76.6.D333   001.64   81-21691
ISBN 0-07-015071-0   AACR2

Text set in English Times Roman by BYTE Publications.
Edited by Bruce Roberts.
Design and Production Supervision by Ellen Klempner.
Cover Illustration by Robert Tinney.
Production Editing by Margaret McCauley.
Production by Mike Lonsky.
Typeset by Valerie Horn.
Printed and Bound by
Halliday Lithograph Corporation,
Arcata Company,
North Quincy, Massachusetts

Dedication

To my parents for their help and encouragement and to my friends at BYTE *for making this book possible.*

Acknowledgments

I would like to acknowledge the assistance and contributions of those who aided in the preparation and publication of this book. Gregg Williams supplied the structured flowcharting notation and the appendix describing it. Bruce Roberts provided continuous feedback regarding the content and structure of the material. Ellen Klempner designed the book, the reference card insert, and helped with the cover design. Robert Tinney provided the cover artwork, and Ed Kelly, Chris Morgan, Virginia Londoner, and Gordon Williamson gave me the opportunity to write the book.

Table of Contents

Microcomputer Operating Systems

Preface

Over the past five years I have read countless books on how to design microcomputer systems and have read a number of books explaining the intricate details of operating system design. All of the microcomputer books introduced the topic of system design from the hardware point of view. All of the operating system books assumed that the reader had access to an IBM 370 and had no interest in the physical hardware design of the computer.

This book introduces the concept of microcomputer system design from the software end rather than discussing the familiar details of hardware design.

The material begins with a brief overview of the technology and some of the indespensible terminology associated with modern microprocessor designs. The material is presented in an evolutionary fashion, describing how operating systems came about on large computers, and how they have been adapted for the microcomputer environment. The bulk of the book describes the features and facilities of an operating system that looks a great deal like the disk operating system (DOS) in common use on most microcomputers today. The remainder of the book expands on this type of operating system by describing multiprogramming, multiprocessing, and networking.

This material presents the concepts involved in operating systems design and illustrates many aspects of currently available systems.

1:
Introduction

What is an operating system? In general, an operating system is any program or group of related programs whose purpose is to act as an intermediary between the hardware and the user of a computer. In the case of a small microprocessor application—a development or evaluation system with about 2 K bytes (2048) of programmable read-only memory (PROM) and a small amount of random access memory (RAM)—the operating system may consist of little more than a set of service subroutines and a simple set of commands that allow the user to load or dump memory to or from an external storage device, to modify bytes, and to test application programs.

A more sophisticated operating system may have a disk-controller interface and some form of memory management. The highest level of operating system discussed in this book includes such features as multiprogramming (running multiple independent programs on a time-slice basis), bank-selected memory, a hard-disk controller interface, and random track-sector allocation. Multiprocessing (running multiple microprocessors in parallel with some level of interaction) is also discussed.

Then why does one need an operating system? If the microcomputer in question has a hard-wired front panel, there is theoretically no need for a control program. The user may enter and modify instructions and data in binary on rows of switches. This method is somewhat time consuming and is always clumsy. After some experimentation with this method, the user inevitably comes to the conclusion that there has to be an easier way. The user begins to wonder why the microprocessor can't do all the routine tasks, since it is sitting idle anyway. This is how operating-systems concepts evolved on larger computers. In this book I attempt to define what features are useful or necessary for several levels of operating systems.

In Chapter 2 the role of operating systems in microcomputers is considered. Several different sizes of systems are examined to determine what features are needed for each application.

In Chapter 3, the small-system monitor is discussed in detail. In Chapter 4, the medium-to-large-scale system and such topics as data management and disk-space reclamation are considered. Chapter 5 covers multiuser and multiprogramming environments and the considerations that must be made when designing an operating system to handle more than one application at a time. The concept of multiprocessing is introduced in Chapter 6; loosely and tightly coupled systems as well as distributed networks of microcomputers are also discussed.

In Chapter 7, memory management is covered, including linear address spaces, bank switching, and virtual memory. Chapter 8 covers the machine-independent environment, and Chapter 9 covers system utilities. In Chapter 10, user interference with the system is discussed. Chapter 11 concludes by laying out the design parameters of an operating system and discussing what features should be included and why.

Appendices I and II provide a short-form reference to the Control Program for Microcomputers (CP/M) and UNIX operating systems, their philosophies, and internal organizations.

Microcomputer Hardware and Terminology Overview

Microcomputer architectures are relatively simple compared to those of minicomputers and large mainframe computers. In this book, 8-bit microprocessors are dealt with, although most of the concepts apply equally well to the newer 16-bit microprocessors. Some features that are available only on 16-bit architectures are also discussed.

Central Processor Organization

A typical 8-bit microprocessor has an internal architecture similar to that in figure 1.1. The arithmetic-logic unit (ALU) performs all arithmetic and logical data manipulations. There are generally some internal holding registers, or at least an accumulator, which are used to hold intermediate results from the ALU. Other registers such as an index register may be provided as a way of setting up memory addresses or *pointers*. The instruction register is a single-byte buffer that holds the current machine instruction as obtained from memory. (The instruction register is generally not accessible by the programmer.) A program counter (PC) that always points to the current instruction byte in memory is also present.

The internal bus of the microprocessor is interfaced to the external bus of the system, which is buffered and distributed throughout the microcomputer on a system bus. The external bus consists of an address bus (usually 16 bits wide or greater), a data bus (8 bits wide on an 8-bit microcomputer), and control signals such as READ, WRITE, MEMORY-REQUEST, I/O REQUEST, WAIT, and so on.

These control signals are used by main memory and input/output (I/O) ports to determine if the central processing unit (CPU) is "talking" to them. Most microprocessors have at least one interrupt input. An interrupt is a way of forcing the CPU to stop what it is doing and jump to a predefined memory location to execute a special sequence of instructions. Often keyboard or serial inputs are set up on an interrupt basis to allow asynchronous external devices (such as a keyboard) to force some kind of high-priority action on the part of the microprocessor. This saves the programmer the trouble of periodically "polling" the input to see if data is available. When the microprocessor is reset (by means of hardware), the first action is to fetch an instruction from memory. The PC (program counter) is set to zero on most microprocessors, so the start-up instructions must be in the first few bytes of memory (this is not always the case, but that is not important at this point in the discussion). Wherever execution is to begin, the instructions must be present before resetting the CPU. This can be done with a hardware front panel or by placing read-only memory at the starting location. The CPU loads the contents of location zero into the instruction register and decodes it under the assumption that it is an executable instruction (operation code or opcode).

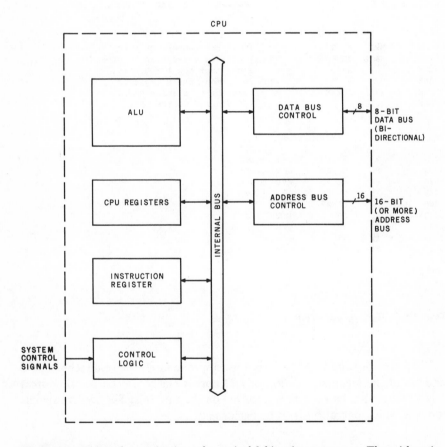

Figure 1.1: *Internal organization of a typical 8-bit microprocessor. The arithmetic-logic unit (ALU) performs all logical functions, whereas the control logic coordinates all activities.*

If the instruction is more than one byte long, the CPU continues fetching bytes and incrementing the PC and then executes the entire instruction. Except for the case of jumps (often referred to as branches) or calls, the PC is incremented and the process repeats. Jumps or calls cause control to be transferred to the specified memory address. This means that the address found in the instruction (or in a register specified in the instruction) is loaded into the PC. This cycle repeats until a HALT instruction is executed or until power is removed.

```
0000H    MVI    B,0FFH            ;Load the number 'FF' into the
                                  ;B register.
0003H    JMP    0020H             ;Branch to location 0020.
0006H    OUT    23H               ;Output the A register to
                                  ;port 23H.
0008H    RET                      ;Return to calling program.


0020H    MVI    A,10H             ;Load the number 10H into
0022H    CALL   0006H             ;call the subroutine at 0006.
0025H    INR    A                 ;Increment the A register.
0026H    DCR    B                 ;Decrement the B register.
0027H    JNZ    0022H             ;Branch to location 0022.
002AH    HLT                      ;If done, Halt the CPU.
```

PC	A	B	INSTRUCTION		
0000	?	?	06 FF	MVI	B,0FFH
0003	?	FF	C3 00 00	JMP	0020H
0020	?	FF	3E 10	MVI	A,10H
0022	10	FF	CD 06 00	CALL	0006H
0006	10	FF	D3 23	OUT	23H
0008	10	FF	C9	RET	
0025	10	FF	3C	INR	A
0026	11	FF	05	DCR	B
0027	11	FE	C2 22 00	JNZ	0022H
0022	11	FE	CD 06 00	CALL	0006H
0006	11	FE	D3 23	OUT	23
--	--	--	--	---	
--	--	--	--	---	

Figure 1.2: *Flow of execution.*

All memory and I/O operations use approximately the same scheme; the address of the memory location or I/O port is placed on the 16-bit address bus and the 8-bit data is sent or received on the data bus. The control signals indicate which operation is to be performed.

Memory Organization

The memory of a microcomputer is classified in two main categories: read/write and read-only. Memory chips (integrated circuits) exist that contain as many as 65,535 bits per chip, and this capacity is constantly being improved. If a particular memory chip is organized as 16,384 bits × 1, then it will take eight chips in parallel to achieve 16 K bytes of memory that is 8 bits wide. If a 16-bit microprocessor is used, 16 memory components in parallel must be used. Figure 1.3 shows a typical memory board for an 8-bit microcomputer. Note that in computer terminology, 16 K means 16,384, not 16,000. Therefore, a "K" is 2^{10} or 1024, which is more useful and convenient than 1000.

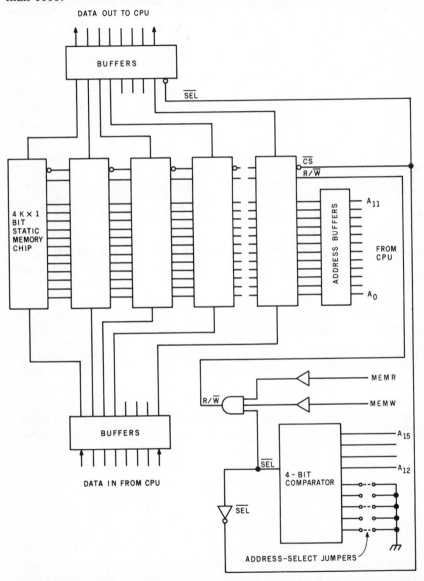

Figure 1.3: *A typical 4 K-byte memory board. Address decoding is handled by the 4-bit comparator. The select line (SEL) goes high (1) when a valid board address is detected. Memory read (MEMR) and memory write (MEMW) are gated with SEL to obtain a single signal, which is high for read and low for write. Chip select (CS) is active low.*

Read-only memories (ROMs) are further subdivided into mask ROMs, programmable ROMs (PROMs), and erasable programmable ROMs (EPROMs). (The acronym PROM is commonly used to refer to ROMs, PROMs, and EPROMs in general.) EPROMs are generally used in prototype or small-run quantities, since they are more expensive to manufacture and may be field programmed and later erased by ultraviolet light. They are ideal for development since they can be easily erased if program errors are detected. PROMs are identical to EPROMs except they cannot be erased. PROMs are available that are pin-for-pin compatible with EPROMs so that software and hardware developed with EPROMs need not be changed when the application goes into mass production. PROMs usually use a fuse-link technology—each bit is a silicon "fuse" that blows when certain voltages are applied. Once the fuse has blown, the information cannot be erased. ROMs are used for high-volume applications and only after extensive testing has been done to ensure that the data and programs are correct. ROMs are made by encoding the data (bit pattern) onto a "mask" that specifies a layer of the silicon chip itself. Thus the bits are manufactured directly into the chip.

ROMs, PROMs, and EPROMs are available in many sizes ranging from 128 × 8 bits to 8 K (8192) × 8 bits. This capacity is rapidly growing. Note that most ROMs, PROMs, and EPROMs are designed to be 8 bits wide on the chip. This is convenient since one of the primary uses for PROMs is in start-up programs and mass-production electronics, where package count becomes critical. PROMs are also available in 16 K × 1 bit arrays as well as countless other sizes.

Software Concepts

The most convenient way of programming microcomputers is with an assembler language or a high-level language such as Pascal or BASIC. In this text, 8080 assembler language with extended mnemonics for the Z80 (where needed) is used to present examples. All algorithms are presented with a structured single-path flowcharting technique (see Appendix III). High-level languages are often easier to use when developing large programs, but compilers don't often produce efficient object code, and this results in a loss of overall speed and efficiency.

Data Types

Tables, lists, and other constructs are built out of primitive data types—specifically, bytes and pointers. A byte is defined as a group of 8 bits. A bit can be either a one or a zero. This means that the range of values that are possible within a byte is 0 to 255 or 00 to FF in hexadecimal (base 16). The computer is concerned only with the ones and zeros, not with what the bits mean in context. Thus, a 41H (meaning 41 in hexadecimal) or 65 in base 10 can mean the number 65, the American Standard Code for Information Interchange (ASCII) character A, or the packed decimal number 41, and so on. The bit pattern of this byte is 01000001, which could be interpreted as a series of status flags or status bits. When the bit is on (one), the flag is set. When it is zero, the flag is off or reset. Using bits to represent on/off values saves much space in memory.

Other constructs include the *string*, which is a series of data bytes in sequential ascending order in memory. The string usually contains character data and some kind of terminator character to indicate the end of the string. Alternately, the length of the string may be put in a byte at the beginning of the string.

```
Assembler input:
                    TEXT: DB    'THIS IS A CHARACTER STRING',0
                    MSG2: DB    'THIS STRING ENDS WITH A CR',0DH
                    MSG3: DB    'THIS STRING ENDS WITH A $'
                    MSG4: DB    49,'THIS STRING CONTAINS A '
                          DB    'HEADER BYTE FOR THE LENGTH'

Basic statement:    TEXT = "THIS IS A STRING ASSIGNMENT IN BASIC"
```

Figure 1.4: *String types.*

Note that in figure 1.5, the first few strings have different terminator characters. This is generally up to the programmer or follows the conventions used in the system in question. A second format involves putting a leading byte on the string that contains the length of the string, counted in bytes. To access the string in the assembler, a pointer (equal to the start address of the string) would have to be loaded into a CPU register. The string could then be processed as needed.

```
Assembler input:
                    LXI   H,MSG2    ;Load address of MSG2
                                    ;into the HL registers.
                    CALL  DMSG      ;Call the "Display-
                                    ;Message" subroutine.

Basic statement:    PRINT TEXT
```

Figure 1.5: *String handling.*

In figure 1.6, the address of MSG2 is loaded into the HL-register pair, and a "display-message" subroutine is called. This subroutine accesses each byte of the string and outputs it to the console device until it finds the carriage-return byte (0DH). Then it returns to the calling program.

```
Assembler input:        DMSG: MOV A,M      ;Get character from (HL)
                              CPI ODH      ;is the character a CR?
                              RZ           ;if so, return to caller
                              CALL CO      ;Output character in A
                              INX  H       ;Increment HL pointer.
                              JMP DMSG     ;Get next character.
```

Figure 1.6: *Display-message subroutine (DSMG).*

Figure 1.6 gives one possible version of the display-message (DMSG) routine written in 8080 assembly language. This subroutine first gets a character, then tests to see if it is a carriage return (the terminator code used in this example), and then calls the console-output (CO) subroutine (console-output must not disturb the HL registers). Then the HL register pair is incremented, and the process is repeated for the next character. Figure 1.7 gives the equivalent of the DMSG subroutine in structured flowchart notation. See Appendix III for a complete description of this notation.

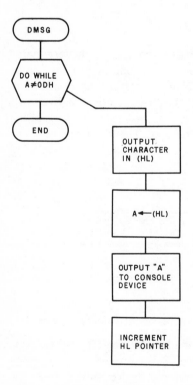

Figure 1.7: *A structured flowchart of the display-message subroutine.*

2:
What Should an Operating System Do?

Before actually writing any portion of the operating system, it is extremely important to take a long look at the hardware and software requirements of the desired microcomputer system. Many times, designers spend too little time planning and realize halfway through the development process that their design did not perform as expected or that the hardware chosen for the application would not handle the processing load placed on it.

This chapter details both the small system and the medium-to-large system and puts into perspective all the design requirements that must be addressed. Subsequent chapters present detailed discussions of each element of the operating system.

The Small System

A "small system" is defined as any microcomputer that has between 1 K and 8 K bytes of memory. A further characteristic is that its external storage (if any) be no more sophisticated than cassette tape. Typical applications for such a system might be

- Development system
- Intelligent terminal
- Controller
- Slave processor

In the case of the controller and the slave processor, it may be difficult to decide what should be in the operating system and what should be in the application program. The general rule for all operating systems design is:

If the function is used frequently or by many different application programs, it should probably go in the operating system.

Establishing a Framework

The easiest way to begin designing an operating system is to list what functions the microcomputer is to perform. It can be assumed that there will be some form of simple input and output, such as a serial or parallel keyboard input and printer output. Electrically, there is no difference between a keyboard and some other input (i.e., another computer) as long as the microcomputer in question "sees" an input port. Similarly, the printer output port may actually be a connection to another computer, a modem, or other device. The important point is that all inputs and outputs should be listed and their general characteristics taken into account when deciding what the operating system will be responsible for.

Starting with simple input and output routines, the primitive functions of the operating system can be built up. The second functional level of the operating system controls external storage. If cassette or paper tape is to be used, input and output subroutines must be written and included in the operating system. This does not mean only character-in and character-out, but such functions as search-for-file and read-header-information. Another function that may be required is a host computer or dial-up interface. This interface may function either on the primitive I/O level (turning the microcomputer into a terminal) or on a slightly higher level as an external storage device. In the latter mode, the host computer becomes the equivalent of a cassette tape recorder with the ability to upload or download data to the microcomputer. In this mode of operation, the microcomputer's operating system may have a boot-load (start-up) procedure that reads bytes from the host computer and places them in memory at a predetermined starting point. The microcomputer then executes the program that has been sent to it.

Support Routines

Depending upon the application, other subroutines may be required. If the input ports are interrupt driven, routines must be provided to properly service an interrupt and return the data from the input device. Interrupts may also be used to establish a counter/timer. The microcomputer hardware may be set up to generate interrupts every 10 milliseconds, for example. The subroutine that gains control when the microcomputer is interrupted is responsible for accessing and incrementing a memory location every 10 milliseconds. The value of this memory location may be accessed by the application program at any time.

If the microcomputer is to have some form of monitor (a term used to describe a simple operating system with some sort of command interpreter that can recognize simple commands), it is necessary to build up a set of character-string and table-search functions.

For example, a subroutine is needed to display error messages and operator prompts. Generally, the subroutine will be called with the address of the ASCII error message in a CPU register. Another commonly used subroutine is one that displays the two-digit hexadecimal representation of an

8-bit quantity in a predetermined CPU register. When the subroutine is called, it examines the contents of the register and outputs (using the console-output subroutine) two characters corresponding to the two 4-bit nybbles in the register.

Other useful subroutines include a routine that outputs a carriage return and a line feed, a routine that reads a two-digit hexadecimal number and places the 8-bit result in a CPU register, and a routine that clears the video display on a video board or causes a form feed (advances to a new page) in a printer terminal.

The next higher level of the operating system is responsible for recognizing and servicing requests made of it. If the microcomputer has an operator's console, it must respond in some legible and comprehensible fashion. Since it is easier for a human operator to deal with the operating system if it accepts mnemonics, a look-up table must be incorporated into the operating system and a search-table routine must be written. The operating system must look for table entries, and, if found, it must transfer control to that part of itself that handles the function. If the mnemonic is not found, an error message should be issued and appropriate action taken to prevent the user from crashing the system.

The operating system must also be capable of servicing requests made from the application program. This may be as simple as providing a series of jump vectors starting at a known location, or may be as complex as having the application program call a single entry point and provide a function number and other quantities as needed. The operating system must (in the latter case) recognize which function the application program has called for and whether the appropriate input quantities are available. If conditions are not right, the operating system must return with an error code in a register or should at least set CPU flags (such as zero or carry) to indicate that something has gone wrong.

Medium to Large Systems

When designing microcomputers with more memory and external or mass storage, the same factors should be considered as in small systems with the addition of

- Minifloppy-disk or full-size floppy-disk storage
- Memory management
- Multiuser or multiprogramming considerations
- Hard-disk storage
- System utilities
- Multiprocessing
- High-level language support
- Hardware independence

Floppy-disk storage is the standard external storage device of the industry. Most operating systems (other than primitive monitors) have some form of floppy-disk interface. The primitive routines required when communicating with a floppy-disk controller include

- Set track and sector
- Read controller status
- Send command to controller
- Go to Track 00 on drive
- Read a byte of data
- Write a byte of data
- Set memory buffer address
- Read (and write) a sector
- Select drive (and side, if double sided)

The interface software can get fairly complex, depending on how smart the controller hardware is.

Memory management is not too important in systems with only one user, but if two or more people are trying to access the microcomputer at a time, each user must be allocated specific areas of memory and must be prevented from accessing any memory outside his or her assigned areas.

Multiuser or multiprogramming systems can also get quite complex, depending on the number of functions each user is allowed to perform. The operating system must be responsible for task switching, saving the current-status and CPU registers of each user, and task prioritization. If memory management is used, a listing of what blocks of memory are available to each user must be established. Another common approach is to have bank-selected memory, with one 48 K-byte memory segment for each user and a 16 K-byte common area for the operating system. The common area holds the entire operating system and tables for memory allocation, task switching, and all I/O routines. When a task is activated, the table must indicate which bank of memory the task is assigned and must issue the appropriate hardware commands to select that bank.

Hard-disk subsystems are rapidly coming down in price and are becoming physically smaller while holding more information. Generally, the controllers used with a hard disk are quite sophisticated; they use direct memory access (DMA) for speed. Software-interfacing requirements are similar to those of a floppy disk.

It is often desirable to have some transient application programs that may be loaded from disk to perform certain utility (housekeeping) functions that are quite necessary but infrequently used. It would be wasteful, for example, to include a disk-formatting routine in the resident portion of the operating system when it is used perhaps once a week. Similarly, routines for copying files and compacting disk space are infrequently used. These programs are generally kept on disk as program files and are called up and executed on demand. Other useful utilities include a disk-file status report, which lists allocation maps for files on a disk; an error-recovery program, which may be used to retrieve and fix data on bad sectors of a disk; and a system diagnostic package.

Multiprocessing is defined as two or more computers operating in some closely coupled fashion. Special software must be written to handle the interaction between microcomputers to optimize their operation. In a loosely coupled arrangement, there may only be two parallel ports connecting the microcomputers, and their interaction may consist of little more than sending messages back and forth.

A more sophisticated multiprocessor may have shared memory and shared task execution. This means that if one processor is busy, the other can execute a program that the first had started to work on. If one CPU stops functioning, the other can continue execution, thereby preventing the entire system from going down.

If the microcomputer is to run a high-level language, it may be desirable to have commonly used subroutines such as floating-point math and string manipulation included in the operating system. If the floating-point routines are implemented entirely in software, they will be fairly slow. If they are isolated and put in the operating system, they may later be upgraded to drive a floating-point processor circuit, a piece of hardware that performs floating-point arithmetic at much greater speeds. The operating system could be upgraded to use the faster hardware, and the application program would not have to be modified.

This brings us to hardware (machine) independence. A well-designed operating system should be fairly hardware independent so that application programs do not have to be altered to run on another piece of hardware using the original operating system. If, for example, the program was written on operating system X and machine Y, it should not have to be modified to run on machine Z just because machine Z has 32 K instead of 16 K bytes of memory and uses a different console device or a different disk controller.

3:
The Small-System Monitor

In this chapter the simplest of all operating systems—the monitor—is discussed. *Monitor* is a term used to describe an operating system/command language combination that historically allowed the user to "monitor" the CPU, the registers, and the memory as an application program was executed. Originally, monitors were little more than software "front panels," replacing the old-style hard-wired front panels made up of lights and switches. Later, more and more functions were added, making them much more versatile and useful. Another step in the evolution of monitors was the separation of I/O services from the command processor portions of the system. This enabled the user to call standard I/O or other service subroutines without having to duplicate those subroutines in each application program.

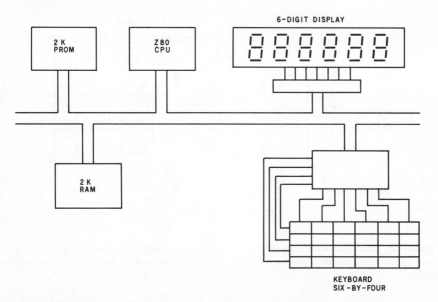

Figure 3.1: *A typical Z80 microcomputer evaluation system. It includes a monitor in a 2 K PROM, 2 K bytes of RAM, a six-digit numeric display, and a six-by-four, 24-key keyboard input.*

The Evaluation System

The first hypothetical system that will be dealt with consists of a Z80 (or similar) microprocessor, 2 K bytes of RAM, 2 K bytes of PROM, a six-digit numeric display, and a four-by-six array of keys (figure 3.1). This kind of microcomputer is commonly referred to as an evaluation system. It has limited input and output, no external storage, and only a small amount of memory. Just as its name implies, it is for evaluation—experimenting with the instruction set of the microcomputer, the speed of the processor, and the price-performance characteristics of a system based on the microprocessor. For the noncommercial user, an evaluation system is one purchased to learn more about microcomputers without spending a great deal of money.

First we must set up the driver routines for the keyboard and display. This requires some analysis of the hardware and its function.

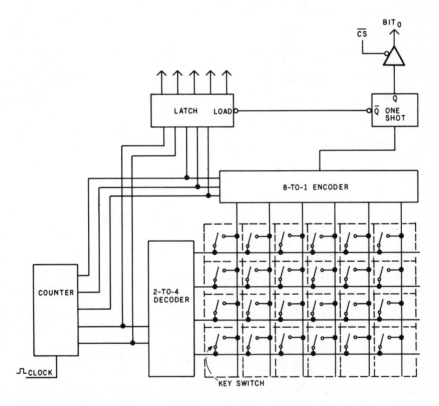

Figure 3.2: *The keyboard array (six-by-four) is scanned by a counter circuit at left. Each key is checked individually for closure. When one is detected, that address is latched.*

The Keyboard

Figure 3.2 shows the keyboard interface. Several components are used to automatically scan the keys and generate a five-bit code at the input port. The microprocessor is able to read a status port to determine when a key has been depressed. In this example, the status port is at port address 00H, and the five-bit keyboard data may be read from port address 01H. Bit 0 of the status port will be high (one) when a key has been depressed. Reading port 01H will automatically reset the status bit to zero.

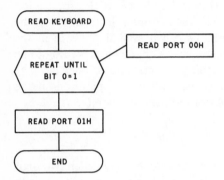

Figure 3.3a: *The software read routine for the circuit in figure 3.2.*

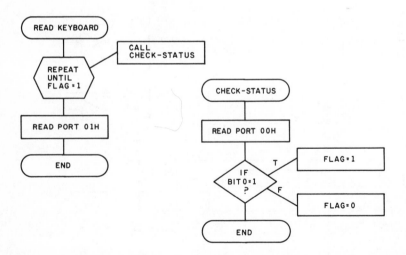

Figure 3.3b: *A more generalized read routine. The check status subroutine sets a flag to indicate if a character is available.*

Figure 3.3a shows a typical subroutine used to read the keyboard port. In this form, the status check portion of the routine is done first, continuously looking for a keyboard input. The disadvantage of this method is that it is often desirable to check for a keystroke without actually waiting for one. If the microcomputer is performing operations in real time, one doesn't want to stop everything just to wait for a keystroke. A good example of this would be a stopwatch program. If the keyboard read routine was entered and it kept looking for a keystroke, the system would be "trapped" in the subroutine until someone hit a key. The solution (shown in figure 3.3b) is to have a separate subroutine that checks the status bit and returns with a flag set (typically the zero flag). Then, if new data is ready, the application program can perform the actual read. The read routine, in turn, resets the hardware status bit. If the status routine is called several times in a row without calling the read routine, it indicates that a character is waiting to be read. This is a useful feature if one is running several tasks at once (such as refreshing a display) when it would interfere with other operations if the keyboard-read routine were to keep control until the status bit was set.

The Six-Digit Display

Figure 3.4 shows the organization of the six-digit display. Each two-digit group is assigned as one 8-bit port. This allows the display to be updated with three output instructions. For example, the first two digits are assigned to port 10H, the second two to port 11H, and the third to 12H.

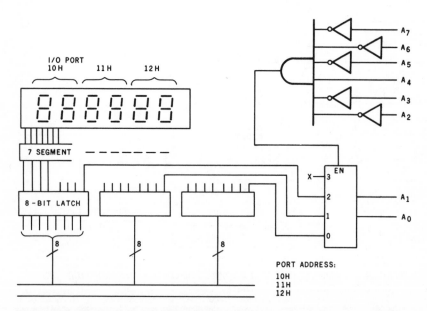

Figure 3.4: *The hardware support for the six-digit display. Port address 10H, 11H, and 12H latch up the three pairs of digits. Thus each pair of digits can be written with one-byte output to the appropriate port.*

Several approaches might be taken to update the display, but it really depends on the application. If a clock program is the end product, it would be simple to treat each group of two digits as a separate entity. If the end use of the display is to show memory addresses and contents of memory, it might be more efficient to update all of the display at one time.

An example is shown in figure 3.5a. The first four digits are used to display the hexadecimal equivalent of a 16-bit memory address. The last two digits display the contents of the memory address referenced. A subroutine that will handle this function is diagramed in figure 3.5b. The first subfunction is to break the address in B into two parts: the most significant byte and the least significant byte. Each byte is output to the appropriate port (10H and 11H). The second subfunction is to put the contents of the memory location pointed to by B into another register (A). Then the contents of A are sent to port 12H.

This example represents only one possible application; it is necessary to consider the requirements of each application and to design display drivers accordingly. A more generalized form of the the routine in figure 3.5b would be to put each two-digit pair in a separate register (or memory location) and output them separately. Figure 3.5c shows another possible display technique—one byte per display digit. Figure 3.5d shows a display driver that outputs the string of digits represented in memory as a string of six bytes (using only the lower four bits of each byte). If one is dealing with decimal quantities, this subroutine can be called after a conversion routine has taken a 16-bit binary number and generated a six-digit base-ten number in memory.

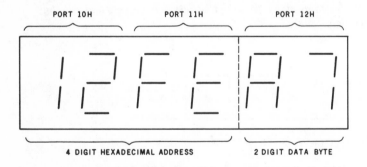

Figure 3.5a: *This display shows the results of the algorithm in figure 3.5b. The address is in B. The data is found at (B) and is displayed to the right of the four-digit address.*

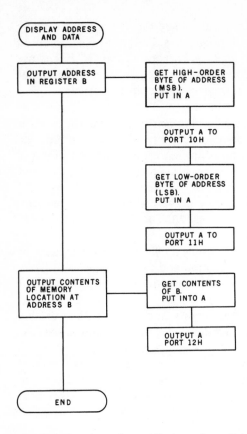

Figure 3.5b: *A routine to display a four-digit hexadecimal address and two-digit data byte on a six-digit display.*

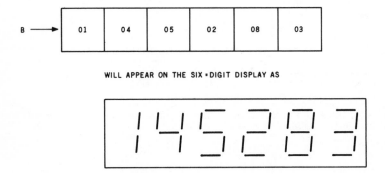

WILL APPEAR ON THE SIX-DIGIT DISPLAY AS

Figure 3.5c: *A possible display technique in which B points to a string of six digits (one per byte) that is to be displayed on the six-digit LED display. Figure 3.5d shows the algorithm to accomplish this.*

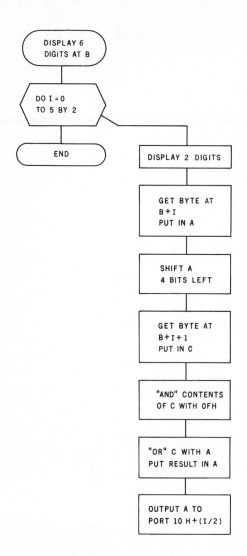

Figure 3.5d: *This routine displays the six digits found at address B.*

Establishing a Framework of Service Subroutines

After defining the input and output drivers, it is necessary to decide on some memory assignments. In the hypothetical development system in figure 3.1, the PROM memory is located at the bottom of the address space—from 0000H to 1FFFH. The RAM area extends from 2000H to 3FFFH.

First, because the power-on reset hardware causes the CPU to "wake up" with the PC initialized to 0000H, at least the start-up portion of the monitor must be at location 0000H. Figure 3.6 shows the memory organization of the development system. A standard approach to this problem is to put a series of jump vectors starting with one generally called COLD START.

This can be followed with warm start, console input, console output, cassette input, cassette output, and whatever else is needed.

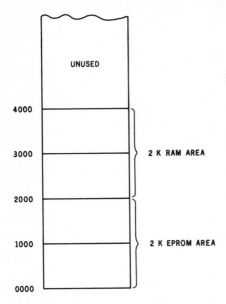

Figure 3.6: *Memory organization for the evaluation system.*

There is no restriction, of course, on where the individual subroutines must be located; some operating-systems designers put the main program first, followed by the utility subroutines. Others put the subroutines first, then the body of the monitor. Figures 3.7a and 3.7b show these two configurations.

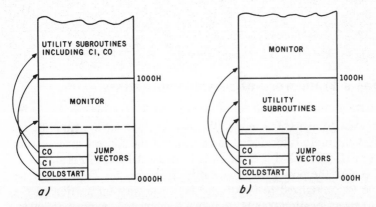

Figure 3.7: *Two possible internal organizations for the monitor. In (a), utility routines are placed at the end. In (b), they are at the beginning.*

Assuming that for this version, keyboard-in and display-out are needed as the primary I/O routines, we can proceed with the designing of a suitable command language.

Implementing High-Level Commands

First one must list what functions are going to be needed in the monitor. If it is for writing and testing simple programs in machine language, some form of hexadecimal-data input and output is required. In the example used here, part of this has already been written. Following is a generalized list of commands that are found in other monitors:

- Display memory
- Modify contents of memory
- Execute at a specified memory address
- Set breakpoints
- Increment/decrement through memory (when displaying or altering)
- Perform a block move of memory
- Input from and output data to I/O ports

Before writing the monitor, one must decide how the keyboard is to be organized, that is, what functions are to go on the keytops and where they should go for ease of use. Figure 3.8 shows one possible arrangement.

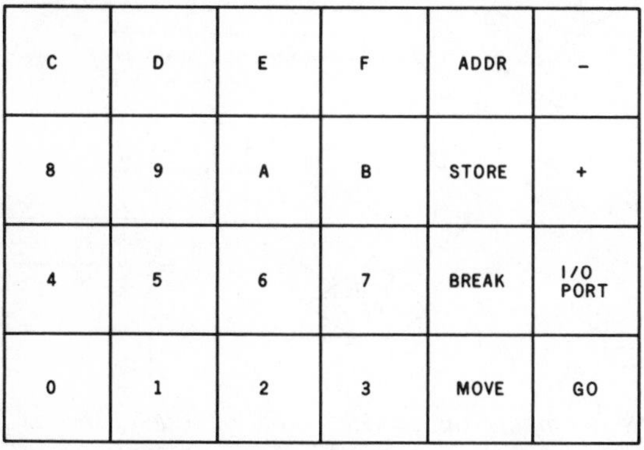

C	D	E	F	ADDR	–
8	9	A	B	STORE	+
4	5	6	7	BREAK	I/O PORT
0	1	2	3	MOVE	GO

Figure 3.8: *Evaluation-system keyboard layout. The choice of keyboard layout and function is entirely up to the programmer.*

If more functions are needed than there are keys on the keyboard (or if more are added at a later date), a shift key can be used to get to a second set of keys. Figure 3.9 shows a simplified top-down structure for the monitor. The problem with this design is that it uses in-line compare instructions and hence is not very flexible. A more efficient table-driven design is shown in figure 3.10.

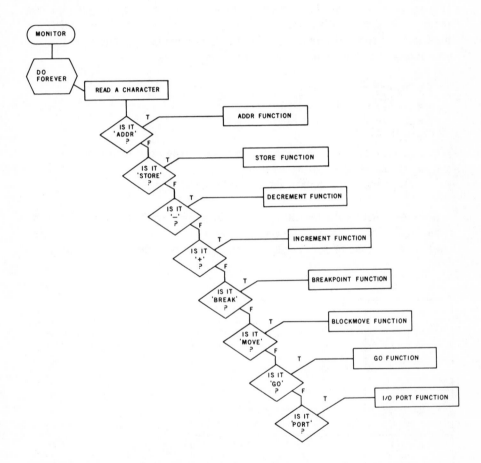

Figure 3.9: *Flowchart of a simple "compare and branch" monitor. Each function is written as a subroutine. When the function is completed, execution continues at the DO loop, causing a new character to be read.*

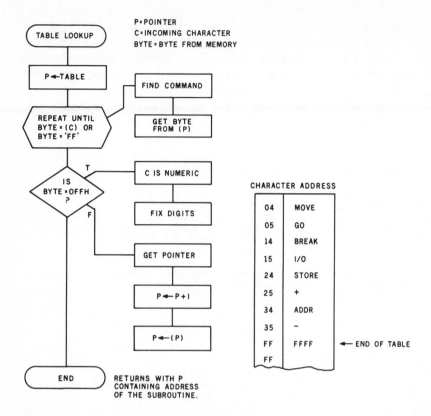

P = POINTER
C = INCOMING CHARACTER
BYTE = BYTE FROM MEMORY

CHARACTER	ADDRESS	
04	MOVE	
05	GO	
14	BREAK	
15	I/O	
24	STORE	
25	+	
34	ADDR	
35	−	
FF	FFFF	← END OF TABLE
FF		

Figure 3.10: *Single-character table look-up routine.*

In figure 3.10, each command character (the hexadecimal number that matches what is sent by the keyboard) is stored in a table, followed by the address of the routine that handles that function. The table can be terminated by a series of FFH bytes, which can (if a sufficient number of them are left at the end of the table) be replaced with additional commands. This can be done because most PROMs' normal "erased" state has all bits turned on, hence FFH. Thus new commands can be added to the PROM monitor without having to erase and reprogram the PROM.

The algorithm listed in figure 3.11 is the 8080/Z80 assembler version of figure 3.10. The first step in figure 3.11 is to initialize the HL-register pair (P is used in figure 3.10) with the address of TABLE. At the label search, the first byte of TABLE is loaded into the A register (equivalent to BYTE in figure 3.10). The keystroke is in the C register and is compared to the contents of the A register. If they match, a zero condition is flagged and the JZ (jump on zero) causes control to be transferred to GOTIT. If the condition is not met, execution continues with the three INX H instructions, which increment the pointer (HL) to the next table entry. After incrementing, control is transferred to SEARCH, where the cycle is repeated until either the keystroke matches a table entry, or the end of the table is found.

If the table entry does match, the INX H instruction at GOTIT moves the HL pointer to the lower half of the jump table address and the byte is loaded into the E register. A second INX H and a move instruction load the high-order byte into the D register. The single instruction XCHG causes the HL and DE register pairs to be swapped. With the jump address now in HL, the PCHL instruction causes control to be transferred to the address in HL.

```
;
;      Enter with keystroke in C-register.
;
;
SEARCH:     MOV   A,M         ;Get the byte at (HL).
            CPI   OFFH        ;if FF, we are done.
            JZ    NUMERIC     ;end of table. look for number.
            CMP   C           ;if same as character in C reg,
            JZ    GOTIT       ;we have it.
            INX   H
            INX   H           ;if not, increment to next table
            INX   H           ;entry and try again.
            JMP   SEARCH
;
NUMERIC:    MOV   C,A
            CALL  TRANS       ;Translate to proper numeric value
            MOV   A,C
            JMP   ---         ;Go to numeric handler as needed.
;
GOTIT:      INX   H           ;Point to lower half of address
            MOV   E,M         ;get lower half
            INX   H
            MOV   D,M         ;get upper half
            XCHG              ;put address in HL registers.
            PCHL              ;jump to the address found in table
```

Figure 3.11: *Z80 single-character table look-up routine.*

If an end-of-table (identified by an FFH byte in the first byte of the last table entry) condition is encountered, the input keystroke is assumed to be numeric (i.e., from the 0 to F keypad). Depending on the layout of the four-by-six keypad, the codes for the 0 to F keys could match one for one, meaning that the binary code returned for the 9 key would be 01001 (or 9 in decimal). However, because of the layout of the keypad in this example, the key codes do not correspond to the digits directly. Figure 3.12 shows the relationship between keypad codes and internal codes.

LABEL ➞	C	D	E	F	ADDR	–
ADDRESS ➞	30	31	32	33	34	35
	8	9	A	B	STORE	+
	20	21	22	23	24	25
	4	5	6	7	BREAK	I/O PORT
	10	11	12	13	14	15
	0	1	2	3	MOVE	GO
	00	01	02	03	04	05

NUMERIC TRANSLATE TABLE

KEYPAD	OUTPUT DIGIT	KEYPAD	OUTPUT DIGIT
00	00	20	8
01	1	21	9
02	2	22	A
03	3	23	B
10	4	30	C
11	5	31	D
12	6	32	E
13	7	33	F

Figure 3.12: *Keyboard function mapping.*

A similar table-search algorithm may be used to recognize and translate these key codes. Figure 3.13 shows this algorithm in structured-flowchart form. Figure 3.14 is the 8080/Z80 version of figure 3.13. Here again, P is set to point to the start of the translate table, and the first byte is tested for a match. If there is no match, P is incremented twice to move to the next table entry (this table has two bytes per entry), and it tries again. If the end of the table is reached without a match, an FFH byte is found, causing an error condition to be established. In this example, the carry flag is set with the STC instruction, and control is returned to the calling program.

If a match is found in the table, P is incremented once, and the second byte of the table entry is loaded into the C register, replacing the keycode received from the keypad.

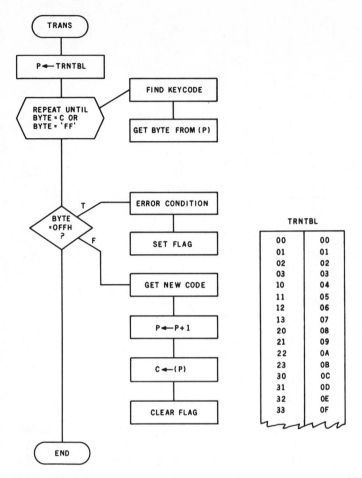

Figure 3.13: *This routine translates an incoming keyboard key value into the correct internal value.*

```
TRANS:    LXI    H,TRNTBL    ;point to start of the table
;
TT1:      MOV    A,M
          CPI    0FFH        ;if FF, we are at end of table
          JZ     ERR         ;error condition
          CMP    C
          JZ     FOUND       ;if (A) = (C)  then we have it
          INX    H
          INX    H           ;if not, point to next table entry
          JMP    TT1         ;and try again.
FOUND:    INX    H
          MOV    C,M         ;replace code in C register
                             ;with the correct internal code.
          RET
;
ERR:      STC                ;if end of table encountered,
          RET                ;set carry flag and return.
```

Figure 3.14: *Translate subroutine for SEARCH in figure 3.11.*

The ADDR Command

This command, within the framework of the hypothetical monitor, allows the user to enter a new four-digit memory address to view and/or modify data. The syntax is

ADDR 0 0 0 0

where ADDR is the single keystroke command, and the four zeros are the four digits of the address. When the ADDR key is depressed, the algorithm in figure 3.10 searches the jump table and finds the address of the module that handles the reading of the four-digit address. Figure 3.15 shows the algorithm for a typical ADDR command.

Figure 3.15: *The ADDR function of the monitor. It reads in four digits and builds an address that is also displayed on the left four digits of the six-digit display.*

The ADDR flowchart shown in figure 3.15 is actually quite simple. First, the four digits are read in one at a time and translated to the internal representation using TRANS from figure 3.13. Each digit is ANDed with the current address register, after the address is shifted left four bits to make room for it. This way, the six-digit display can be updated one digit at a time, causing the four-digit address to appear to walk across the display, calculator style. When the last of the four digits has been entered, the last two display digits show the contents of the new memory location. After the function is completed, control is transferred to the restart point of the monitor by a jump rather than a return instruction. In this example, the restart point would be the keyboard-in call just prior to the first statement of figure 3.10.

The STORE Command

The STORE command allows the user to modify the contents of memory at the current address (shown in the first four display digits). Normally whenever a numeric digit is entered, it is checked by the command algorithm to see if it is a command, then is translated to the appropriate internal code, and is ANDed into a temporary location in memory. When the STORE key is depressed, the contents of that memory location are written into the actual memory location shown on the display. This is provided as a safety measure, allowing the user to reenter the two digits until they are correct before storing the data. STORE does nothing else but update the contents of memory at the displayed address.

The Increment Command

This command (referred to as " + ") does the same thing as STORE, except it also increments the address pointer and updates the display. Figure 3.16 shows this command.

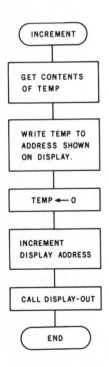

Figure 3.16: *The increment command. It increments the address and redisplays it (and the contents of memory at the address) using the DISPLAY-OUT routine.*

The Decrement Command

This command (referred to as " – ") merely decrements the address pointer and redisplays the address and contents of memory. No store operation is involved. Figure 3.17 shows the decrement command.

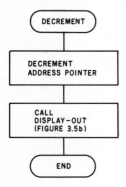

Figure 3.17: *The decrement function. This one simply decrements the address pointer and redisplays six digits.*

The MOVE Command

The MOVE command is used to perform block moves of data from one area of memory to another. The syntax of the command is as follows:

MOVE 0 0 0 0   0 0 0 0   0 0 0 0

The first four digits after the MOVE keystroke define the source or starting point of the move. The second four are the destination address, and the last four specify the length of the block to be moved. Requiring multiple entries would be difficult without some form of prompting. Otherwise the user would not have any feedback on each of the three parameters. A common way of doing this is to display some kind of mnemonic on the six-digit display. Since the only possible display characters are 0 through F, we must approximate. The display character for the number five looks like an *S*, which will stand for source. The lower case *d* character is already available, and a number 1 can be used to simulate an *L* for length. The important point here is to have some kind of prompt; the actual characters are not as important as the fact that they appear on the display. In this case the three prompt characters are made to appear across all six digits while the monitor is awaiting the next input. Figure 3.18 shows the MOVE command input sequence.

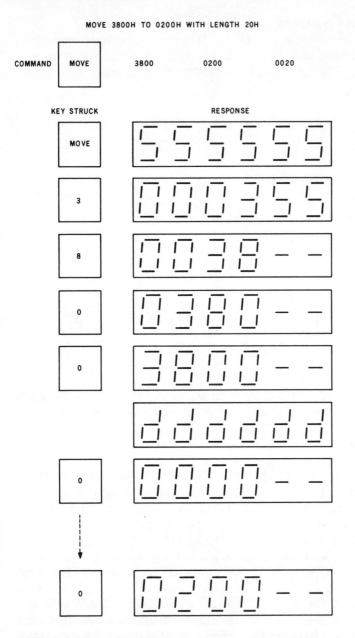

Figure 3.18: *An example of the MOVE command. Function ends with address display pointing at destination.*

Note that as each four-digit number is entered, the display is updated and shifted across, just as on a calculator display. After each entry, there is a momentary pause, then the next prompt appears. Figure 3.19 gives the flowchart for the MOVE command.

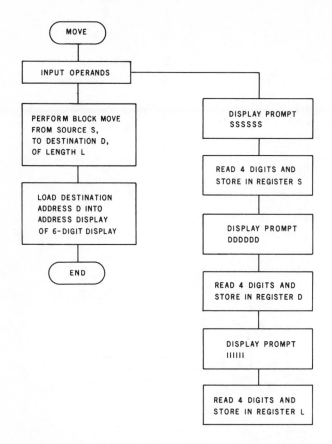

Figure 3.19: *Flowchart of the MOVE command.*

The PORT Command

This command presents some problems. Optimally, two functions should be provided: input port and output port. Since the port commands are not as frequently used, it often does not seem worthwhile to take up two keys on the keyboard when other commands are more important. One way of setting up this command is to have the monitor display the current value of the port (on input) and wait for a two-digit response to be output to the specified port address. If the user does wish to perform the output portion of the command, it may be aborted by striking any non-numeric key. Again, the monitor should provide a prompt when waiting for the input data. Figure 3.20 shows the flowchart for the port command.

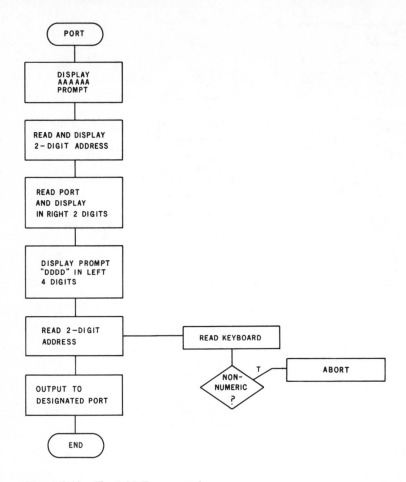

Figure 3.20: *The PORT command.*

The Breakpoint Command

This command is actually part of a larger set of functions called debugging facilities. It is given here because it presents some important ideas and is useful even by itself. First, the purpose of the command is to set a breakpoint or stopping point in a program that is being tested. This allows the programmer to run part of a program or subroutine and stop at any point to examine its function. It is a very important debugging tool. There are several prevalent philosophies concerning how a breakpoint should be implemented. One technique is to replace the actual instruction at the specified address with a jump (or call) instruction. The bytes that are overwritten can be saved elsewhere and later restored when the breakpoint is removed. Another technique involves hardware modifications that cause an interrupt whenever a new instruction cycle is started. This approach may be inherently easier in terms of programming and debugging, but it requires special hardware and is not dealt with here.

The first approach—replacing the instruction with a jump instruction—is discussed here because it is conceptually the simplest to work with. The first step is to describe the sequence of events surrounding the use of the command. The programmer has entered part of a program to test, and it is not working as desired. The programmer then enters the command BREAK 0 0 0 0, where BREAK is the key on the four-by-six keypad, and the four digits following it represent the address at which the breakpoint is to be inserted. Figure 3.21 shows a sequence of instructions and the effect of the breakpoint command. Typically, the breakpoint jump transfers control to a portion of the monitor that saves all registers and allows the programmer to view them to determine what the troublesome program was doing.

```
BEFORE:     0100   LXI    H,200H
            0103   MOV    A,M
            0105   CPI    0
            0107   RZ
            0108   CALL   CONSOLE$OUT
            010B   INX    H
            010C   JMP    0103H
            010F   ---

Command:    BREAK 0103

AFTER:      0100   LXI    H,200H
            0103   JMP    MONBK    <--- Jump to BKPT program.
            0107   RZ
            0108   CALL   CONSOLE$OUT
            ----   ---
```

Figure 3.21: *The effect of the BREAK command.*

Note that in figure 3.21 the jump instruction has overwritten 3 bytes, including the next instruction. As soon as the breakpoint is "found" (i.e., executed), the first action of the breakpoint handler is to rewrite the old instructions over the breakpoint jump. This ensures that the program executes correctly when the user tries to continue where it left off. The other problem is that if more than one breakpoint is present at one time (or if the programmer indiscriminately goes around inserting breakpoints), their locations will be forgotten, and there will be no hope of tracing execution. Also, if more than one breakpoint is inserted, the monitor must be smart enough to keep track of all of them and the 3-byte blocks displaced by each one.

Figure 3.22 shows the BREAK command. This version only supports one breakpoint at a time. To prevent the user from crashing the program, a new breakpoint is inserted before the last one is removed, and the previous one is automatically removed. Figure 3.23 shows the breakpoint-handler routine. Since this is a rather primitive handler, the contents of the CPU registers are written to a save area in memory so they can be manually viewed by the programmer.

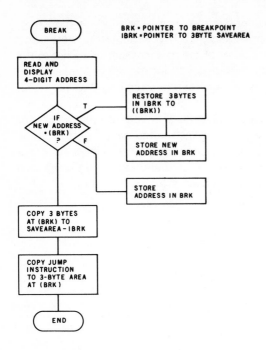

BRK = POINTER TO BREAKPOINT
IBRK = POINTER TO 3BYTE SAVEAREA

Figure 3.22: *The BREAK command.*

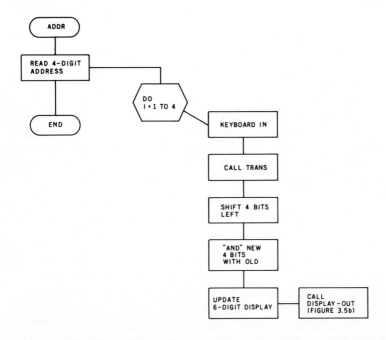

Figure 3.23: *The breakpoint handler. This routine is called when the breakpoint-jump instruction is encountered.*

The GO Command

This is a simple but important feature of a monitor. Its purpose is to allow transfer of control to the application program that the user has entered. The form is GO 0 0 0 0, where the four digits represent the address to begin execution.

The Development System

A more sophisticated microcomputer (shown in figure 3.24) includes a full alphanumeric keyboard, a memory-mapped video display, and a bi-directional serial interface for external communications.

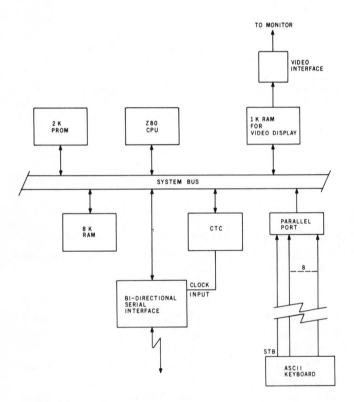

Figure 3.24: *The development system.*

The Keyboard

An ASCII-encoded keyboard (see Appendix V) generates a seven-bit character code and a strobe signal. The keyboard (shown in figure 3.25) itself has an onboard large-scale integration (LSI) circuit that scans the array of keys (usually 64), including shift, shift-lock, and control keys and generates appropriate ASCII character codes that may be read through the parallel port on the development system.

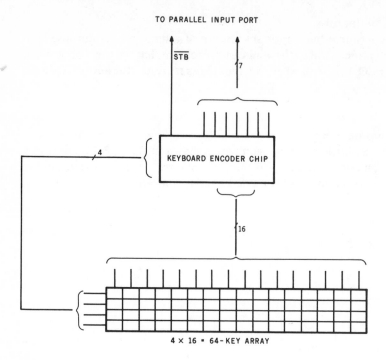

TO PARALLEL INPUT PORT

$\overline{\text{STB}}$

KEYBOARD ENCODER CHIP

4 × 16 = 64-KEY ARRAY

Figure 3.25: *The keyboard.*

The Video Display

The video display described here and used in the examples is referred to as a memory-mapped display. This means that the microcomputer can address it as main memory. Typically the display is organized as 64 characters per line by 16 lines or as 40 characters by 24 lines. In the former case, the total number of characters displayed on the screen is 64 × 16 or 1024—exactly 1 K byte of memory. In the latter case, 40 × 24 is equal to 980, which does not quite use up an entire 1 K byte. Since 1 K byte will easily handle either format (and since it is quite difficult to get memory in units smaller than 1 K anymore), the video display used here will have 1 K byte of memory. In all further discussion and examples, I will use the 64 × 16 format.

Since ASCII codes require only seven bits of data, the eighth bit is often used in video displays to determine whether the character is displayed as white on a black background or black on a white background. Normally, if the bit is zero or off, the background is black.

Since the video display circuitry must continually refresh (redisplay) the monitor or television display, it must read the contents of the 1 K byte of screen memory. This is accomplished through simple arbitration logic. The purpose of this is to decide whether the microprocessor or the video display refresh logic may access the screen memory at any given instant. Generally the microcomputer is given priority—meaning that the video display has occasional black "flecks" or streaks one scanline wide and perhaps an inch long (depending on the video display used and the time it takes the microcomputer to perform the memory access). Since most video display circuits are designed to blank (black out) the signal when the microcomputer is in control, the streaks are almost invisible to the human eye. If this is unacceptable, most video display circuits can be modified to allow the microcomputer to access the screen memory only during a retrace (when the electron beam is moving invisibly across the screen to a new scan line).

Figure 3.26 shows the block diagram of a typical video display circuit. Also in figure 3.26 is a diagram of the screen display of a 64 × 16 video display. Note that the memory address is set to A000H. If the screen is to display 1024 characters, the last character on the display is at memory address A3FFH.

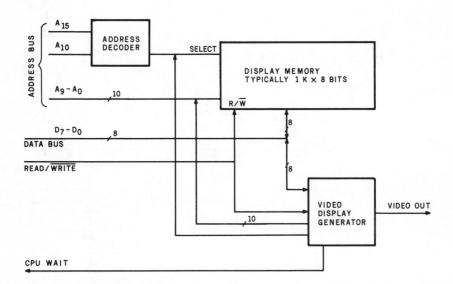

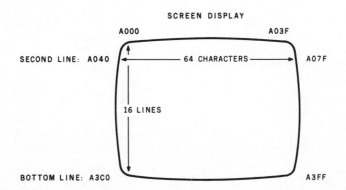

Figure 3.26: *The video display circuit.*

Figure 3.27 shows the algorithm for a simple video display (commonly referred to as the console) driver subroutine. It accepts any ASCII character and responds to carriage return, line feed, and form feed. All other control characters (nonprintable ASCII characters such as ETX, SOH, NUL) are ignored.

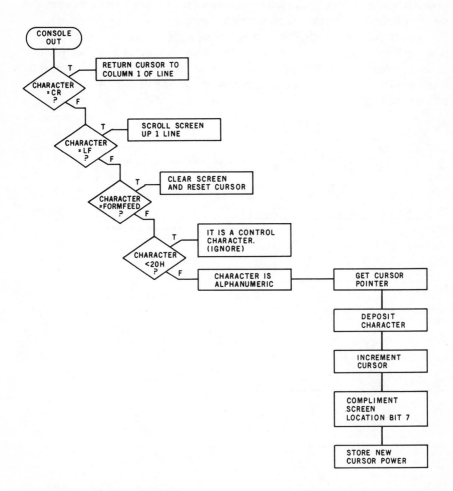

Figure 3.27: *The console-driver routine.*

Figure 3.28 shows this algorithm in operation. In figure 3.28b, the subroutine was called with a character value of A. Note that the cursor (white-box character used to denote current position on the screen) has moved over to the second column. Upon examination of the algorithm in figure 3.27, you can see that the character-display section loads the cursor pointer (points to the video screen memory address of the cursor) and deposits the character value into that memory location, overwriting the old cursor character (the white box). Next it increments the cursor memory address by one, causing it to point to the next screen column. To display the new cursor location, it complements bit 7 of the data byte at that memory address. Next it must preserve the memory address of the new cursor location, which is stored as the new cursor pointer.

Figure 3.28c repeats the process described in the last paragraph. The character B is displayed on the screen, and the new cursor is in column 3. In figure 3.28d, a carriage return is the input character. Again the cursor pointer is loaded, but this time there is no printable character to deposit on the screen. Instead, we must get rid of the cursor on the screen. This is accomplished by loading the character and complementing bit 7 to reverse the background. The character (white box) then becomes black. Instead of incrementing the cursor memory address, we load a new constant—the memory address of column 1 of the line. This address is stored as the new cursor pointer, and the bit 7 of the character in column 1 is complemented to display the new cursor location.

Figure 3.28e shows what happens when a line feed is sent to the console driver subroutine. Here the screen must be scrolled (rolled up one line to simulate a printer terminal). Bit 7 of the cursor location must again be complemented, but the cursor pointer need not be updated. A subroutine that performs a block move must be called to copy the entire screen down 64 characters in memory. This has the effect of rolling it up one line. The top line (from address A000H to A040H) disappears off the top of the screen. The contents of the bottom line move up one line, but the bottom line itself is not altered. Thus a second loop is needed to deposit blanks from A3C0H to A3FFH. After the bottom line is cleared, the cursor location must be redisplayed on the bottom line.

The only other control character recognized by the algorithm in figure 3.27 is the form feed. This simply clears the screen and resets the cursor pointer to A3C0H. Other control characters could be added, such as backspace, which would decrement the cursor pointer, or HT (horizontal tab), which would move the cursor across the screen to fixed positions every nth character.

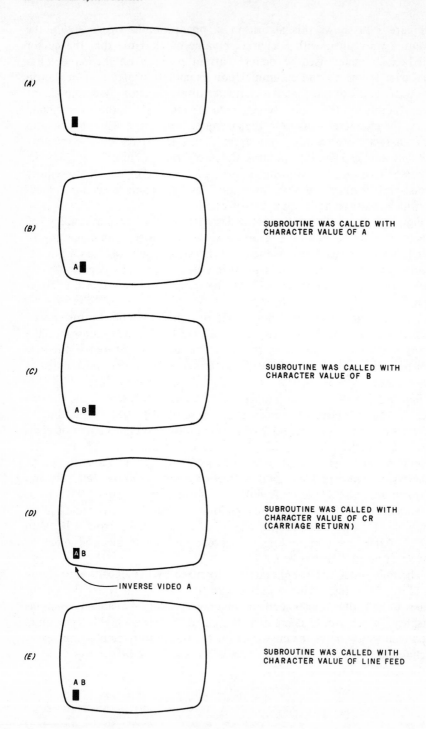

Figure 3.28: *Console-driver algorithm in use.*

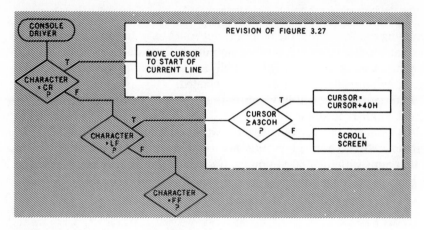

Figure 3.29: *Revised version of the routine in figure 3.27.*

Note that the algorithm in figure 3.27 allows cursor movement only on the bottom line of the display. Conventional video display terminals generally start at the top of the screen and work their way to the bottom before scrolling the display. Figure 3.29 shows how the algorithm in figure 3.27 might be modified to accomplish this. The only differences are in the shaded box. When a carriage return is the input character, the cursor is returned to column 1 of the current line, rather than to column 1 of the bottom line. When a line feed is the character, a test is made to see if the cursor is on the bottom line. If so, the screen is scrolled. If not, the cursor pointer is moved to the same column on the next line. This is easily accomplished by adding 64 (the line length) to the cursor pointer. When a form feed is detected, the screen is cleared as in figure 3.27, but the cursor pointer is reset to A000H rather than to the start of the bottom line.

Another useful feature is cursor addressability. This means that when a control character (such as ESC or 1BH) is received, the next 2 bytes (or perhaps two CPU registers) contain the line and column numbers of the new cursor location. This feature is advantageous when setting up formatted screen displays. The algorithm is shown in figure 3.30.

Designing a Command Language

When I designed my first monitor for a cassette-based system, I did so without an assembler or any development tools. Hand assembly of even the shortest program is no easy task. The project took about 200 hours, 75 percent of which was devoted to the routine task of hand assembling and loading in the program.

A simple monitor, contrary to popular belief, is not hard to write. A few months ago, I bought a Z80-based S-100 CPU board for a consulting project. The monitor supplied with it was set up to work with a serial terminal, which would not work in this particular application. I spent several hours attempting to disassemble the monitor, but could only locate a portion of the code that handled console input and output; the manufacturer obviously did not want a user to disassemble its monitor. Thus I had to start from scratch to get a monitor that would do what I wanted.

I started with two utility subroutines. One converts two-digit ASCII decimal numbers to single 8-bit numbers in a CPU register. The other takes an 8-bit number and converts it into two hexadecimal digits in ASCII. In approximately two hours, I wrote a monitor that was virtually identical to the one that came with the Z80 computer. If I were to write one as complex as the one I had hand assembled years ago, it would probably take 20 to 25 hours.

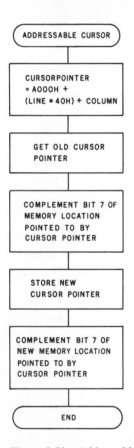

Figure 3.30: *Addressable cursor routine.*

A Simple Video-Based Monitor

One should first define what the monitor is to do. Starting with the evaluation-system monitor as a model, one needs a memory view/modify command, an execute command, a port examine/modify command, a block-move feature, and some sort of debug facility.

The Memory-Display Command

A common format for a memory display on a video screen is shown in figure 3.31. The address is shown on the far left, followed by eight bytes and a group of eight characters off to the right showing the ASCII interpretation of the eight bytes. If the byte has no ASCII representation, a period or some other character is put in its place.

The procedure for the memory-display routine is shown in figure 3.32. Note that it consists of two simple DO loops. The first DO loop starts with P set to ADDR, the starting address of the memory block to be displayed. It immediately outputs a carriage return and a line feed, to start a new line. Then the memory address in P is displayed in four hexadecimal digits. The second DO loop level starts with Q set to the current value of P.

```
d100
0100 0E 10 21 54 00 CD 58 32 23 E5 F5 CD 10 32 F1 E1  ..!T..X2#....2..
0110 C3 08 02 05 C9 79 2A FE DF 01 49 E8 FE 0D CA EA  .....y*...I.....
0120 E8 FE 0C CA AD C0 FE 0B CA CE E8 FE 0A CA AB E8  ...............
0130 FE 0E CA DC E8 FE 08 CA 3B C3 FE 18 CA FC E8 FE  ........;......
0140 07 CA 51 E8 FE 17 CA 30 E9 FE 7F CA 3B C3 CD B5  ..Q....0....;...
0150 C1 C3 00 C0 D1 C1 2A 20 EF F9 E1 79 C9 20 FF F1  ......* ...y. ..
0160 D1 C1 E1 C9 C9 2A FE DF CD 0A C3 2A FE DF CD 0A  .....*.....*....
0170 C3 C9 2A FE DF CD 3B C3 C3 50 E8 2A FE DF CD 55  ..*...;..P.*...U
0180 C0 7E EE 80 77 C9 AF 80 F8 23 23 23 7E B8 D8 AF  .~..w....###~...
0190 81 F8 23 23 23 7E B9 D8 2B 2B 2B 2B 2B 2B E5 C5  ..###~..++++++..
01A0 D5 CD 55 C0 D1 C1 7E EE 80 77 E1 E5 23 23 70 23  ..U...~..w..##p#
01B0 23 23 71 E1 C3 00 C0 23 23 46 23 23 23 4E C9 2A  ##q....##F###N.*
```

Figure 3.31: *Memory-display output format. Each line in this example has 16 bytes, with a display of the ASCII character representation to the right.*

First the value of the memory location at the address in Q is loaded into a CPU register and is converted to two-digit hexadecimal represented in ASCII. These two characters are output to the video display with the console-driver subroutine. For readability, a space (ASCII 20H) character is output after the two-digit number. The innermost DO loop iterates from P to P + LNS − 1 or from P to P + 7 in this case. The next DO loop repeats this sequence of bytes, but displays them as characters instead of two-digit hexadecimal numbers. If the byte is found to be a printable ASCII character (between 20H and 7FH), then it is output directly to the video display. If it is outside of this range, a period or some other character is output instead.

The next iteration of the P loop will set P to ADDR + 8. Again the value of P is displayed as a four-digit hexadecimal number, and the next line of eight bytes is displayed.

The Memory-Examine/Modify Command

Although the memory-display command is useful for seeing the big picture, it is still necessary to be able to examine individual bytes and, if necessary, alter their contents. One standard (if somewhat unimaginative) way is to enter the examine command followed by a hexadecimal address.

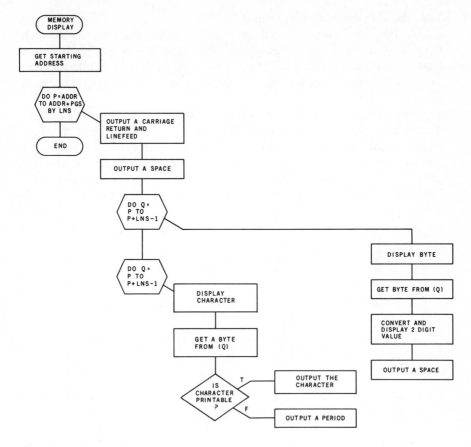

Figure 3.32: *Memory-display routine.*

The monitor displays the address, followed by a two-digit hexadecimal number representing the current contents of the memory location. If the user does not want to alter the contents, he or she may enter a carriage return, hit the space bar, or hit some nonhexadecimal character. If any one- or two-digit number is entered, the number is deposited in the place of the old number. Normally, after the user hits carriage return, the address is incremented, and the process is repeated. Some other character such as a period or the escape key might be used to abort the examine command. The algorithm is shown in figure 3.33.

Other Commands

The port input and output commands for the development system are similar to those described for the evaluation system. The input port command expects to find a two-digit hexadecimal number representing the port address. It then reads the port and displays the result as another two digit hexadecimal number.

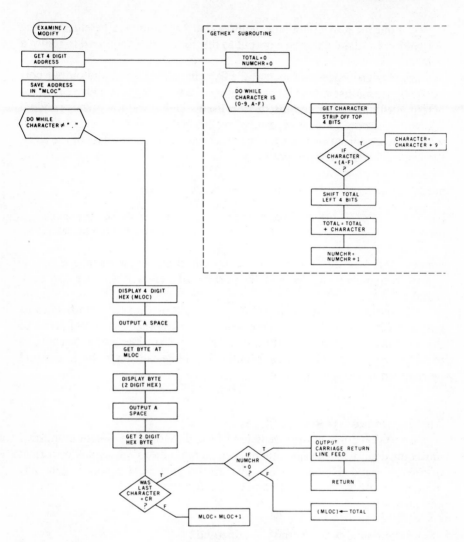

Figure 3.33: *The memory examine/modify command.*

The output port command requires that two numbers be entered—the port address and the data to be output to the port. It does not need to return a number.

Some microprocessors such as the 8080 have only input and output port instructions that use immediate addressing. That is, the port address is in the byte immediately after the instruction itself. This does not permit random addressing of ports. However, a simple solution does exist. The monitor must write its own subroutine using a few bytes of memory. In the case of the 8080, the instruction sequence might be

```
address opcodes label   instruction     comment

0A00    D3XX   OUTR     OUT port        ;Output to the port
0A02    C9              RET             ;Return to the monitor
```

where "port" is the address of the output port. To work properly, the "port" byte must be loaded with the port number entered with the port command.

The monitor would then load the accumulator with the data byte to be sent and CALL OUTR. The same sequence of instructions would apply to the input instruction as well—but the D3H byte at 0A00H would be changed to DBH. In the latter case, the subroutine would be called and the data would be returned in the accumulator.

The Command Syntax

Up to this point in the discussion of the development-system monitor, I have only dealt with the function of each command, not the syntax or format of the command. Having a video display and an ASCII keyboard generally implies a more sophisticated command interpreter. A common syntax for commands is

< Command > < operand1 > < operand2 > . . .

where the command is mandatory and the operands are optional. The command can consist of a single character or a string of characters. An alternate (and much simpler) command format accepts single-character commands and then prompts the user for the operands. This format is actually advantageous; it prompts the user, making it easy to remember which operands are needed for each command. The structured flowchart for a prompting monitor is shown in figure 3.34.

The flowchart in figure 3.34 shows what is probably the most primitive monitor possible. Commands are prompted by displaying the menu, and operands are prompted by displaying a message prior to each keyboard input. The following is a sample sequence:

```
Prompting Monitor Version 1.0

    D - Display memory
    E - Edit bytes in memory
    I - Input from a port
    O - Output to a port

Enter a command: E
Enter a four-digit address: 1A23

    1A23 FB
    1A24 23 45
    1A25 00 01
    1A26 .

Prompting Monitor Version 1.0

    D - Display memory
```

and so on.

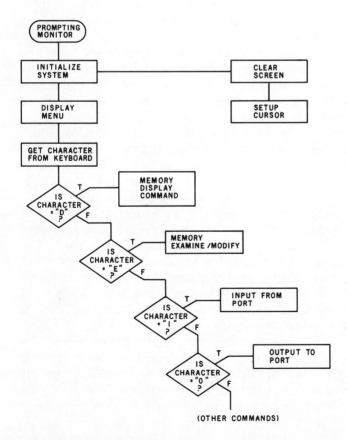

Figure 3.34: *A prompting monitor.*

In the previous example, the menu is first displayed, followed by the "Enter a command:" prompt. When the E command is entered, the monitor transfers control to the examine/modify module and displays the "enter four-digit address:" prompt. Next each memory location is displayed after the address is printed. If the user enters a valid hexadecimal number, it is deposited into the address just displayed. If the character is a period (or other abort key such as control-c), control is returned to the top of the monitor, where the menu is redisplayed.

A more sophisticated command interpreter has a command buffer where a string of characters is read in, allowing for backspace and other editing functions. When the carriage-return key is hit, the entire buffer is scanned for a command and operands. Although this kind of command syntax is very widely used, it requires some additional error checking and is generally more complicated.

Figure 3.35 shows a buffer input routine. The first character code checked for is the backspace. If one is found, the CPNTR is decremented, and the last character (the one being deleted) is redisplayed to show that it no longer is present. Although it is common to redisplay the deleted character on terminals with no way of backspacing (a printer terminal, for example), there is no reason why you cannot send a backspace to the terminal device and get rid of the deleted character.

The second character code checked for is the carriage return. When one is detected, the carriage return is deposited in the buffer, and control is returned to the top level of the program, since the repeat-until loop is now satisfied. The next step is to restore the CPNTR (reset it to the start of the buffer) and return to the main program.

The third check is for a line feed. In the case of a printer terminal, where it cannot backspace, the input line may get messy if a lot of backspacing is done. The solution to the problem is to redisplay the line as it is in the buffer.

If none of the three special characters are found, the input character is put in the buffer at CPNTR, and CPNTR is incremented by one.

Now the problem is finding the command in the string. It may not be in the first byte of the buffer. Scanning for the command involves checking each character to see if it is a printable alphanumeric (A-Z, a-z, 0-9). The search is continued until one is found (this is assumed to be the start of the actual command). If the monitor allows only one-character commands, the next task is simple, in fact, identical to the prompting monitor described earlier. If the command consists of more characters, it will probably be necessary to search a table of commands.

Once the command is found and control is transferred to the appropriate module, routines similar to GETHEX must be devised to scan for the first valid hexadecimal digits and ignore everything until the operand is found. If no operands are present (if a carriage return is encountered), an error code should be returned, and the appropriate action should be taken to terminate the command.

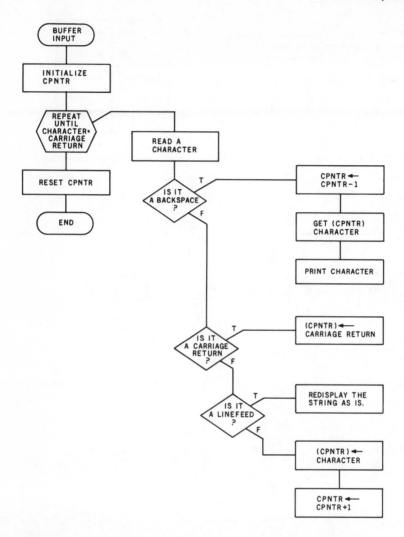

Figure 3.35: *Buffer input routine.*

Commands Longer Than One Character

It is often desirable to have commands that are longer than one character. A multiple character name is generally easier to remember, and if there are many commands, it allows greater flexibility in selecting names for commands.

Figure 3.36 shows the procedure for recognizing longer commands. First the pointer T is initialized to the start of COMM, the command table. P is initialized to the start of BUFF, the command to be searched for. FLAG and ERR are set to zero. The procedure is repeated until FLAG is set to one—meaning that the command has been found.

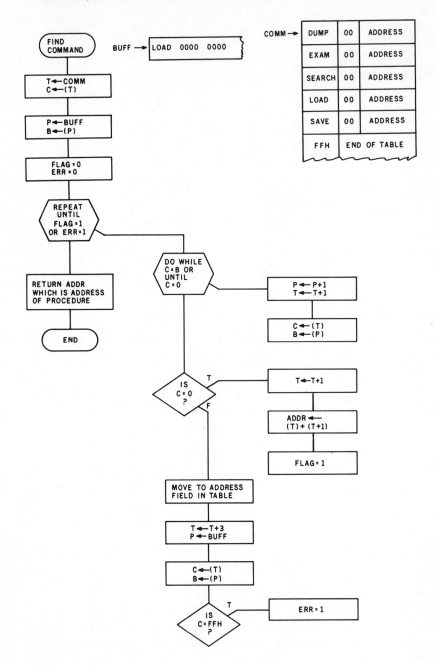

Figure 3.36: *Recognizing multicharacter commands.*

The DO loop is repeated as long as C equals B (meaning that it is on the right track), or until C equals 0 (the end of a command was found, and there is a match). Note that a DO WHILE loop tests its condition at the beginning, not the end. C and B are then compared, and if they are found to be equal, P and T are each incremented by one. C and B are then set to the new character values, and the loop ends. Returning to the top of the DO loop, C is again compared to B.

```
                     ;
                     ;
                     Find:
0000 AF                      xra    a
0001 324400                  sta    Err        ;Err = 0
0004 324500                  sta    Flag       ;Flag = 0
0007 210002                  lxi    h,Comm     ;T <- Comm
000A 114800                  lxi    d,Buff     ;P <- Buff
000D 1A          Rept:       ldax   d
000E BE                      cmp    m          ;is C = B?
000F CA3100                  jz     Same       ;yes
0012 7E                      mov    a,m
0013 FE00                    cpi    0          ;is C = 0?
0015 CA3600                  jz     Czero      ;yes
0018 23          Findz:      inx    h          ;locate the zero
0019 7E                      mov    a,m
001A FE00                    cpi    0
001C C21800                  jnz    Findz      ;continue
001F 23                      inx    h
0020 23                      inx    h
0021 23                      inx    h          ;T <- T + 3
0022 114800                  lxi    d,Buff     ;P <- Buff
0025 7E                      mov    a,m
0026 FEFF                    cpi    0FFH       ;is C = 0FFH?
0028 C20D00                  jnz    Rept       ;if not, repeat
002B 3E01                    mvi    a,1
002D 324400                  sta    Err        ;Err = 1
0030 C9                      ret               ;done.
                     ;
0031 23          Same:       inx    h
0032 13                      inx    d
0033 C30D00                  jmp    Rept       ;so far so good. continue.
                     ;
0036 23          Czero:      inx    h          ;T <- T + 1
0037 5E                      mov    e,m
0038 23                      inx    h
0039 56                      mov    d,m        ;get address from the table
003A EB                      xchg              ;swap de, hl
003B 224600                  shld   Addr       ;save in ADDR
003E 3E01                    mvi    a,1
0040 324500                  sta    Flag       ;flag = 1
0043 C9                      ret               ;done.
                     ;
0044 00          Err         db     0          ;error return flag
0045 00          Flag        db     0          ;set flag if successful
0046 0000        Addr        dw     0          ;save area for address
                     ;
0048             Buff        ds     70         ;command buffer
                     ;
                     ;
0200 =           Comm        equ    200H       ;pointer to command table
008E                         end
```

Figure 3.37: *8080 command search subroutine.*

This procedure repeats until C is not equal to B, or until C is equal to zero. In the first case, when C is found to be different from B, there is a no-match situation, and it must go on to the next command in the table. The pointers must again be set up for a new command. T is incremented by two, and P is reset to BUFF. Finally, a test is made to check for the end of the command table. If the end is found, there is an error condition, because no match was made. The routine terminates abnormally.

In the second case in which C is found equal to zero, the routine has successfully matched a command (to the last character) and must retrieve its address. T is incremented by one, and the address is loaded into ADDR. After FLAG is set to one, the routine terminates normally. Figure 3.37 shows a typical 8080 assembler program based on this procedure.

Using a Bi-directional Serial Interface

In the examples given in this book, I usually use a parallel keyboard and memory-mapped video display as the console device, because the interface required is more complicated in terms of hardware and software. Many systems use a serial-interface port connected to a serial video display terminal (VDT) or possibly a serial teletype or other printer terminal.

A serial interface consists of a universal asynchronous receiver/transmitter (UART) or a universal synchronous-asynchronous receiver/transmitter (USART) and some level conversion circuits to change transistor-transistor logic (TTL) (logic 0 = 0 v, logic 1 = 5 v) to RS-232 levels (logic 1 = −12 v, logic 0 = +12 v). The purpose of the serial interface is to convert parallel data to serial and vice versa. When a byte of parallel data is sent to the UART, it is shifted bit-by-bit sideways and sent down a single wire to the receiver. The receiver takes each bit as it comes in and converts it back to the original parallel data.

This allows data to be transmitted over a pair of wires (signal and ground) or over a telephone line by means of a modulator/demodulator (modem) that changes the ones and zeros into two audible tones.

Initializing the UART

There are several different types of UARTs and USARTs on the market, and they all have special initialization sequences, but they all require basically the same information. The UART must be told what data format to use and the number of bits to transmit (selectable from 5 to 8 bits). The data format includes the number of stop bits (1, 1½, or 2) for asynchronous operation and other information for synchronous operation. The data rate is usually determined by the clock rate of the clock input line of the UART. Normally this line is derived from the system clock rate (or some fraction of that rate) or from a counter-timer circuit in the system. If the counter-timer can be programmed under software control, the user may initialize it by sending bytes to the counter-timer port. This procedure varies from computer to computer and is fairly hardware specific—hence I will not pursue the matter here.

Sending Data to the Serial Interface

Once the UART has been initialized, data may be sent to it by outputting to the I/O port assigned to the UART circuit. Generally a status (input) port is available to check on the UART's current status. Bits within the byte indicate such things as transmitter ready, receiver ready, overrun error, parity error, and buffer full. The program must check for these and react appropriately. Figure 3.38 shows a typical serial-output routine. The TX RDY bit indicates whether the transmitter portion of the UART is ready to send another byte. If it is zero (in this example), the repeat condition is met, and processing continues. If it is one, the test is repeated until it goes to zero. This procedure works for serial input also. The status-test loop must check the RX RDY bit, and instead of outputting a byte, an input from the UART must be done.

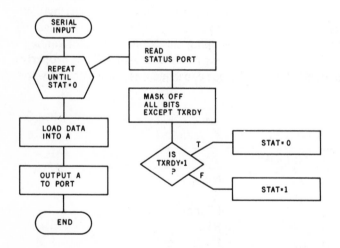

Figure 3.38: *Serial-output driver. This routine needs the status port until the TXRDY (transmitter ready) bit is on, and then it outputs the data byte.*

Adding External Storage

After I bought my first microcomputer and successfully entered and ran some simple programs, I started looking for some form of external storage. At the time, disk drives were still expensive and hard to locate, but the Kansas City standard cassette interface was becoming quite popular. I bought an interface card that had a UART and the modem circuits set for the Kansas City standard frequencies. The circuit only ran at 300 bits per second—slow compared to modern cassette interface standards.

A typical cassette interface uses a serial interface similar to the UART circuit described in the last section. In fact, the procedures described previously and shown in figure 3.38 work perfectly in this application.

Defining a Protocol

In its most primitive form, the cassette interface may be used like a paper-tape reader/punch, with no error checking (other than the parity bit) and no header bytes. A well-defined protocol writes data on a tape in blocks, with header and trailer bytes on each block, a file name, and the length (in bytes) of the file. This permits some fairly sophisticated error checking and greatly enhances a tape operating system.

A typical protocol (one that I designed for my Kansas City standard interface) is shown in figure 3.39. The block starts out with a string of nulls, followed by some STX characters (ASCII start of text). Next comes the file name in eight characters. Another STX character separates the file name from the load address, which is two bytes long, yielding a 16-bit address. Another STX is included, followed by the length or number of bytes of data coming. After the data (1 to 255) bytes are an ETX (end of text) byte, a checksum byte for error detection, and some more nulls. The advantage of this protocol is that it has some error checking and is fast. The disadvantage is that some bytes such as the load address fields or length are not properly error checked, which could have disastrous consequences if a bit or two were dropped in transmission.

BYTE	RECORD	
0 - 7	0	Nulls.
8 - 9	02H	STX.
10 - 17	8 chars.	Filename.
18 - 19	02H	STX
20	L	Load address.
21	H	
22	02H	STX.
23	0 - n	Record length (number of bytes of data).
24 - n		data (n) bytes.
$n + 1$	03H	ETX.
$n + 2$	CKS	Checksum.
$n + 3 - n + 7$	00H	Nulls.

Figure 3.39: *One possible cassette-interface data protocol.*

The Intel Hex—ASCII Format

Intel Corporation developed a protocol that has become an industry standard—the Hex-ASCII format, named because it is made up of a string of ASCII characters, with the data represented as two-digit hexadecimal numbers. This provides a lot of redundancy in transmission. Each byte is sent as a two-digit hexadecimal number encoded in ASCII. Figure 3.40 shows the Intel format.

The disadvantage of this format is that it takes approximately twice as long to send any block of data because each byte is sent as two ASCII characters. The main advantage is that it is reliable, and all the characters sent are printable characters.

BYTE	FIELD
1	Record identifier. ASCII colon (:).
2 - 3	Data byte count (values called n below).
4 - 7	Load address.
8 - 9	Unused (set to zeros).
10 - $(2 \times n + 10)$	Load data.
$2 \times n + 11, 2 \times n + 12$	Checksum byte
(CR, LF)	Records may be terminated by a carriage return and a line feed.

Figure 3.40: *Intel hexadecimal ASCII data format.*

Terminal Emulation

It is possible to make a video-based microcomputer emulate an intelligent terminal. This allows the user to access time-sharing computers that have cross-assemblers or compilers that may be used for software development. The procedure for a simple terminal emulator is shown in figure 3.41.

The emulator in figure 3.41 is extremely simple; it first initializes the serial interface, then enters a loop in which any character received from the serial interface is displayed on the console and any character received from the keyboard is sent to the serial interface. This assumes that the host computer is operating in full duplex mode. Full duplex means that the host computer echoes each character back to the terminal (in this case, the development system). Half duplex means that the host does not echo characters; the terminal is responsible for echoing each character locally. Full duplex is useful in situations in which the integrity of the transmission line is in question.

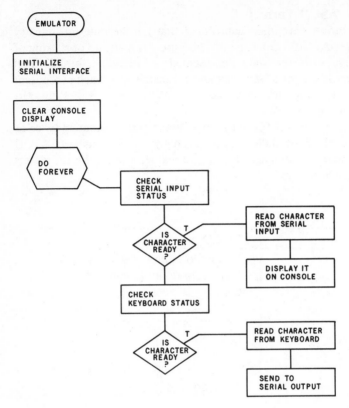

Figure 3.41: *A simple terminal emulator. This program emulates a "dumb terminal."*

Uploading and Downloading

A further enhancement to the terminal-emulation concept is uploading and downloading of data. In a sense, this is quite similar to the cassette storage technique described earlier. The host system may be used to save programs or data in the development system's memory. Conversely, programs may be developed on the host system using a cross-assembler or compiler that generates code for the particular microprocessor instruction set. Many cross-assemblers will generate hex-Intel format files that may be sent to the development system—if a hex-Intel loader is present in the terminal emulator. For example, the terminal emulator might be used (as a terminal) to develop a program and test for syntax errors. When the user is ready to test it, he or she might enter a command to transmit the file to the microcomputer. Immediately after hitting carriage return (to terminate the command), the user must place the microcomputer in the reader mode to accept the program as it comes to the serial interface. Typically, the terminal emulator watches for some special character (such as Control-L) and jumps to the hex-Intel loader procedure. Figure 3.42 shows a modified version of the terminal emulator with this feature.

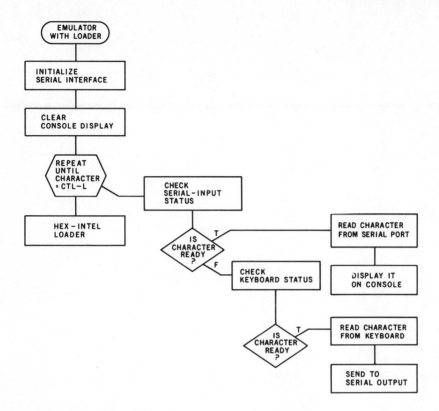

Figure 3.42: *Terminal emulator with hex-Intel loader feature.*

Uploading is accomplished in a similar way. The host computer is set up (a file is opened and put in the text input mode). A sequence of bytes (perhaps 32 bytes per record) is converted into the hex-Intel format, and then each byte is sent. At the end of each record, a carriage return and line feed are sent, and then the user goes to the next line. Some host computers operate on an XON, XOFF protocol, where XON means "I'm ready for a new line of text," and XOFF means "Don't send any more until you see the XON character." This allows the host to catch up, or in a time-sharing environment, it may be working on someone else's program. The uploader procedure must then be able to check for XON and XOFF (or whatever protocol the host uses) and wait for the ready signal.

4:
Medium to Large Systems

This chapter deals with the type of system that is now commonplace—the disk operating system (DOS). Figure 4.1 shows a typical medium-sized microcomputer that consists of a CPU, memory, and a console device, as in the development system. The difference is in the amount of memory (typically 16 K to 48 K bytes) and the type of external storage (at least a 5.25 inch minifloppy-disk drive). A single-density minifloppy disk will hold about 70 K bytes of data, and any number of disks may be used. Considering even this meager amount of disk storage combined with the fast access speed of disk drives (compared with tape drives), you can readily see the implications of low-cost disk technology.

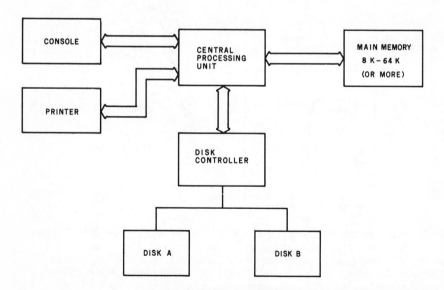

Figure 4.1: *A typical medium-sized microcomputer system.*

The System Environment

As shown in figure 4.2, the DOS is broken into several sections, starting with the nucleus (NUC), which handles resource allocation and access to I/O interfaces. The disk input/output (DIO) section supervises and controls user access to the disk drives. The byte-oriented input/output (BIO) section provides low-level subroutines used to access byte-oriented devices such as the console, tape-drive interface (if present), printer, and so on. The command interpreter (CINT) section may be considered to be an application program, because when it is in control of the system, it uses the resources made available through the NUC. Figure 4.3 shows the structural hierarchy of the DOS. Note that the application program (AP) may be the CINT and that the CINT can be transient (only in memory when needed).

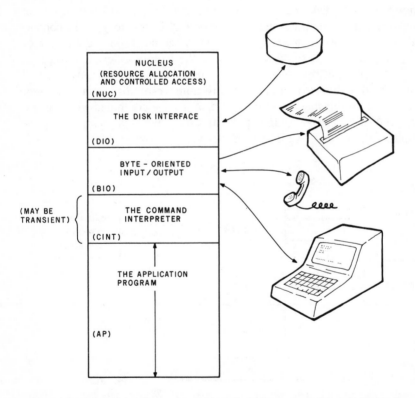

Figure 4.2: *The disk operating system (DOS). The operating system is broken into several segments. The nucleus (NUC) is the coordinator of all activities in the system. The byte-oriented input/output (BIO) and disk input/output (DIO) are hardware dependent, whereas the NUC and the command interpreter (CINT) are hardware independent. The application program (AP) area is available for the user's program.*

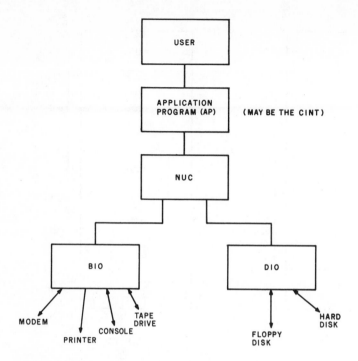

Figure 4.3: *The DOS. The BIO handles "character" I/O devices, whereas the DIO handles block-oriented devices like disks.*

Deciding Where to Put the DOS in Memory

Figure 4.4 shows the two common placements of the DOS in memory. There are many reasons for either placement, with advantages and disadvantages to each.

The low-memory version in figure 4.4a is convenient because the entire DOS is contiguous. This has a hidden advantage, because some absolute addresses and jumps cannot be moved around from version to version or if memory size changes. This feature is easily accommodated with the low-memory version. Secondly, if the system has 32 K bytes of memory and an additional 16 K bytes are added, the operating system need not be relocated in memory. The application program area (APA) will grow to the top of available memory and will not have to be moved from its starting address. Note that the APA can extend down to the lower limit of the CINT section, because the CINT is not needed when an application program is running.

The major disadvantages of the low-memory version are that the BIO and DIO sections cannot be easily expanded if more functions are added. If the BIO or DIO grows in size, the upper limit of the DOS will be increased, squeezing the APA. If programs are assembled or compiled at an absolute address, they will have to be recompiled at a higher address—clearly not a desirable feature.

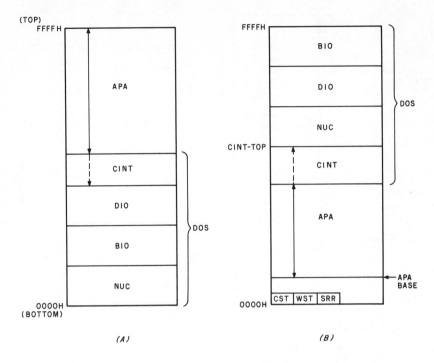

Figure 4.4: *Two locations for the DOS. The operating system can be organized in a number of ways. The NUC may start at the top or the bottom.*

The high-memory version in figure 4.4b is desirable because application programs are always loaded at the base address (APA BASE) and may extend up to the top of the CINT if necessary. The base of the NUC is the actual base of the DOS (excluding the CINT). If the BIO and DIO are increased in size, some space must be left at the top for their growth. Usually an extra 1000 bytes are left at the top for the system stack and other device-interface routines. Alternately, the whole DOS may be moved down to allow for an increase in its size.

The major disadvantage of the high-memory version is that the entire DOS must be relocated (all internal addresses must be added to an offset constant) to a higher memory address if more system memory is added.

The disadvantage of the low-memory version is easily overcome if all application programs are assembled or compiled into a relocatable object-code format rather than an absolute format. That is, the AP may be placed at any starting location in memory at load time and will execute properly. This is the standard approach used on larger computers and is a necessity in multiprogramming environments. Thus, for compatiblity and the capacity to upgrade to a multiuser environment, the relocatable format is the most desirable.

This still does not answer the question of low memory or high memory, however. If relocatable object modules are used for all application programs, then the relocatable format might as well be used for the DOS, making the problem somewhat academic. The only reason it is discussed is for the case of the absolute load address environment.

The Nucleus

The NUC is responsible for controlling access to the many devices attached to the system. Regardless of what the application program wants to do, it must go to the NUC and request service. To make the interface as straightforward as possible while still keeping it generalized, many currently available operating systems have one system subroutine that I will refer to as the system resource request (SRR) call. The SRR is placed in memory at a location that will never change from computer to computer—probably in low memory. When the SRR is called, it must be told what services are requested and must be given either data or a pointer to the data to be operated on. The requested function is selected by a number placed in a CPU register. Figure 4.5 is a typical list of functions.

NUMBER	FUNCTION
0	Perform a warm start.
1	Read a character from the console device.
2	Send a character to the console device.
3	Read a character from user device 1 (tape).
4	Write a character to user device 1 (tape).
5	Read a character from user device 2.
6	Write a character to user device 2 (printer).
7	Select disk.
8	Create file.
9	Open file.
10	Close file.
11	Delete file.
12	Read a block from file (sequential).
13	Write a block to file (sequential).
14	Read a block (random) (finds block).
15	Write a block (random) (finds block).
16	Read a byte from file (sequential).
17	Write a byte to file (sequential).
18	Rename file.
19	Write protect a disk.

Figure 4.5: *System resource request (SRR) functions for the hypothetical DOS.*

For example, if the AP wanted to read a character from the console, it would load the function number one into a CPU register (probably the accumulator) and would call the SRR. The SRR would return a character in some other register (depending upon the conventions set up by the NUC and the designer of the operating system). If the AP wished to open a disk file with the name DEMOPROG, it would have to set up a pointer to the character string DEMOPROG and load the function number nine into the accumulator. The SRR would then be called and would return with a status code indicating whether the open function was successful or not. If the file existed on the specified disk, the SRR might return a zero. If the file did not exist, the number one might be returned. If the disk drive was not turned on, or if the disk had been removed from the drive, different error messages might result. Although this requires the programmer to be more careful in his or her error-handling strategy, it also provides better control over the system environment.

NUC Functions

Figure 4.6 shows the internal organization of the NUC. The jump vectors in low memory are there for a reason. Many microprocessors have certain functions dedicated to low memory. The 8080/Z80 uses eight locations as restart or interrupt vectors. Also, it is quite common to have the CPU restart (reset) address at 0000H. Thus, in this example, the cold-start (system-start-up) jump vector is placed at 0000H. For convenience, the warm-start (CINT reload/reentry) vector is also put in low memory after the cold-start vector. The entry to the NUC is made available as the SRR call. This is the only way to request services from the NUC.

In figure 4.7a, the SRR (after saving all CPU registers) indexes into the SRR command table to get the address of the subroutine that will service the AP request. Figure 4.7b shows a typical indexing technique. Figure 4.7c is the same example implemented in 8080/Z80 assembly language.

Next, the SRR loads the address found in the table into a 16-bit register and jumps to the subprogram at that address. When the function is completed, the subprogram must jump to a common return module, which restores the CPU registers and returns to the application program.

The BIO Section

The BIO is responsible for all byte-oriented devices such as the system console, the printer, and tape drive (if available). When the NUC receives a request for service, it scans a table for the function number and transfers control to a lower-level routine that handles the actual I/O operation. These lower-level routines are located in the BIO and DIO sections. The start of the BIO contains a series of jump vectors that refer to all subroutines within the BIO. Figure 4.8 shows the internal layout of the BIO.

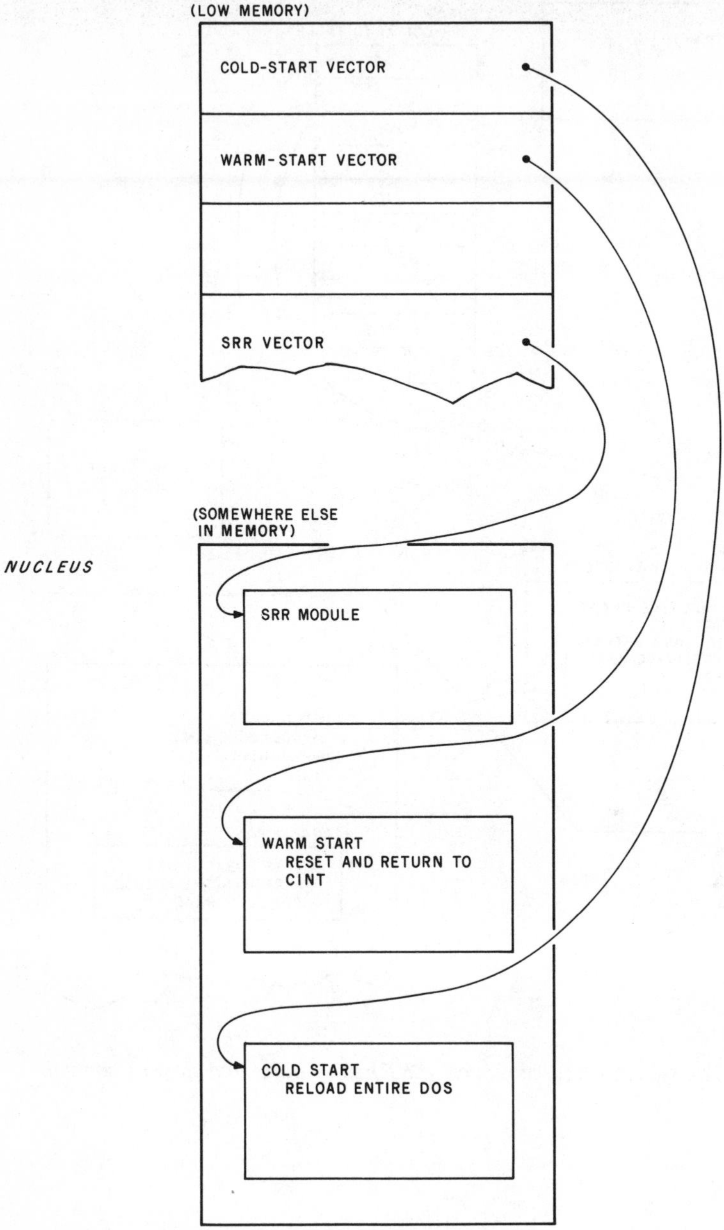

Figure 4.6: *The nucleus (NUC).*

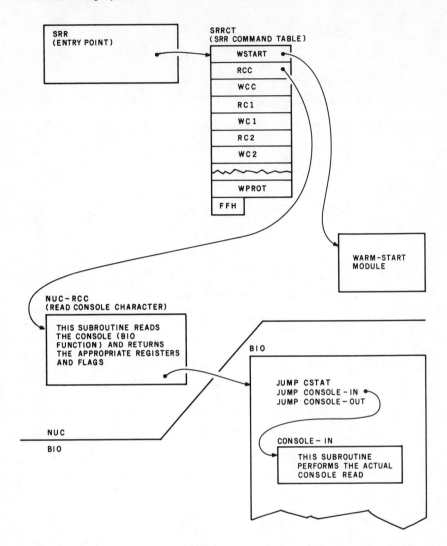

Figure 4.7a: *The system resource request (SRR) entry point and flow of control.*

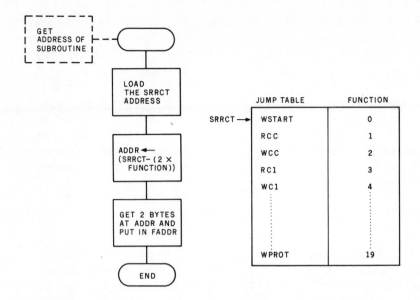

Figure 4.7b: *Indexing into the system resource request command table (SRRCT).*

```
; On entry, the C register must contain the function number
;
    LXI    H,SRRCT    ;load table address
    MVI    B,0
    DAD    B          ;SRRCT + function#
    DAD    B          ;SRRCT + (2 x function#)
    MOV    E,M
    INX    H
    MOV    D,M        ;get address in table into DE registers.
    XCHG              ;move it to HL registers.
    PCHL              ;jump to the address.
```

Figure 4.7c: *8080/Z80 example of indexing into the SRRCT.*

JMP	Console Status.
JMP	Console In.
JMP	Console Out.
JMP	User device 1 input.
JMP	User device 1 output.
JMP	User device 2 input.
JMP	User device 2 output.
JMP	User device 1 input status.
JMP	User device 2 input status.

Figure 4.8: *Internal layout of the BIO.*

The NUC may either call the BIO routine (via its jump vector) or may prefer to call a subroutine within itself to check for special conditions. For example, it might be wise to first check the status of the console before actually calling the console-read routine. If a character is not entered by the user within a reasonable period of time, the NUC might have better things to do than repeatedly checking a status bit. This strategy applies equally well to all input devices, since they have the opportunity to "hang" or bring to a halt all activity on the system. This may not seem useful on a single-user system, but when running a background task or in a mulitprogramming environment, it becomes critical. This will be discussed in greater detail in the section on multiprogramming.

The DIO Section

The DIO is considerably more complex than the BIO. The DIO must handle all the mechanical details of the disk drive, which is substantially more involved than a simple tape drive. Figure 4.9 is a block diagram of a disk controller. Most controllers are wait-state driven, meaning that they put the processor into a wait state until they are ready to proceed. However, some controllers can be run in an interrupt-driven mode, in which they signal the CPU when the disk is ready to transfer data to or from the microcomputer.

The disk-controller chip performs many timing and control functions that previously required dozens of integrated circuits. It is responsible for loading and unloading (raising and lowering) the read/write head of the selected disk drive and track seeking (finding the requested track on the disk). It must also perform the serial-to-parallel and parallel-to-serial data conversions when information is transferred to and from the disk. Other capabilities include error-code checking, error generation, and IBM 3740 format soft-sector recording. When a sector of data is being read or written, the data rate of the disk is synchronized with the CPU by inserting wait states (hence the name wait-state controller) until the controller is ready for the next byte of data. On full-size (eight-inch) disk drives, the data rate is one byte every 32 microseconds, or 31,250 bytes per second. On 5.25-inch disk drives, the data rate is one byte every 64 microseconds, or 15,625 bytes per second.

Data is recorded on a floppy disk in tracks and sectors. Figure 4.10 shows how tracks are organized on disk. An eight-inch disk has room for over twice the number of tracks as a 5.25-inch disk. A track is divided into sectors with a gap or unrecorded space between sectors. Two types of disk formats, the hard sectored and the soft sectored, are in general use. Hard-sectored disks have index holes wherever a new sector starts. Thus if a disk is "formatted" for 10 sectors, there will be 10 holes in the disk in a concentric circle where the single hole is in figure 4.10. The holes are located by a small light source and phototransistor mounted above and below the hole in the disk enclosure. Hard-sectored disks are easier to program for because the programmer does not have to be concerned with finding the sector. The disadvantage is lack of flexibility. The disk controller shown in figure 4.9 can be configured (by changing the software and a few jumpers on the board) to operate on either minifloppy-disk or full-size floppy-disk drives, with up to 26 sectors per track. This also means that one can write programs that will read nonstandard disk formats. This is not possible with a hard-sectored format.

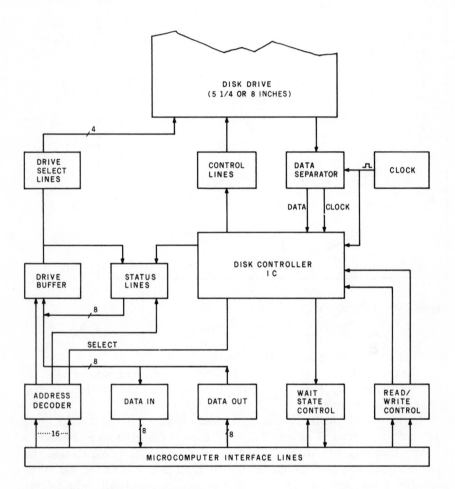

Figure 4.9: *A floppy-disk controller.*

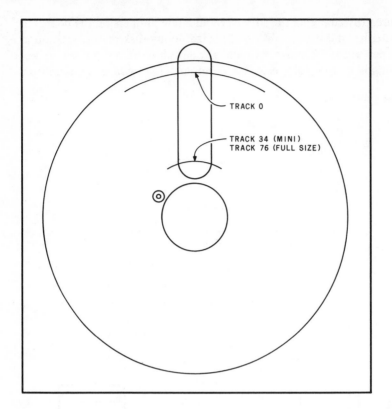

Figure 4.10: *A floppy disk.*

Reading and Writing a Sector of Data

The two most important functions of the controlling software are sector-read and sector-write. Figure 4.11 gives the structured flowchart for a typical sector-read subroutine.

In figure 4.11, the first action of the subroutine is to select the disk drive and track to be read. This information is usually stored in several reserved memory locations within the DIO. Next, the hardware is told to find the specified track and position the read/write head over it. The software then loads the destination memory address (referred to as ADDR) into a CPU register and loads the BYTE-COUNT (128 bytes per sector in this case) into another CPU register. After outputting a READ command to the controller, the CPU enters a loop that repeats until BYTE-COUNT reaches zero. Each iteration of the loop gets one byte of data from the controller and deposits it in memory. The ADDR pointer is incremented to the next memory location and the BYTE-COUNT is decremented. BYTE-COUNT is then tested for a zero condition. If zero, the subroutine waits for a not-busy signal from the controller and then checks for errors. If no errors are found, a normal return is performed.

A sector-write is nearly identical, except data is taken from memory at the address in ADDR and is sent to the controller by way of the output port.

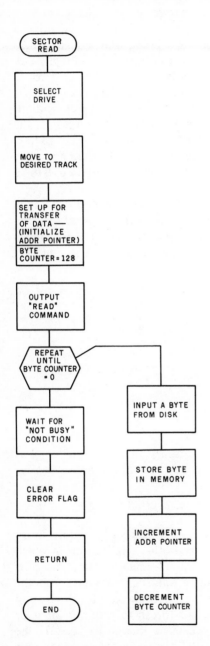

Figure 4.11: *Sector-read routine.*

Drive and Track Selection

In the previous example, the details of disk-drive and track selection were left out. The box in figure 4.11 that says "select drive" is actually a subroutine in and of itself. Select drive checks to see if the requested drive is already selected. If it is, a normal return is taken. If not, the new drive is selected (by outputting the drive number to a port), and a delay of 35 milliseconds is performed to allow the read-write head to settle into place. A check is made to be sure that the new drive is ready. If not, an error is reported to the calling program. If the new drive is ready, the track address is read from the disk to inform the software of the current disk-head location.

The second box in figure 4.11 is another subroutine that checks for the current location of the disk head and moves it to the requested track address if necessary. It also checks to see that the requested track and sector addresses are valid (within the allowed range of 0 to 34 for minifloppy drives or 0 to 76 for full-size drives).

Although other functions are required by the NUC for full control of the disk drives, these subroutines provide the majority of the required services. Figure 4.12 shows the internal organization of the DIO. The NUC-DIO interface will be discussed in greater detail in the data-management section.

JMP	Select-Disk
JMP	Set-Track
JMP	Set-Selector
JMP	Set-Memory-Address
JMP	Read-Sector
JMP	Write-Sector
JMP	Format-Track
	[Body of DIO]

Figure 4.12: *Internal organization of the DIO.*

Interrupt-Driven Disk Controllers

Most floppy-disk controller boards have provisions for interrupts. Interrupts are useful in multiuser environments and other applications in which the CPU must service requests from several sources. In a wait-state controller (as described earlier), the CPU is forced into a wait state until data from the disk is ready. This can seriously degrade the performance of an operating system. In larger computers, the CPU is not forced to wait for input or output devices. The I/O interfaces are intelligent enough to perform the required operations and then inform the CPU that the data is ready or that the operation has been completed. In the case of a disk controller, the CPU might issue a seek-track command and wait for an interrupt to occur, indicating that the desired track had been found. While waiting for the track to be found, the CPU might be able to execute several thousand instructions of another program. The same concept may be applied to almost all disk I/O operations. Figure 4.13 shows the sector-read process as it might be coded if interrupts are used.

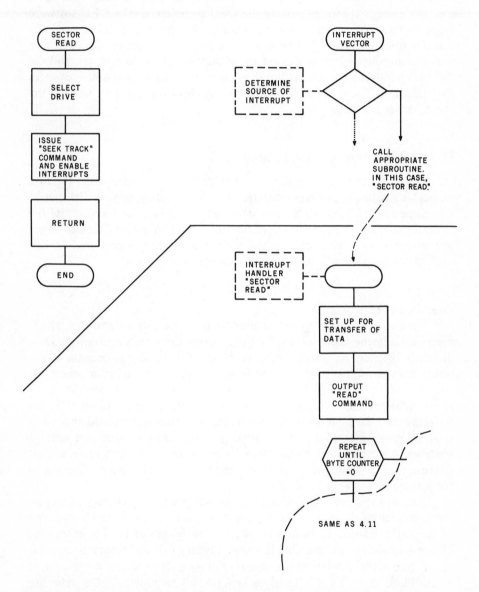

Figure 4.13: *The interrupt-driven version of the sector-read routine in figure 4.11.*

DMA Controllers

DMA controllers have additional circuitry that accesses system memory as if it were the CPU. This is accomplished by disabling the processor while the operation (i.e., memory-read or memory-write) is being performed. This allows the controller to transfer large blocks of data directly into main memory at high speed, bypassing the CPU completely. The CPU software requirements are greatly reduced because the controller takes over the transfer function. The CPU need only load some registers on the controller that contain the desired track and sector address, the load address, and the desired operation. The controller then takes over the system and completes the operation. The processor can then simply check a status port to see if the function has been completed.

Data Management on a Floppy Disk

The method of storing data on a floppy disk (or hard disk, for that matter) is a prime consideration in terms of system efficiency. A disk can be viewed in several ways: as a glorified cassette interface, as a sequential-file allocation device with a directory of files, as a random-access (track or sector allocation) device with a directory, or as a random-access device with multiple directories or a hierarchy of directories.

Sequential Allocation

The cassette-interface method and the sequential-file allocation methods are essentially the same, except that the former does not necessarily have a directory of files. As shown in figure 4.10, a floppy disk is organized into tracks (concentric circles) and sectors (equal-sized segments of a concentric circle). Each track and each sector is addressable through software. Thus, the sector-write routine in figure 4.11 could be used along with a simple DO loop to record data on a floppy disk, and the sector-read routine could be used to read the data back. Figure 4.14 shows a typical cassette-style data-storage routine using the sector-read/sector-write procedure in figure 4.11. Note that the read routine would be identical except that the sector-read routine would replace the sector-write routine.

A more advanced sequential-allocation scheme has a directory of files on the first track of the disk. Each entry in the directory has the name and type of a file, the starting track and sector, and the length of the file in sectors. Figure 4.15 shows one possible implementation of this directory structure.

Figure 4.15a introduces the directory entry in the form of a file control block (FCB). Each FCB is 16 bytes long (in this example). If 128 bytes are stored in each disk sector, then eight FCBs will fit in one sector. Figure 4.15b shows the entire disk directory as a series of sectors in track one. When the nucleus needs to find a file on the disk, it consults the directory by reading it one sector at a time. The procedure in figure 4.16 shows how to search the directory.

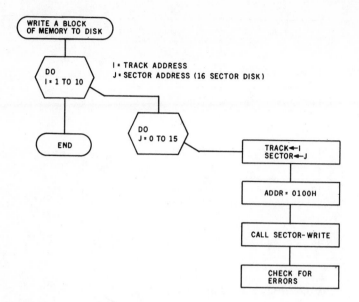

Figure 4.14: *Writing a floppy disk.*

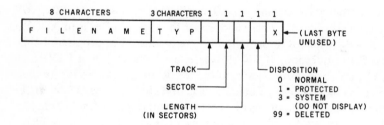

Figure 4.15a: *One possible design for the file control block (FCB).*

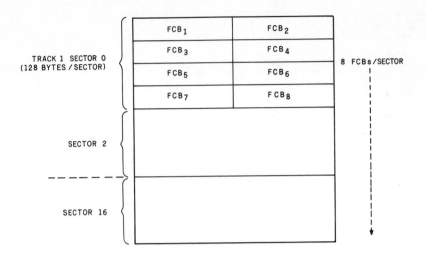

Figure 4.15b: *The disk directory (16 bytes per FCB).*

In figure 4.16, the DO-WHILE loop checks for the file name and file type, which are found by indexing into each FCB. The starting address of each FCB is computed by looping from 0 to 128 (the sector length) in steps of 16—the FCB length. Since the base address of the sector buffer is in ADDR, ADDR + J + K (where K is the byte index) gives us the appropriate fields within the FCB in question. If FNAME is equal to NAME and FTYPE is equal to TYP, the loop terminates, and the test is made again to insure that the file name has indeed been located. This is done because the DO-WHILE may terminate on the loop portion (I = 0 to 15) without ever finding the file name. If the names are found to match, the FCB attributes such as TRK, SCTR, LENGTH, and DISP are loaded from the ADDR + J area, and a normal return is taken. If the test fails, an error code 1 is loaded into the accumulator (or other designated register), and control is returned to the calling program.

Sector Mapping

A typical problem with the slower floppy-disk drives (primarily the minifloppies) is that if a sector is located and read, the disk will have moved beyond the next sector before the software can get around to reading it. Thus each sector-read (or write) takes an entire revolution of the disk. The solution to this problem is sector mapping. Figure 4.17 shows the internal mapping of sectors in both a normal disk and a sector-mapped disk. Notice that in figure 4.17b, each logical sector is mapped three sectors in the clockwise direction compared with the previous logical sector. This offset of three sectors gives the software time to catch up without having to wait for each revolution of the disk. This technique is somewhat more useful in a sequential sector-allocation disk format. If random sector allocation is done, the more random the allocation, the less useful sector mapping becomes.

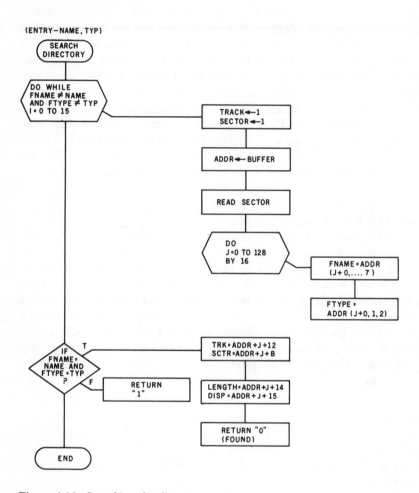

Figure 4.16: *Searching the directory.*

Random Allocation

Sequential sector allocation has its problems. When a file is deleted, the directory entry is flagged, indicating that the file is gone, but the space used by the file is still unavailable. To reclaim it, one of two approaches may be used. First, if a new file is created, the CREATE function of the NUC could look for deleted files before adding new files at the top of the directory. If the new file (of predetermined size) fits in the space of the old file, everything is fine. If the new file is smaller, some space is wasted with no way of reclaiming it. If more files are deleted and new ones created, eventually the entire disk will consist of files with unused gaps between them. This process is called *fragmentation*. A solution to this problem is to compact the disk every so often. A procedure for doing this is discussed in the section on reclaiming space.

The solution to the sequential-allocation problem is random allocation. Any unit of space may be allocated to a file on a random basis, meaning that a file may be spread over the entire disk. The FCB must then maintain a list of sector allocations so the file can be read sequentially. Not only sectors but also tracks or other units of space may be handled just as easily.

Figure 4.18 shows an example of a sector allocation system. Since a diskette can have more than 256 sectors, this example uses a two-byte field for each sector pointer in the FCB. When a file is created, an FCB is added to the directory. No sectors are allocated to the file until something is written into it. When this happens, the NUC looks in the directory to find an unallocated sector and then adds it to the list of sectors assigned to the file.

Keeping Track of Available Sectors

The NUC must have some way of finding unallocated sectors. Two common schemes are discussed here. First, to reduce the waste of fragmentation, a list of holes or gaps could be kept. Figure 4.19a shows a typical list that corresponds with the allocation map in figure 4.18. As new sectors are allocated, the list of holes is updated to reflect those changes. Also, when files are deleted, the entire file can be listed as a single hole. The disadvantage of this scheme is that the list is difficult to generate from the FCBs in the directory. It would probably have to be kept on disk and loaded into memory while the disk is logged into the system.

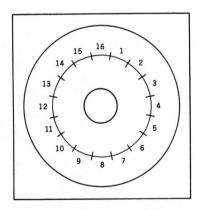

(A)

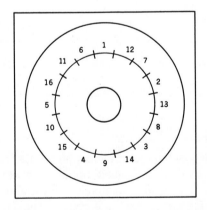

(B)

Figure 4.17: *Sector mapping schemes for a 16-sector disk.*

FCB
(32 BYTES TOTAL)

8	3	1			SECTOR MAP	(16 BYTES)							
FNAME	FTYPE	5	E_X	0010	0002	0003	0006	0007					
FNAME 2	FTYPE2	7	E_X	0001	0004	0005	0008	0009	000A	0015			

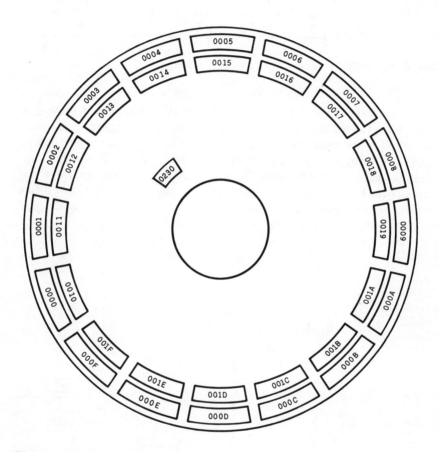

Figure 4.18: *Random sector allocation.*

SECTOR #	LENGTH OF HOLE
0000	0001
000B	0005
0011	0004
0016	0220

Figure 4.19a: *Keeping track of available sectors in a diskette-allocation map.*

	OF	0E	0D	0C	0B	0A	09	08	07	06	05	04	03	02	01	00
00	0	0	0	0	0	1	1	1	1	1	1	1	1	1	1	0
01	0	0	0	0	0	0	0	0	0	0	1	0	0	0	0	1
02	0	0	0	0	0	0	0	0	0	0	0	0	0	0	0	0
03	0	0	0	0	0	0	0	0	0	0	0	0	0	0	0	0

Figure 4.19b: *A "0" bit indicates an unallocated sector.*

The second common organization is shown in figure 4.19b. A bit map of sectors is kept in memory for each disk that is active and logged in. A zero in a bit position indicates that the sector is unallocated. This map is easily constructed from a list of FCBs in the directory. Figure 4.20 shows a procedure for generating a bit map. Updating this map is quite easy; one just calculates the bit position (from the sector address) and changes the bit to a one if the sector is going to be used. If the sector is being returned to the pool of unused sectors, changing the bit to zero is all that is required.

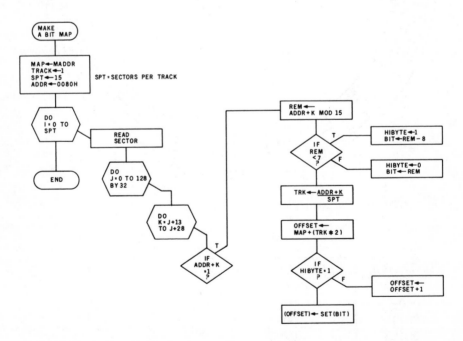

Figure 4.20: *Generating the bit map in figure 4.19b.*

Extents

Using the FCB example in figure 4.18 makes it possible to have files of up to only 16 sectors (2048 bytes at 128 bytes per sector), which is not much. To allow for larger files, one could have a much longer FCB. If a disk has 560 sectors, that would mean having a 580-byte FCB—clearly not very efficient. The standard solution to this problem is to have dummy FCBs following the first FCB, each with 16 sectors of the file. The NUC must be intelligent enough to know when it has reached the end of the first FCB so it can issue a search for the next one. This process can continue up to any reasonable number of FCBs (with 560 sectors maximum, this would mean 35 FCBs). The number of extents is placed in the first FCB of a group in the EX field in figure 4.18. Note that in most systems, allocations are done on blocks of sectors rather than individual sectors to save space in the directory and make addressing and allocating easier. If sectors are allocated in blocks of eight, then each FCB would have room for 16 blocks of eight sectors or 16 K bytes of file space. With this arrangement, a maximum of four extents would then be possible with a 560-sector disk.

Extending a File

In a sequential allocation system, files cannot readily be extended because there are other files in the way. You would have to move up all files on the disk the required number of sectors and then update the directory to reflect the shift. In a random allocation method, files can be extended by simply allocating more sectors and adding the sector addresses to the end of the list of sectors in the FCB. If the FCB is full, the NUC must create an extent FCB and change the first FCB to reflect the number of extents. This method of extending a file is probably the most straightforward, uncomplicated procedure available.

Reclaiming Disk Space

Some disk housekeeping is always necessary. As discussed in previous sections, holes or gaps will eventually show up on a disk. This space is wasted unless it is properly reclaimed and redistributed. In a sequential allocation environment, gaps in the disk must be closed to produce one large block of free space at the high end of the disk. This is accomplished by moving all files down toward sector zero and then updating the directory to reflect their new positions. The procedure in figure 4.21 will accomplish this.

In a random allocation environment, the task becomes trivial because the allocation mechanism used to keep track of available sectors does the job for itself. See figure 4.19.

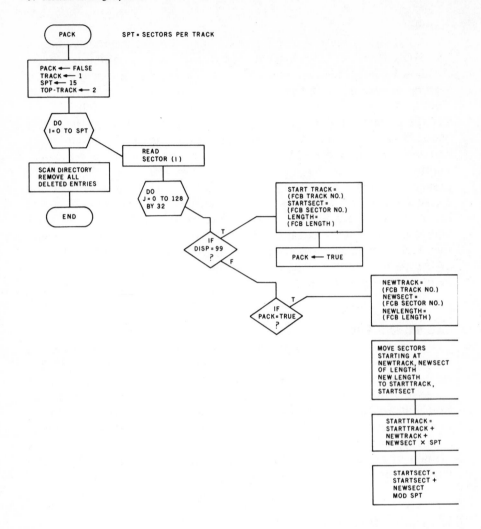

Figure 4.21: *Reclaiming space in a sequential allocation environment.*

The Console Command Interpreter

The Console Command Interpreter (CINT) is actually an application program operating in the APA and using the resources of the DOS. As shown in figure 4.22, the APA can extend up to the top of the CINT or, in other terms, to one byte less than the start of the nucleus. The reason for this is obvious: when an application program is running, there is no need for the CINT. The NUC, BIO, and DIO are all that are needed if the program is to access disk or byte-oriented I/O.

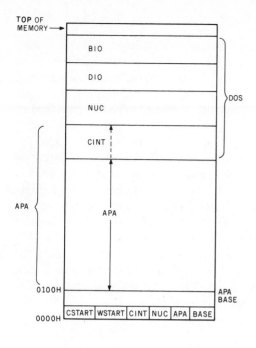

Figure 4.22: *The command interpreter (CINT). The application program area (APA) bottom is APA BASE. The APA top is NUC minus one.*

The Functions of the CINT

The purpose of the CINT is to monitor the DOS and to allow the user to control the system through it. It acts like the development-system monitor discussed in Chapter 3. For purposes of hardware independence, the CINT is restricted to using resources provided through the NUC.

Implementing Commands

A wide variety of services must be available through the CINT so that the user will not have to write programs to perform routine tasks. Some of these include allocating space for a new file, deleting old files, executing application programs, listing the contents of the directory, copying files and disks (discussed in Chapter 9), and printing files. Some of these functions will be used quite frequently, but others, such as copying a disk, may be used only once a week. It is important to decide which commands are to be resident within the CINT and which commands or functions can be called from disk when needed. The latter are often referred to as transient commands.

Handling Transient Commands

Transient commands are system functions that must be loaded when needed, such as disk copy, file copy, and print file. Transient commands can also be application programs written by the user. As long as the program is in a standard format (such as hex-Intel or straight binary data) the DOS does not care if it is a user program or a system command. The file-type field of the FCB is used to distinguish executable application programs from other types of files on disk. The file type could be TRN for transient, COM for command, or AP for application program. When the user enters a command on the CINT, it first looks at its internal resident command table for built-in functions. If it is not found there, the CINT starts searching the disk directory for file names with a file type of TRN (if TRN is the established file type for a transient command or a user program). If it finds a file with a file name equal to the command and the correct file type, it loads the file into the APA and jumps to the start of the APA. If the user creates a program using the assembler program and editor and then wishes to make it into a new command, he or she needs only to put TRN in the file-type field. The procedure in figure 4.23 outlines this search sequence.

Recognizing Operands

Some commands require operands, just as the development-system commands require operands. A common technique is to copy the input command string (less the command at the beginning) into a buffer that will be available to the application program (or resident command) when it takes control. In addition, the CINT might look at the input command string for file names (or what look like file names) and set up file-control blocks for the AP to save it the trouble. In this case, the CINT would scan for sequences of characters that do not start with numerics and for blanks between groups of characters to determine where each file name begins and ends. This procedure is not critical, but merely aids the AP and the programmer.

The Application Program

When loaded, the application program resides in the APA and can extend up to the top of the CINT. To be fully hardware independent, the AP must use only services provided by the NUC and obtained through the SRR, as described in the section about the NUC. The AP has some duties and responsiblities to the system. First, it must not extend above the upper limit of the CINT or, conversely, the lower limit of the NUC, as this will probably result in crashing the system. Secondly, it must observe the protocol of the SRR and not attempt to bypass it, as this will result in a lack of hardware independence. Sometimes the SRR must be bypassed when dealing with hardware that the NUC does not have responsibility for. For example, if the AP uses a specialized video display or graphics board, the operating system may not have the facilities needed to deal with it, so the user must fend for himself. If the hardware conflicts with the operating system, or if the required hardware addresses are not in the same place in all versions of the system, the user should write the software so that it can easily conform to variations in the hardware. In the case of a memory-mapped video board, the AP should be written so that the address of the video board can be changed in one location, rather than having to recompile or reassemble the entire program to make the change. The best approach to this dilemma is to follow the advice of Chapter 2: if the function is used frequently or by many different application programs, it should probably go in the operating system.

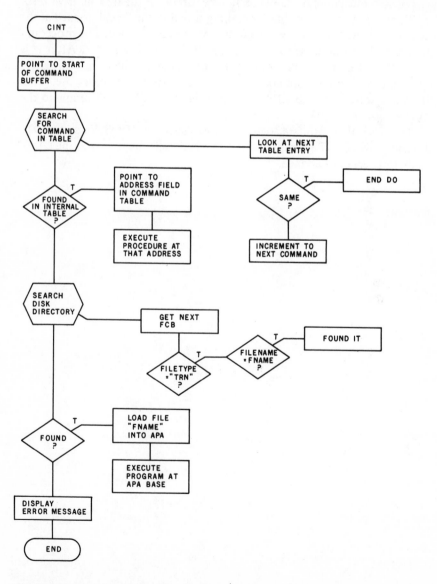

Figure 4.23: *CINT command interpreter section.*

Loading the DOS

When the microcomputer system is powered on and reset, the operating system must be loaded in from disk in order to begin execution. This means that some program—a "loader"—must be in memory after the computer is powered on. The process of loading the system is called the initial program load (IPL). A slang term for it is boot-loading, from the idea of "pulling the DOS on by the bootstraps." Usually, some PROM software is placed on the disk-controller board, which, when given control, loads in the first several tracks (which must contain the DOS in its entirety) of the disk in drive zero. The IPL program is responsible for making sure that the DOS is loaded at the correct address and that it is given control after being loaded. The procedure in figure 4.11 can be used to read in the DOS sector by sector. After it is loaded, the IPL transfers control to the NUC, where an initializer subprogram sets up the pointers and jump vectors in low memory (i.e., cold start, warm start, jump to CINT, jump to NUC, SRR), then jumps to the entry point of the CINT.

The CINT then prints a log-on message such as "DOS Version 1.00" and displays the CINT prompt character, which tells the user that the CINT is ready to accept commands.

5:
Multiuser and Multiprogramming Environments

Until recently, no well-designed multiuser operating systems were available for microcomputers such as the 8080/Z80, 6502, or 6800. There are actually some good reasons for this delay. Most 8-bit microprocessors simply do not have the facilities to handle multiple users in an efficient manner. Secondly, even though multiuser operating systems are now available, the response time is slow. This does not mean that the concept should be abandoned. On the contrary, there are many circumstances in which multiuser or multiprogramming systems would be most efficient and cost effective.

Interrupt-Driven Systems

To begin the discussion of generalized multiprogramming, I will describe a more primitive form of multiuser operating system that uses interrupts. As explained in Chapters 2 and 3, several levels of interrupts may be used in most microprocessors. Generally, hardware on the CPU board is used to prioritize these interrupt levels, giving higher priority to certain external stimuli than to others. Figure 5.1 shows the hardware of such a system. When an interrupt is detected on line three, for example, the hardware looks to see if an interrupt has come in from any level higher than three. If a higher one is in progress, the hardware will wait until the current level has completed its task (until the CPU acknowledges) and then allow the lower level interrupt to be processed.

A simple multiuser system could be designed using this scheme. If each user terminal were connected to an interrupt level, each character coming from the terminal would cause an interrupt to occur. The interrupt-handler software would then be responsible for adding the character to the buffer of incoming characters from that terminal. An interrupt-driven system might be used in a process-control environment, where timing is crucial. Even if the response time is slow, at least the user has the satisfaction of knowing that all incoming characters will be received without incident.

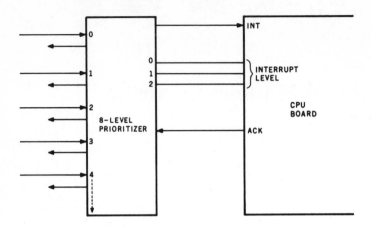

Figure 5.1: *Prioritized interrupts.*

Several programming strategies are possible when using the above hardware. First, each character can be fed to a buffer, and upon receipt of a carriage return, the entire line is processed at once. Secondly, a circular or first-in-first-out (FIFO) buffer can be used. In this case, the application program tests a flag that indicates when a character has been received and placed in the buffer. In either case, several processes are running concurrently.

Some Definitions

Before proceeding, I should clarify the definitions of some terms. A *multiuser operating system* is one that can service the requests of more than one user or programmer at once. This does not mean that the users are being handled simultaneously. Each user or programmer is serviced within a short time frame before control is passed to another user. Since this process is happening at high speeds, the individual users do not normally notice these delays.

A *multiprogramming environment* is similar to a multiuser environment, except it implies a more sophisticated approach to the problem. Instead of just servicing several users at once, it may also run background programs that run independently of a specific user.

Multitasking is another term for multiprogramming.

A *background job* or program is one that is hidden from view and runs in a low-priority mode. A background job can be any normal program that does not need user prompting or assistance and often needs to run for a long time.

Time-sharing refers to one form or another of multiprogramming.

A *task* is essentially the same as an application program, although a task need not be a full-fledged program. It may be a subroutine or subprogram that an application program started for its own use.

Generalized Multitasking

A multitasking operating system must perform duties in addition to those described in Chapter 4. Since there may be several programs running in the machine, devices such as consoles, printers, and disks have to be allocated or assigned to a program. If this is not done, each program will attempt to use the same devices, causing havoc. Also, the DOS must be responsible for switching from one program to another. Each program must have an opportunity to execute, or the program is said to be "locked out" of the machine. To the user, it would appear that the computer had lost track of him or her, or that the machine had gone down.

To accomplish this, two methods are used, either independently or in conjunction. First, interrupts may be used, but in a more efficient manner than described earlier. One interrupt line is connected to a counter circuit that generates a pulse every 10 milliseconds (an arbitrary figure). Every time an interrupt occurs, control is transferred to the NUC, which determines (by priority scheduling) which program should get control next. The second method requires less complicated hardware, but is more dangerous. Since virtually all programs use some form of input or output, control is gained when the application program uses the SRR vector. The SRR is written with a built-in trap for the program scheduler. The desired I/O operation is performed, but instead of returning to the calling program, control is transferred to the next program waiting in line.

The second method is more dangerous, because if the application program gets into an infinite loop, control will never be returned to the NUC, so all other users will be locked out, perhaps forever. The solution is to combine these two methods. The result is a reliable mechanism for gaining control from an application program.

Transfer of Control

When either an interrupt occurs or the SRR is called, the NUC regains control of the system. First it must save all registers and status flags of the application program. Normally this is done by saving them on the application program's stack. Once they are pushed onto the stack, the stack itself must be protected. It is immediately apparent that one cannot simply pass control to the next AP, because the last AP's stack would be vulnerable.

The solution (on most microprocessors) is to retrieve the stack pointer and save it in a fixed-memory location. Since other vital information about each task must be kept, it would be convenient to have it all in one place for easy reference. A *control block* or table refers to such a group of related pieces of information. In this case, the control block will be called the task-control table (TCT). Normally I distinguish between control blocks and control tables in that tables contain information about many tasks or application programs, but blocks contain information specific to a particular task.

Each TCT entry contains the task identification number, its status, the entry point (or starting address) of the task, and a save area for its stack pointer (see figure 5.2). The last field shown in figure 5.2 is the task I/O block (TIOB) pointer. Its function will be discussed later. The current-task indicator (CTI) is a pointer to the currently active task in the system. It enables the NUC and SRR to locate information and pointers within the TCT when I/O functions are requested.

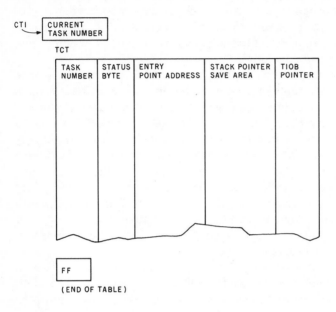

Figure 5.2: *The task-control table (TCT).*

When the SRR gains control, it first completes the requested I/O operation and then transfers control to the multitasking dispatcher program. The dispatcher first saves all CPU registers and flags on the application program's own stack. Then it looks at the CTI to find out which task was last in control (see figure 5.3). Once it has the address of the TCT entry for that task, it computes the location (within the table entry) of the stack-pointer save area. It then copies the stack pointer (the application program stack pointer or APSP) into this save area.

After the current status of the task (reflected in the contents of the stack and the stack-pointer save area) has been carefully preserved, the dispatcher is free to find new work for the system. The second field of the TCT, the status byte, keeps track of several useful bits of information (see figure 5.4).

The status byte contains a bit that indicates whether the task has been stopped by the user. By console command, the user or operator of the system may suspend a task for any length of time. The task is still in memory, but it will never execute. The dispatcher will skip over it each time it looks for work to do. Although it is possible to establish a priority scheme, it would serve no purpose in this example. Priority scheduling is useful only if tasks can be put into a wait state while I/O operations are being performed. I have chosen not to allow it in this example.

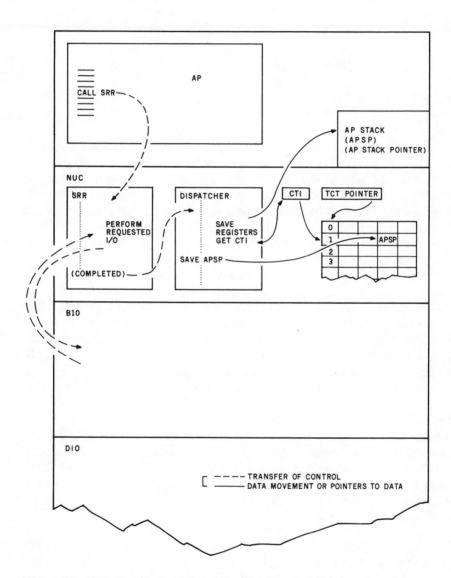

Figure 5.3: *Transfer of control and data movement within the system resource request (SRR), dispatcher, and task-control table (TCT).*

```
bit 0
    1 ⎫
    2 ⎬    Task Priority.
    3 ⎭
    4
    5
    6
    7        Task is suspended if 1.
```

Figure 5.4: *The TCT status byte.*

To prioritize tasks, bits 0 to 3 could be used to hold a number from 0 to 15, where 15 was the highest-priority task. Whenever the dispatcher got control, it would look at the priority bits. The task found with the highest priority would always get first choice at control of the system. If the task were waiting on I/O or had been suspended by the user, the dispatcher would go on to the next highest priority task, and so on. It becomes obvious that if a task could never be suspended (except by the user), only the highest priority task in the system would ever be allowed to execute.

Several other prioritizing schemes are possible, even if I/O waits are not used. The simplest form of prioritizing is called round-robin scheduling. In Figure 5.5, each task is given its turn, without playing favorites. If a task has been suspended, it is simply ignored by the dispatcher. If there are 10 tasks, this system gives each task one time unit for every 10 units, assuming that only a 10-millisecond timer is involved in task switching. If use of the SRR causes task switching, it would cause uneven time units.

The second method of prioritizing tasks makes use of the relatively even time units of the timer interrupts, but would work equally well with only the SRR-dispatcher calls. All priorities of all active tasks are summed. In figure 5.6, the total is 65. Thus for each 65 time units, (either 65 × 10 milliseconds, or 65 SRR calls, or some combination of both), tasks zero and one will each get 15 time units, while task six will only get one time unit out of 65. This form of scheduling will work on any system with any arrangement of dispatching. If a task is suspended, the total of the task priorities must be updated.

Allocating I/O Devices

Each task must communicate with input and output devices. If each task merely assumed that the system console or printer were available for exclusive use, the results would be disastrous. The output would be a confusing mix of characters from each task. The NUC must in some way control the allocation of I/O devices on the system. This is most easily accomplished by establishing a logical/physical-device reference table for each task.

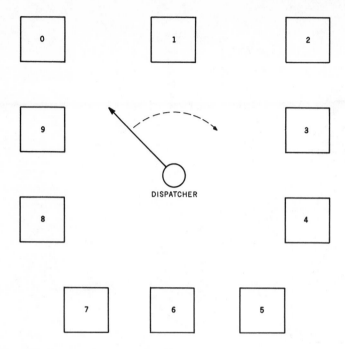

Figure 5.5: *Round-robin scheduling.*

TASK #	PRIORITY
0	15
1	15
2	14
3	12
4	5
5	3
6	1
	65 Total of Priorities

Figure 5.6: *Time-unit priority dispatching.*

In the TCT (see figure 5.2), the TIOB entry is a pointer to the task input/output block. As shown in figure 5.8, the TIOB has three fields for each entry: the function number (as shown in figure 4.5), the device code, and the reference name. The device code tells the SRR which physical device the function number is mapped into. More than one function number (or logical device) may map into a physical device under certain circumstances. The name field allows the user to refer to a device by name, such as CIN or PRTR.

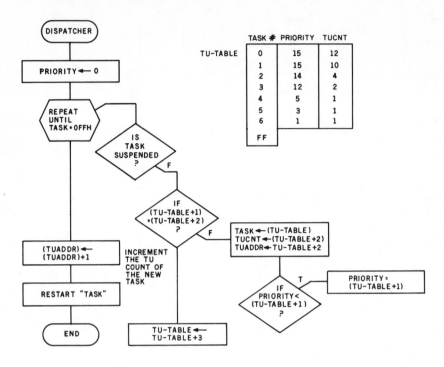

Figure 5.7: *Priority-scheduling algorithm.*

Ideally, when a task wishes to allocate a device (such as the console), it should have a way of referencing a specific console, without having to refer to the actual physical device. The name field allows the programmer to open a device (or disk file) by generic name without bothering with numbers. The open function then allocates the device, ensures that the TIOB table entries are correct, and then returns the function number assigned to the device. The programmer is then responsible for keeping track of the assigned function number.

The System Device Table

The NUC must have some way of knowing which devices are available and how to access them. The system device table (SDT) in figure 5.9 is one possible implementation of this concept. The device number is the assigned physical device number referred to by the TIOB-device-number entry. The status byte indicates to the NUC what the device is capable of and whether it is already allocated to another task. Bit zero indicates whether the device is shareable (as in the case of a disk drive), bit one tells if the device is to be used for input, and bit two indicates if it can be used as an output device. If both input and output are allowed, the device-driver subroutine must have some way of knowing which function has been requested when called. This is usually accomplished by loading a CPU register with a code number. Bit three tells the NUC if the device has been opened by a task, and bit four indicates if the device is defined to the system or not. Bit four is present to allow a device to have an "off-line" status without removing it from the table. For example, if a printer were down for repairs, the system could be told with a console command that that device was undefined, preventing users from allocating it. The task-number field is updated when the device is opened or allocated by a task.

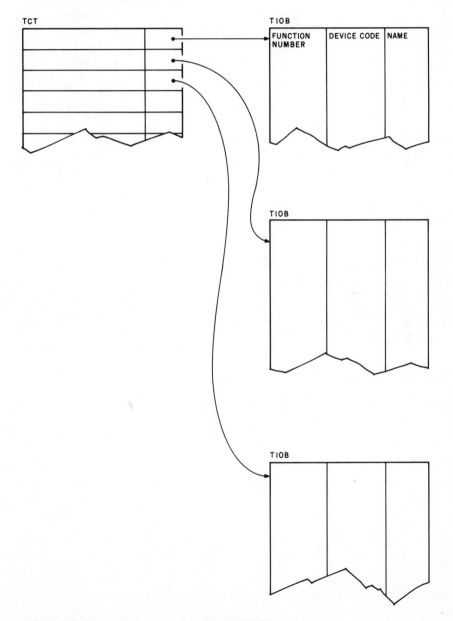

Figure 5.8: *The task input/output block (TIOB).*

SYSTEM DEVICE TABLE

SDT	Device #	Status	Task #	Device Name	Device Driver Address	Description
	0			CON		Console 0
	1			CON		Console 1
	2			CON		Console 2
	3			CON		Console 3
	4			CON		Console 4
	5			CON		Console 5
	6			PRTR		Printer 0
	7			PRTR		Printer 1
	8			DISKA		Disk drives
	9			DISKB		Disk drives
	10			DISKC		Disk drives
	11			DISKD		Disk drives

STATUS:

bit 0 : 1 = Shareable 0 = Nonshareable
1 : 1 = Input
2 : 1 = Output
3 : 1 = Device is opened
4 : 1 = Device is defined
5 : Undefined
6 : Undefined
7 : Undefined

Figure 5.9: *System device table.*

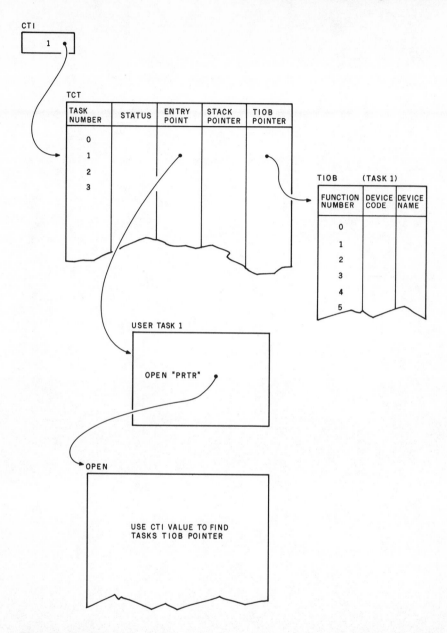

Figure 5.10: *Opening a device.*

6:
Multiprocessing Environments

As the last chapter illustrates, multiprogramming allows more than one program to run on a given machine at one time. The programs are said to be running concurrently, but this is not really the case. Each program is taking its turn as the processor grants it time on a millisecond-by-millisecond basis.

Multiprocessing is a technique whereby multiple computers are connected together to split up the work load on a more or less even basis. There are two major organizational structures for a multiprocessing system. *Loosely coupled* systems consist of a group of computers connected together with serial or parallel data links, allowing data and files to be transferred from one system to another. *Tightly coupled* systems are computers tied together so that they share one or more resources intimately.

Loosely Coupled Systems

Figure 6.1 shows a typical loosely coupled system. Each processor has its own memory and disk drives, and they communicate with each other by serial data links. The communication paths may be local (within the room or building) or over a telephone line or other medium.

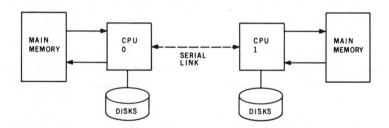

Figure 6.1: *A loosely coupled microcomputer system. Each CPU has its own memory and disks. A serial or parallel link allows them to communicate.*

The major advantage of this form of multiprocessing is that it can be used to distribute the work load of a centralized facility. Each office or user has an independent computer that is more or less autonomous. Only when the user requires additional resources that are not available locally does he need to communicate with the master or central system.

Tightly Coupled Systems

Figure 6.2 shows a tightly coupled system. Here both processors share a block of 8 K bytes of memory. This common block allows information to be transferred from one processor to the other at a much higher data rate.

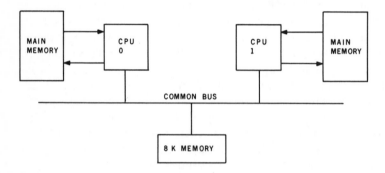

Figure 6.2: *A tightly coupled system. Each CPU has its own memory, but a portion of it is shared between the CPUs to allow for communication on a high level.*

For example, the common memory may contain a message to processor B to start running a program that is located in a file on processor A's disk drive. To get to the program, processor B leaves a message for A's NUC, asking it to open the disk file. Next it asks for the first sector or record of the program to be loaded into the common area. Block by block, it is transferred to B's main memory. Once loaded, it begins to execute normally. The A processor services all requests of B as if B were another task running on A (see figure 6.3).

Another configuration would allow more memory to be shared between the two processors—perhaps all of it. Then each processor would have access to all TCT and TIOB tables. Once a task had been loaded and readied for execution, a TCT-status byte flag could be set, indicating which processor was to execute the program.

It is also possible to have the task "float" between processors. A flag bit is set indicating if the task is being executed by a processor. If neither processor is running it when the TCT is scanned by either processor, that processor may take on the task and begin executing it.

As discussed earlier, one task may wish to allocate an I/O device owned by another processor. The SDT and the TIOB can be modified to indicate which processor the device is attached to. Then messages can be placed in common memory to transfer the request from one processor to the other.

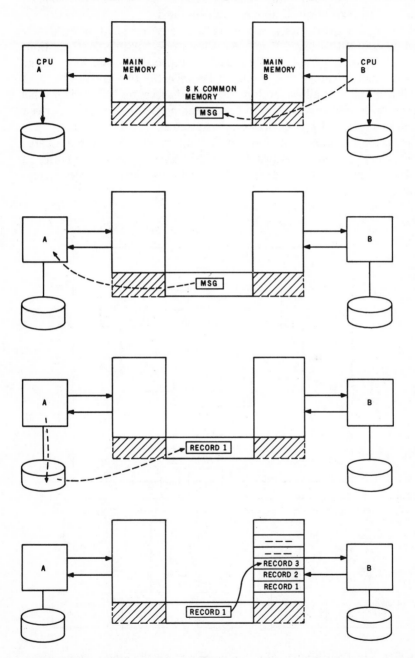

Figure 6.3: *Example of message handling on a tightly coupled system. The message block is deposited in common memory. The destination processor can then read the message.*

Distributed Networks

Distributed data processing is defined as a collection of processors that are interconnected in such a way as to decentralize resources and provide an environment for execution of application programs.

Distributed networks may be composed of any combination of loosely and tightly coupled systems. Figure 6.4 shows one possible configuration. The master consists of a tightly coupled multiprocessor that has a large amount of main memory that is shared between the two CPUs. The I/O arbiter is a circuit that allows both processors to access all I/O devices. This configuration is 100 percent symmetrical, meaning that either processor can access all memory and I/O devices on the system.

The major advantage of this system is that if either CPU develops hardware problems, the remaining processor will be able to continue running all programs, although at a slower rate. This feature greatly enhances system reliability.

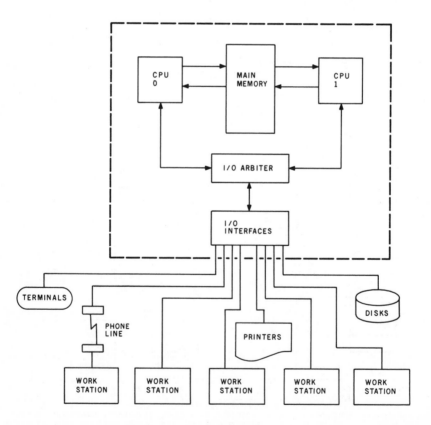

Figure 6.4: *Internal organization of a dual processor. An I/O arbiter allows both CPUs to have controlled access to all I/O devices.*

Figure 6.4 also includes some "work stations," which are actually complete processors with memory, disk, and other optional I/O devices. Each can run in a completely stand-alone mode. When the user requests services that are not available locally (i.e., on the work station) the work station can request assistance from the master. For example, a work station without a printer could send its printed output to the master that might have a high-speed printer. Each work station is considered to be loosely coupled with the master.

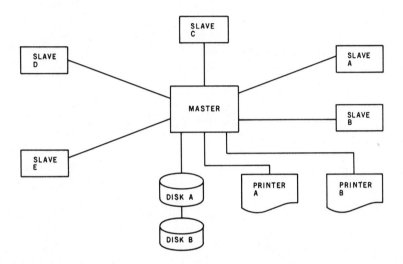

Figure 6.5: *A master-slave distributed system with five slaves and shared resources on the master.*

Distributed networks can have very flexible architectures. Figures 6.5 and 6.6 show common network designs. This particular design is referred to as a *star* network, since all slaves are connected to the master like the rays of a star. Figure 6.7 shows a loop, or ring, architecture. The ring has one main advantage: cables need not be run out to each individual slave. In an office environment, cables can be "daisy chained" from one office to the next, which can drastically reduce the cost of implementing a local network. The ring has some disadvantages, however. If only one of the slaves goes down, the entire ring will collapse.

Figure 6.8a shows a fully interconnected network. This ensures that all processors can communicate with all others. Of course, this case is even more expensive than a simple star network. In general, if you want at least one redundant path to each slave, three connections each is sufficient (see figure 6.8b).

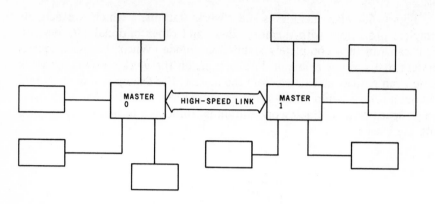

Figure 6.6: *A distributed system with two masters.*

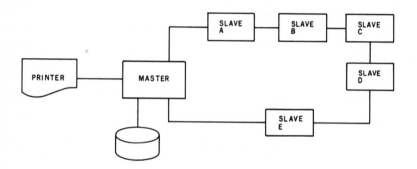

Figure 6.7: *A distributed system with a loop, or ring, architecture.*

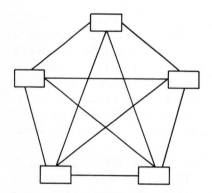

Figure 6.8a: *A fully interconnected network of microcomputers. Each CPU has more than one path to each other one. This is a fully redundant system.*

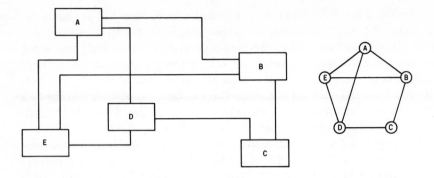

Figure 6.8b: *A partially interconnected system. Each CPU has at least one alternate path to every other CPU.*

Message-Handling Techniques

Connecting one processor to another at first sounds simple: you just run a serial data line between them and start sending data. If you are planning only to transfer short data files at low data rates, this will indeed suit the purpose. If you try to run such a data link at higher speeds, you must take into consideration certain aspects of the host processors. First, if data is

SOURCE	DESTINATION	MNEMONIC DEFINITIONS		
ENQ (05H) ⟶		ENQ −	ASCII	"ENQUERY" COMMAND
	⟵ ACK (06H)	ACK −	ASCII	"ACKNOWLEDGE"
SOH (01H) ⟶		SOH −	ASCII	"START OF HEADER"
SOURCE ID ⟶		MSG LENGTH	MESSAGE LENGTH (0-255 BYTES)	
DEST ID ⟶		STX −	ASCII	"START OF TEXT"
MSG TYPE ⟶		ETX −	ASCII	"END OF TEXT"
MSG LENGTH ⟶		CKS −	CHECKSUM BYTE	
	⟵ ACK (06H)	EOT −	"END OF TRANSMISSION"	
STX (02H) ⟶				
BYTE 0 ⟶				
BYTE 1 ⟶				
− − − −				
BYTE n ⟶				
ETX (03H) ⟶				
CKS ⟶				
EOT (04H) ⟶				
	⟵ ACK (06H)			

Figure 6.9: *A simple message protocol for communication between processors. This protocol was introduced by Digital Research for use with their CP/NET networking software.*

being buffered and stored on disk a record at a time, the act of accessing the disk takes time, but if the source processor simply sends and does not check for an acknowledgment, the destination processor may lose some data while it is busy performing other tasks. Even if interrupts are used, most small systems use disk controllers that disable interrupts before executing critical portions of the disk-transfer software. It is extremely important that the two processors have a protocol for communication that is agreed upon in advance and is strictly enforced. A simple protocol is shown in figure 6.9.

In Chapter 3, I discussed cassette-interface protocols. Message-switching protocols are remarkably similar in nature. The main goal of such protocols is to quantitize data into message "packets" that can be dealt with much more efficiently than a long, continuous stream of data. Also, if multiple processors are between the source and destination, each intermediary processor can use what is called *store and forward* techniques for delivering messages to their ultimate destinations. This means that each processor can allow messages to pile up in the "in-box," waiting for a data link to become available before transmitting the messages. Figure 6.10 shows how this works.

Figure 6.10a shows a typical asymmetrical network in which some processors must send messages through others to reach their destinations. In figure 6.10b, processor C wants to send a message to processor F, but must go through E to get there. Notice that the in-box for processor C (lower center) has a single message waiting, labeled C → F. In figure 6.9, fields were set aside in the message protocol for source and destination processor ID. This allows messages to be sent through intermediaries without someone along the way forgetting the address of the destination. In figure 6.10c, processor E has delivered the message to F's out-box. But some new messages from F and G are coming in also. In figure 6.10d, E has finished the last transmission and is looking for incoming messages. The first one it sees is from G. It transfers the message to C's out-box, because the only way to get from E (current location) to B is via C. When the message reaches C, it will be passed along to B, but this discussion is limited to E. Also notice that another message has arrived from F, making a second entry into the in-box for F. An in-box can have several levels: it just depends on how much buffer space (in main memory) is allocated to message handling. If an in- or out-box is full, the source processor will be told to wait and try again later. In figure 6.10e processor E finally gets around to the F in-box and promptly transfers the first message to C, on its way to processor D, the final destination. Figure 6.10f repeats the procedure, and figure 6.10g transfers the final message. In order for a processor to handle all these complex transfers (without the programmer or user of the system being aware of it), the processor must have some form of interrupt processing. When an interrupt occurs (from any one of a number of sources), the specific interrupt is handled, and then control is transferred to a server task that checks all the in- and out-boxes and makes sure that each byte of data is delivered to the correct destination port.

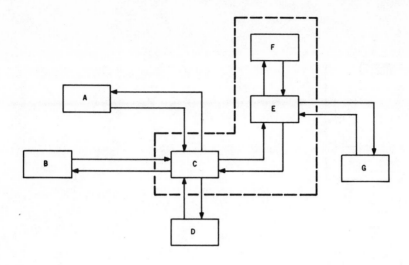

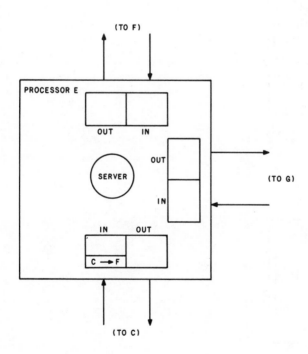

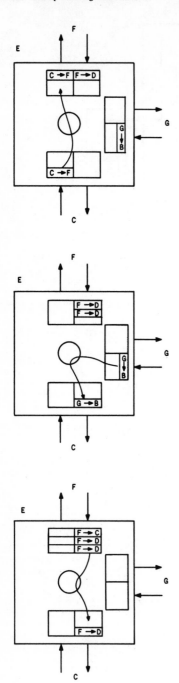

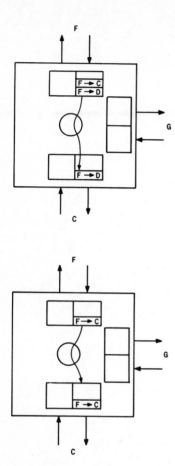

Figure 6.10: *An example of a store-and-forward message-handler system.*

7:
Memory Management

In a single-user single-program environment, the most common memory organization is a simple linear address space ranging from 0000H to a maximum of FFFFH in a 64 K-byte machine (see figure 7.1a). This arrangement requires only very simple memory-management techniques.

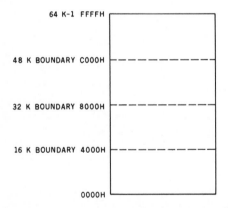

| 64 K-1 FFFFH |
| 48 K BOUNDARY C000H |
| 32 K BOUNDARY 8000H |
| 16 K BOUNDARY 4000H |
| 0000H |

Figure 7.1a: *A linear address space of 64 K bytes.*

As shown in previous chapters, memory is divided into areas, usually with the operating system at the top (see figure 7.1b). To allow user programs in the APA to find the top of the APA, a NUC function can be called, or a pointer can be set up in a known memory location. This pointer points to the address of the NUC minus one. Since the CINT is not required during program execution, it may be overwritten by the application program.

As long as the application program does not extend above NUC minus one, the operating system will be available to service requests made of it.

In a multiprogramming environment, memory must be divided in some fashion so each program has a "partition" large enough to get useful work done. Typically, the available address space is broken into segments called partitions, with the operating system (the NUC, BIO, and DIO) occupying one of the partitions. In a 64 K system there might be three APAs, each with 18 K bytes and a smaller partition for the operating system. The operating system must keep a table of all partitions, and the TCT must have an extra entry indicating the partition number (0, 1, 2) for the task. In a multiprogramming environment, each console must communicate with a different CINT. To maintain continuity, a copy of the CINT can be loaded into each partition, with different device assignments for each. When the user requests a program to be loaded, the CINT will be overwritten with the program as it is loaded in. When a program is terminated, the operating system should automatically reload the CINT into the same partition and then transfer control to it.

Many large computer systems dynamically allocate partitions from a pool of available memory. This approach is usually more efficient than fixed partitions, but it introduces an extra level of overhead on the operating system and usually is counterproductive on a microcomputer. However, other options do exist.

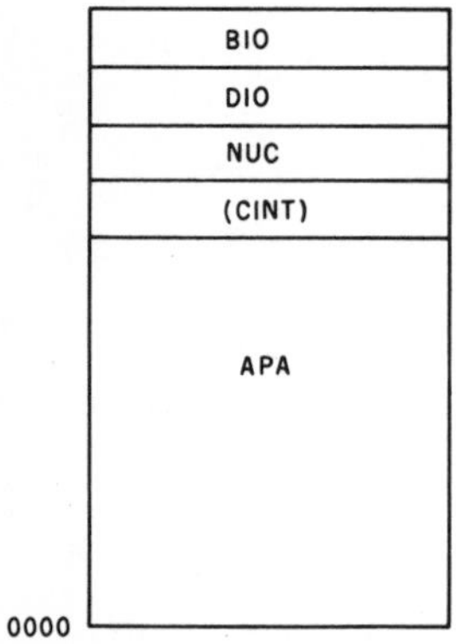

Figure 7.1b: *Arrangement of the operating system in memory.*

Bank Switching

Bank switching allows more than one "bank" of memory in the same range of hardware addresses—but not simultaneously. Figure 7.2 shows one possible arrangement. The 16 K-byte segment at the top is fixed and cannot be switched in or out of the address space. Each bank may hold one segment of the program, perhaps a series of subroutines that are not used very frequently. A switch subroutine is stored in the nonswitched 16 K bank that passes parameters to and from the other banks.

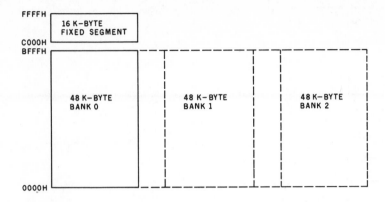

Figure 7.2: *An example of bank switching. Banks are selected by writing the bank address (0, 1, 2) to an output port.*

The other major use of bank switching is in a multiprogramming environment. Rather than partitioning memory for multiple tasks, each task is given its own bank of memory. This makes it more difficult for one program to overwrite or otherwise disturb any other programs and gives the user much greater freedom when designing software packages.

On most current system designs, a bank of memory is selected by sending a byte to an output port. The first three bits of the byte specify the bank to be selected. Three bits give a maximum of eight banks, more than enough for most applications.

Virtual Memory

Virtual memory came about as a way of extending the memory space of large computer systems. One of the first major implementations was the IBM/370. The 360 series has a 24-bit address range that allows for 16 megabytes of main memory. This might seem more than adequate to the microcomputer user, however, some applications on large systems require 10 or 12 megabytes per user. One of IBM's operating systems—MVS—allows for a dozen or more address spaces with 16 megabytes each.

The problem with large memories is that only a small portion of the memory is being used at any one moment. Consider the fact that the CPU can be executing only one instruction at a time. In any given second of wall-clock time, only a few thousand instructions (per task) are being executed (see figure 7.3), and the rest of memory is idle. In a multiprogramming environment in which perhaps three programs are running, only small segments of each are being executed. The reasons for this are obvious: most programs have DO loops that repeat the same segment of code for a relatively long period of time.

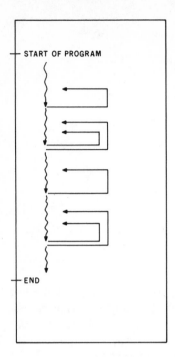

Figure 7.3: *Execution of a typical program with DO loops.*

Rather than wasting a valuable resource, the contents of memory are saved on disk and loaded only when necessary. Figure 7.4 shows how virtual memory works. Note that the real-memory space is not linear, but more closely resembles a checkerboard. Only those portions of the application programs that are in demand are loaded into memory. A page table must be kept so the operating system knows where to locate each program segment. The problem with implementation is that most microprocessors lack the hardware to handle virtual memory efficiently.

Some of the newer 16-bit microprocessors—the 8086 and Z8000 for example—allow addressing of over one megabyte and in some cases up to eight megabytes, giving the user a great deal of address space to work with.

The main disadvantage of virtual memory is that it requires special hardware and fairly fast hard-disk drives to handle demand-paging of memory. Also, with the rapidly decreasing price of memory chips, there is often no need for it. It is presented here merely as a useful concept.

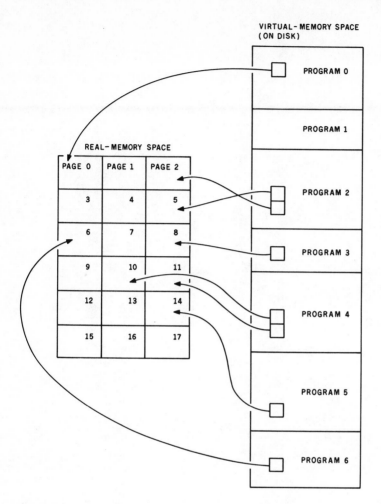

Figure 7.4: *An example of the interaction between real memory and virtual memory.*

8:
The Machine-Independent Environment

In designing software, operating systems, or otherwise, it is important to use standard resource-allocation techniques. This enables programs to be portable over many computer systems, even if a different kind of printer or a different disk format is used.

As discussed in previous chapters, it is desirable to route all I/O and system services through a common subroutine. Each device or function can then be assigned a number, so the application program can gain access to all functions and services in a uniform manner. Note that in Chapters 4 and 5, I have separate NUC calls (separate function numbers) for different devices. This approach can lead to problems. For example, in most high-level languages, the user must issue an "open" before accessing a disk file. What if the input data is read from the console device instead? The open function no longer makes sense. To overcome this (and make the operating system more consistent) it might be wise to require all devices to be formally opened and closed. This also enables the multiprogramming operating system to allocate devices more safely and assure that only authorized users can access them. For example, to open a console input device, the following call might be issued:

```
Open = 10
Devn = 2
In   = 0
Out  = 1
Both = 2
Call  NUC(Open,Devn,Both)
```

This means that the NUC is called, the function is "open file," the device number is console device 2, and it is opened for both input and output. When data must be read from the console, the following statement would be issued:

```
Call  NUC(Read,Devn)
```

The close function is also an important one. In many systems a buffer is maintained by the operating system, which is (in the case of disk) written when it becomes full (typically the buffer is one disk record, or a multiple of one record long). If a program terminates without forcing the last buffer of data to write to disk, some data will be lost. The close function makes certain that the file is properly written and closed, and that the directory entry is updated.

In the case of character or BIO devices, the close function causes the operating system to deallocate the device and make it available to other programs.

Built-In Utilities for High-Level Language Support

Some conversion utilities, math subroutines, or interrupt functions are so commonly used in high-level languages (and assembler-level programs for that matter) that they fall under the category of frequently used system-wide routines and should probably be put in the operating system. For example, most languages use a standard set of floating-point math subroutines for addition, subtraction, multiplication, and division. Depending on the microprocessor, they may have to be done in software using 8-bit arithmetic. Or perhaps a floating-point hardware board is available; this is a circuit card that contains a floating-point math integrated circuit (IC), which greatly speeds up these functions. Therefore, an operating system with built-in calls for math routines can be configured to run them in software or hardware, depending on which extra hardware is available on the system in question. Note that the user never notices the difference, except that the execution time improves with hardware floating point. Also, no changes need be made within the compiler or interpreter.

Base conversions are also useful, since displaying numbers is an integral part of most programs. For example, an 8-bit binary to two-digit hexadecimal notation (see figure 8.1) conversion routine would be by far the most useful conversion in the operating system. Other commonly used conversions include 16-bit binary to decimal, floating-point format to decimal, decimal to 16-bit binary, and four-digit hexadecimal to 16-bit binary (see figure 8.2). Rather than writing and rewriting these (or remembering where the subroutine library is), you can simply include them as function calls in the NUC.

Interrupts

Interrupts can be as much a pain in the neck as they are a useful tool. Most single-user systems have little need for them, unless some real-time processes are going on. Multiprogramming systems generally require them. Without interrupts, CPU intensive programs do not relinquish the processor frequently enough to give the illusion of concurrent activity.

Another common use for interrupts is to update a real-time clock. Some

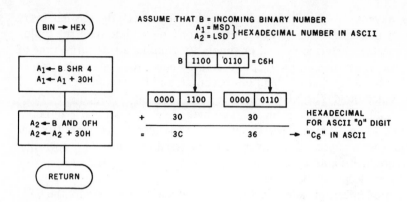

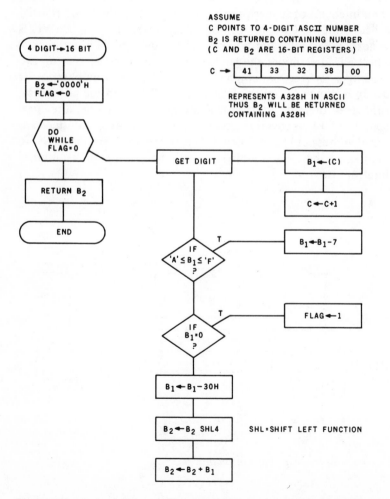

Figure 8.1: *An 8-bit binary to two-digit hexadecimal conversion algorithm.*

Figure 8.2: *A four-digit ASCII to 16-bit binary conversion algorithm.*

systems have a 16.67-millisecond clock that interrupts the system every sixtieth of a second. This gives the user a convenient time base for timing active processes, external events, or simply for running a software "time of day" clock. Each time an interrupt occurs, the operating system can trap it, set a flag indicating that an event has occurred, and then return to the NUC for task scheduling. The NUC in turn sees the flag and increments the time-of-day counter, which has several two-byte fields for seconds, minutes, hours, and so on. Some microcomputers have special counter-timer ICs that will count either up or down from a given starting point. The operating system should be able to manage these counters without the user having detailed knowledge of their operation.

Vectored interrupts allow multiple external devices to interrupt the CPU without conflicting with each other. Figure 8.3 shows a vectored system with four levels of interrupts. When an interrupt occurs, the message is passed bucket-brigade style to the highest interrupt level. If any other levels are active (i.e., an interrupt of higher priority is in progress), the lower priority interrupt is held until the CPU has completed its current task. When VI3 is cleared, the next highest interrupt is issued, and so on until all interrupts are serviced. The CPU determines the source of an interrupt by one of two methods: reading a register that contains the interrupt level number, or by direct hardware methods (as on the 8080 or Z80 CPUs). In the latter case, each interrupt level forces a restart instruction onto the bus when the interrupt is issued. The CPU recognizes any of eight restarts as subroutine calls that call a fixed address in low memory. It is then the user's responsibility to place subroutines at these fixed addresses so that control will be obtained when the interrupt occurs.

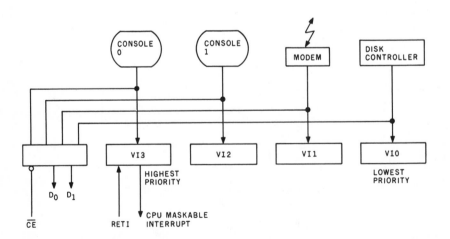

Figure 8.3: *A vectored interrupt implementation.*

9:
System Utilities

Some system functions or utilities are used quite infrequently and really should not be included in the resident portion of the operating system. However, it is important that the user be able to access them in a convenient fashion. Typically, functions such as copy disk, copy file, and format disk are written as transient programs and executed in the APA just as user programs are.

Copy Disk

A disk-copy routine is of great importance on any computer system. It is necessary, in fact, essential, that important disks and disk files be backed up to duplicate disks periodically. Users who do not run backup copies of their disks at least every week are only fooling themselves. Inevitably, the disk will "crash" or develop a bad sector and part or all of the data will be lost. **A backup copy should be made whenever a crashed disk would cause you to lose more keystrokes than you care to reenter.**

In a dual-disk system, a disk-copy routine is quite straightforward: a track (or several) is simply read from disk A and written to disk B. In this case, the user will have to make direct calls to the DIO jump vectors to access the disk on a track-by-track basis.

When only one disk drive is available, the process is somewhat more complicated. Figure 9.1 shows the algorithm for a single-disk copy program. Note that the more main memory available to the copy routine, the faster the routine will execute.

Copy File

A generalized file copy routine or move utility is indispensable. This can be performed quite simply by opening the file in question, reading a record, and transferring it to an output file. If only one disk drive is available, the technique used in the disk-copy routine may be implemented, but instead of tracks, records are copied. Generally, in a 48 K system, files of up to 40 K bytes may be copied in one pass. Longer files will require an extra pass or two.

```
SectorL = 128          ;Number of bytes per sector.
NumTrks = 72           ;Tracks per disk.
NumSctr = 26           ;Number of sectors per track.
Trks.Per.Pass = 12
AbortKey = 03H         ;abort key is Control-C in ASCII

BufferL = (NumSctr * SectorL) * Trks.Per.Pass    ;Buffer length

Define Buffer (Array(BufferL))       ;Define Buffer as
                                     ;an array of length BufferL

Bufptr = ADDR(Buffer)                ;Get address of Buffer
Trk = 1

Do I = 1 to NumTrks/Trks.Per.Pass

    Bufp = Bufptr
    Ntrk = Trk
    Print "Insert Source Diskette, then press any key."
    Input Char
    If Char = AbortKey then END

    Do P = 1 to Trks.Per.Pass
        Call Read(Trk,Bufptr)          ;Get track into Buffer
        Trk = Trk + 1
        Bufptr = Bufptr + (SectorL * NumSctr)
        End

    Bufptr = ADDR(Buffer)
    Trk = Ntrk
    Print "Insert Destination Diskette, then press any key."
    Input Char
    If Char = AbortKey then END
    Do P = 1 to Trks.Per.Pass
        Call Write(Trk,Bufptr)             ;Write Buffer to Track
        Trk = Trk + 1
        Bufptr = Bufptr + (SectorL * NumSctr)
        End
End


Print "Copy Complete"
Stop
END

ON ERROR:  Print "Copy aborted - Bad Read or Write."
Stop
END
```

Figure 9.1: *Single-disk copy algorithm.*

Modifying Device Assignments

If devices are assigned by name in a system (e.g., PRTR, CON, DISK) and if a standard open/close routine is used for all devices, there is no reason why devices cannot be interchanged at will. For example, suppose one wishes all printer output to appear on the system console because the computer does not have a printer. A simple reassignment of PRTR to CON would accomplish this. Typically, a table is maintained in the NUC that is cross-checked for device or function-number assignments. This allows for a generalized mapping of assignments in either a single-user or multiprogramming environment.

System Generation

Generating a new copy of the operating system is done so infrequently that it makes no sense to incorporate it into the actual operating system. In fact, it may not be possible to do so. In some existing operating systems, the system generation or "sysgen" involves only making modifications to the BIO and DIO sections for a given system. In other operating systems, the size or amount of memory available to the operating system must be determined and then the system generated accordingly.

In figure 9.2, a new version of the operating system is loaded, and the user-written BIO and DIO are loaded from disk files in relocatable form. The resultant program (still relocatable) is written back to disk as another file in the user directory. The program then asks if the user wishes to write the newly generated operating system to the system tracks of the disk currently in the drive.

```
-GENSYS              <---- Console Command to invoke Utility

ENTER TOP OF MEMORY PAGE NUMBER: FF
ENTER FILENAME OF USER WRITTEN BIO: UBIO.RLC
ENTER FILENAME OF USER WRITTEN DIO: UDIO.RLC
ENTER DESTINATION FILENAME: OS64

DO YOU WISH TO WRITE THE NEW OPERATING SYSTEM
TO THE SYSTEM TRACKS OF A DISKETTE: Y

DONE.

CONTINUE?: N
END OF GENSYS.
-
```

Figure 9.2: *A sample system generation. GENSYS is the console command to invoke the utility.*

Formatting and Initializing Disks

If the system in question uses hard-sector disks, no formatting is usually required. For all others, some kind of pattern must be written to a disk before it can be used. This involves writing a blank data record for each sector on the disk. Since several different formats are in use, I will not go into detail here. Consult the specifications of the disk controller you are using.

Debuggers and Simulators

Debuggers and simulators are useful programming tools. Often it is nearly impossible to determine what a sequence of instructions is doing unless they are stepped through one at a time. The first method is called the debugger. It is similar to a hardware single-step method in which the hardware stops after each instruction to allow the programmer to look at registers on a front panel display.

The debugger differs from the hardware method in that each instruction is executed, but a breakpoint is placed immediately after the instruction to let the processor regain control after it has executed. The debugger also allows the user to set fixed breakpoints, which are actually jump instructions temporarily written over other instructions at the location of the breakpoint. Figure 9.3 shows this technique. Figure 9.4 shows the execution of the program in figure 9.3 under the control of a debugger.

After the instruction is executed, the original bytes are replaced, overlaying the debugger jump instruction. If the command is given to execute the next instruction, the debugger looks at the next byte, finds the instruction length in an internal table, goes to the byte after the instruction, and again inserts a debugger jump instruction after saving the current contents of those three bytes. In the case of a conditional jump or call, the debugger must test the flags ahead of time, determine the outcome of the jump, and place the debug instruction at the appropriate location.

A simulator is similar to a debugger, except that it does more of the same. Rather than executing each machine instruction directly, the simulator is like an interpreter—it has a table of op-codes and instruction lengths and actually executes a pseudo-instruction set that happens to look just like the instruction set of the microprocessor in question. This approach generally requires more overhead and runs up to 100 times more slowly, but the simulator has better control over the program being executed.

Note that in both cases it is nearly impossible to run real-time programs, interrupts, or high-speed external I/O devices, since both the debugger and the simulator run anywhere from 1 to 100 times more slowly than a normal program.

Memory Dump or Display

A good debugger package should also include a hexadecimal memory-image dump command, which displays the address, eight or more two digit hexadecimal data bytes, and the ASCII or EBCDIC character representation of memory. See figures 3.31 and 3.32 in chapter 3.

A disassembler is also valuable. This is a utility that looks at each instruction or op-code and reconstructs the mnemonic for the instruction that would be used in an assembler. The programmer can then decode instructions without having to look up each op-code in a reference manual. Figure 9.5 shows the use of a memory dump and a disassembler.

```
1100
 0100   MVI   C,10
 0102   LXI   H,0054
 0105   CALL  3258
 0108   INX   H
 0109   PUSH  H
 010A   PUSH  PSW
 010B   CALL  3210
 010E   POP   PSW
 010F   POP   H
 0110   JMP   0208
 0113   DCR   B
```

```
1100
 0100   MVI   C,10
 0102   LXI   H,0054
 0105   CALL  3258
 0108   JMP   A120
 010B   CALL  3210
 010E   POP   PSW
 010F   POP   H
 0110   JMP   0208
 0113   DCR   B
 0114   RET
 0115   MOV   A,C
```

```
1100
 0100   MVI   C,10
 0102   LXI   H,0054
 0105   CALL  3258
 0108   INX   H
 0109   JMP   A120
 010C   NOP
 010D   STA   E1F1
 0110   JMP   0208
 0113   DCR   B
 0114   RET
 0115   MOV   A,C
```

Figure 9.3: *Setting breakpoints with a debugger.*

```
G200
PC=0200 A=00 BC=0010 DE=0000 HL=0000 MVI C,10
PC=0202 A=00 BC=0010 DE=0000 HL=0054 LXI H,0054
PC=0205 A=00 BC=0010 DE=0000 HL=0054 CALL 3258
PC=0208 A=00 BC=0010 DE=0001 HL=0055 INX D
PC=3258 A=00 BC=0010 DE=0002 HL=0056 INX D
PC=3259 A=00 BC=0010 DE=0002 HL=0056 RET
PC=325A A=00 BC=0010 DE=0002 HL=0056 INX H
PC=0208 A=00 BC=0010 DE=0002 HL=0056 PUSH H
```

Figure 9.4: *Execution of the program in figure 9.3 under the control of a debugger.*

```
D300
0300 03 CD 09 03 0D C2 01 03 C9 46 23 7E 23 12 13 05 .........F#~#...
0310 C2 0D 03 C9 3A 67 03 F6 80 47 DB 33 CD 68 03 2A ....:g...G.3.h.*
0320 3E 06 01 93 F9 09 44 4D 21 00 00 39 31 6D 06 D1 >.....DM!..91m..
0330 3E F4 D3 30 7B D3 33 0D 0D 7A D1 D3 33 C2 34 03 >..0{.3..z..3.4.
0340 05 C2 34 03 F9 DB 34 1F D2 45 03 DB 30 32 3B 06 ..4...4..E..02;.
0350 E6 64 C8 21 F9 05 11 FF 05 01 04 00 ED B0 21 FD .d.!..........!.
0360 05 CD 11 04 C3 00 01 00 3A 40 06 4F 0C AF 37 17 ........:@.O..7.
0370 0D C2 6F 03 B0 D3 34 C9 21 44 06 7E A7 C8 CD 96 ..o...4.!D.~....
0380 03 23 C3 7B 03 F5 1F 1F 1F 1F CD 8E 03 F1 E6 0F .#.{...........
0390 C6 90 27 CE 40 27 E5 D5 C5 5F 16 00 0E 02 CD 05 ..'.@'..._......
03A0 00 C1 D1 E1 C9 CD 7B 03 CD CF 03 F5 CD 78 03 F1 ......{......x..
03B0 FE 0D C0 3A 48 06 D3 34 3A 43 00 D3 04 3A 49 06 ...:H..4:C...:I.
```

Figure 9.5a: *Memory-dump output format.*

```
L300
0300    INX   B
0301    CALL  0309
0304    DCR   C
0305    JNZ   0301
0308    RET
0309    MOV   B,M
030A    INX   H
030B    MOV   A,M
030C    INX   H
030D    STAX  D
030E    INX   D
```

Figure 9.5b: *Disassembler output.*

10:
User Interference with the System

A rather popular game at some large computing facilities (especially those on college campuses) is to try to write over or take over other portions of memory, or actually to take control of an entire computer system. This can be accomplished in a number of ways, all of which are moderately difficult but by no means impossible for the determined programmer.

Of course there are many inadvertent ways of writing over someone else's memory, especially in microcomputer or minicomputer environments where system-level protection is not as effective as that on a large computer. On a microcomputer, for example, you need only to start using memory outside of the bounds allocated to the program (in the case of the single-user system, just writing over the NUC) and your program may not last long.

None of the current 8-bit microcomputers have any effective means of protecting memory, although the original Altair design allowed for a memory-protect bit, and even today, S-100 memory boards allow for some kinds of hardware memory protection on a 4 K- or 16 K-byte basis. The disadvantage is that there is no way of controlling it through software. The IBM-360 series has a 4-bit protect key that may be enabled for each 4 K block of memory. Each task (there may be only 16) has a different protect key. When a task requests to read or write into a particular block, the hardware does an automatic check of the protect key and generates an interrupt if the task is not allowed to access that area of memory.

If memory may be protected under software control on a microcomputer, the only feasible way of mechanizing this process is shown in figure 10.1. Note that when the application program is in control, all memory other than the APA is protected. When a call is made to the NUC, the operating system is unprotected and the APA is protected. Actually it is unnecessary to protect the AP unless there is some concern that the operating system is going to harm it.

Memory protection is more useful and important in a multiuser environment. Figure 10.2 shows a typical scenario. When user is in control, all memory not owned by that user is protected; when other users are in control, they can only access their own memories. The operating system usually requires access to all memory, so it unprotects everything while in control.

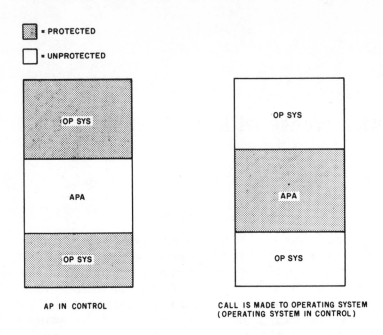

AP IN CONTROL

CALL IS MADE TO OPERATING SYSTEM
(OPERATING SYSTEM IN CONTROL)

Figure 10.1: *Memory protection under software control.*

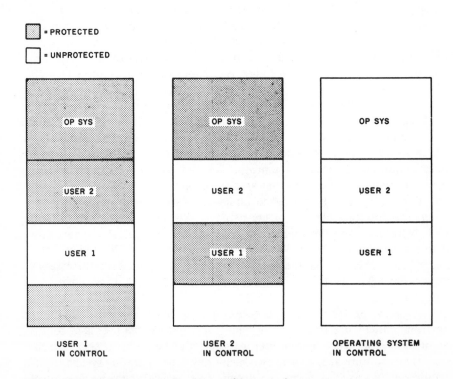

USER 1
IN CONTROL

USER 2
IN CONTROL

OPERATING SYSTEM
IN CONTROL

Figure 10.2: *Memory protection in a multiuser environment.*

Protecting Disk Files

Disk storage may be even more critical than main memory, since it often represents the only valid copy (other than a backup copy of the disk) of each user's data files.

One method of protecting disk files is to give each user a disk drive to do with as he or she pleases. This keeps others from tampering with directories or files on the drive. Secondly, the directory on each disk can be partitioned, with one area for each user's files. Actually, in this case all directory entries can be maintained within the same physical directory, but each has a tag indicating which user it belongs to. The operating system ensures that only authorized users may read a particular directory entry.

Often several levels of protection are desired. The most common ones are: allow write, allow read, allow execute, and allow append. All are obvious except "allow append." This allows another user to write records to the end of a file, but not read or modify the file. This is sometimes useful in a multiuser environment when statistics are being gathered from many users in real time. Figure 10.3 shows a typical disk directory with protection by user number and by function (i.e., allow read, allow write). Figure 10.4 shows what happens when this directory is listed on a console device. Each user only sees his or her files. System files do not appear at all.

USER LEVEL	FILE NAME	EXT	BLOCK	LENGTH	BLOCK ALLOCATION MAP	PROTECTION BITS*
0	GENSYS	EXC				0001
0	BASIC	EXC				0001
0	FORTRAN	EXC				0001
1	FILE	BAS				1110
2	FILE	FOR				1110
4	TEST	EXC				0001
2	FILE	EXC				0001
3	TEST	DAT				1110

*Allow Read, Write, Append, Execution.

Figure 10.3: *A multiuser disk directory.*

```
DIR

Files for User 1:
FILE.BAS

Files for User 2:
FILE.FOR
FILE.EXC

Files for User 3:
TEST.DAT

Files for User 4:
TEST.EXC

System files:
GENSYS.EXC
BASIC.EXC
FORTRAN.EXC
```

Figure 10.4: *User directories.*

Protecting the User from Himself or Herself

This is the most difficult form of protection. In most cases it is impossible to recognize or anticipate a disastrous action on the part of the user. The most that can be done is to check for erasure of all disk files. When in a text editor or word processor, if the user tries to delete the entire edit file (that which is in memory) the operating system can intercept this and issue a verify message. The user must then respond with a deliberate yes or no answer to perform the function.

Another major problem is that of stack overrun. When testing some programs, if a subroutine call is made and then an improper branch is performed, an infinite loop can cause the stack to grow down through memory. Another case is when a subroutine call is made and an extra stack push or pop is performed without a corresponding push or pop to restore the stack pointer to its original position. This causes the return address (of the subroutine call) to be lost. When the RET instruction is reached, it causes control to be transferred to some other part of memory, often with disastrous results. Figure 10.5 shows the above two cases.

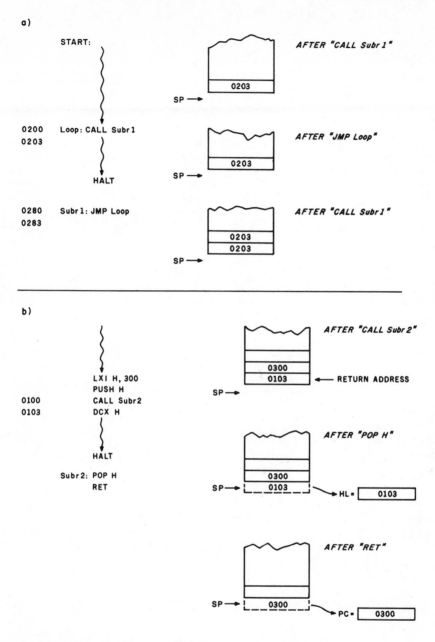

Figure 10.5: *Two methods for ruining the integrity of the stack.*

11:
Tying It All Together

A monitor is really no different from a full DOS; it just has fewer peripheral devices at its command and is generally resident in PROM rather than being loaded from disk. I included the discussion on monitors because I view operating systems in evolutionary terms. The monitor is really just a primitive ancestor of the operating system.

Monitors have the following elements: CINT or command jump table, a large number of accessible utility subroutines, character input and output routines for a terminal, cassette tape interface, telephone interface, and so on.

The major elements of an operating system are the NUC, and the I/O system, which can be further broken down into byte-oriented and block-oriented I/O.

The NUC is responsible for all high-level functions of the operating system such as managing disk directories, controlling access to input and output devices, allocating memory, and in multiprogramming systems, handling task scheduling and synchronization of tasks. All user requests for service or resources are made through the NUC. Forcing all programs to communicate their requests to the NUC also aids in program portability, because the NUC level of the system looks the same on all machines running the operating system, even though the hardware configuration may be quite different.

The BIO section handles all byte- or character-oriented input and output for the NUC. This includes all asynchronous terminal devices, most printers, cassette tape drives, and telephone data links.

The disk-oriented I/O section or DIO section handles all block input and output operations for the NUC. Both the byte- and block-oriented sections are user written to conform to the hardware available on the given system. Some operating systems combine these two I/O sections into one section, but their respective functions remain the same.

The other important elements of the operating system is the CINT, although it is not necessary when running APs. The CINT is essential, however, when attempting to have interactive control of the system. The CINT is really just an AP with no special privileges. Thus the adventurous programmer with special needs could write his or her own CINT, replacing the one provided with a commercially available operating system.

SOFTWARE REQUIRED	APPLICATIONS					
	BUSINESS	SOFTWARE DEVELOPMENT	SCIENTIFIC	EDUCATIONAL	REAL-TIME CONTROLLER	EVALUATION OR DEVELOPMENT
Monitor (Firmware) STD	X	X	X	X	X	X
Operating System	X	X	X	X	X	
Floating Point (Software)	X		X	X		
Uploader/ Downloader		X			X	X
Terminal Emulator		X		X	X	X
Operating System Console Interpreter	X	X	X	X	X	
Copy Disk	X	X	X	X	X	
Copy Files	X	X	X	X	X	
Device Assignment (Generalized)	X	X	X	X	X	
Debugger/ Simulator		X			X	X
Numeric Conversions	X	X	X	X	X	
Real-Time Clock Handler					X	
Priority-Interrupt Handler					X	

Figure 11.1: *Software for typical applications of an operating system.*

Once all major elements of the operating system have been defined, the user must decide what to include in a given operating system. The elements of an operating system can be viewed as a set of building blocks. Some blocks must be present for the structure to support itself, but others are optional and can be used to improve overall system performance in certain environments.

Some typical applications are business, software development, science, education, real-time controller, evaluation or development. Figure 11.1 shows some software options that would improve the performance of the system in each of these cases. Figure 11.2 lists some hardware options that would also improve performance of the systems.

Distribution of systems has always been a problem. It is natural to want to squeeze as much out of a $5,000 system as possible, but even a 4-megahertz Z80 microcomputer is going to be hard pressed to keep up with more than two users. My rule of thumb is as follows: install one microcomputer for every person using one on a full-time basis.

Special Optional Hardware	Business	Software Development	Scientific	Educational	Real-time Controller	Evaluation or Development
			APPLICATIONS			
Floating-Point Board			X		X	
Real-time Clock					X	
Priority Interrupt					X	
Bank-Switched Memory		?				
Memory Protection					X	
DMA Disk					X	

Figure 11.2: *Hardware options for typical applications of an operating system.*

A more quantitized handling is the following: where P_n = percentage of daily time spent on a microcomputer for person n, each individual percentage above 60 should be rounded up to 100.

$$\frac{\sum\limits_{n=1}^{10} P_n}{100} = \text{minimum number of microcomputers for a group of 10 people.}$$

A sample of this algorithm is shown in figure 11.3.

Computer User	Daily Time Spent on Microcomputer (%)	Rounded-up Number (P_n)
P_1	60	100
P_2	40	40
P_3	10	10
P_4	80	100
P_5	90	100
P_6	20	20
P_7	35	35
P_8	42	42
P_9	38	38
P_{10}	50	50
	$\sum\limits_{n=1}^{10} P_n = 465$	$\sum\limits_{n=1}^{10} P_n = 535$

$$\frac{\Sigma P_n}{100} = \frac{535}{100} = 5.35 \qquad \text{Round up to 6 computer systems.}$$

Figure 11.3: *A sample of an algorithm to determine the number of computer systems for 10 part-time users.*

The final determination might depend more on intuition than on calculation, but this formula at least helps in the decision. The point of this discussion should be clear—don't try to put too great a load on too few microcomputers. The real advantage of microcomputers is their inexpensiveness and the fact that each individual has control over his or her own data files.

Appendix I:
CP/M Reference Guide

CP/M (Control Program for Microcomputers) is typical of a class of operating systems currently in widespread use in the market. CP/M also has a number of derivatives including Cromemco (CDOS) and SD Systems (SDOS). CP/M resides at the top of available main memory, with the user or APA (referred to as the transient program area (TPA) by Digital Research) at the bottom of memory. Figure I.1 shows the memory organization of CP/M. CP/M is divided into several modules: the basic disk operating system (BDOS) the basic input/output system (BIOS), and the console command processor (CCP). The labels to the right of the memory map in figure I.1 show the corresponding modules from the discussion of this type of operating system in Chapter 4.

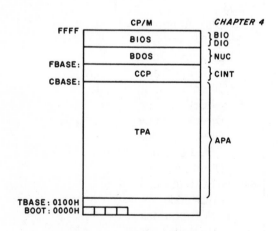

NOTE: TAPE MAY EXTEND FROM 0100H
UP TO THE BOTTOM OF THE BDOS.

Figure I.1: *Memory organization of CP/M.*

The BDOS

The BDOS is equivalent to the NUC in my treatment of operating systems. It is responsible for all management functions including disk-file management, I/O high-level management, and all other function calls available to the user. Table I.1 lists the BDOS function calls available in

		REGISTERS USED (C REGISTER-FUNCTION NUMBER)
0	System Reset	None
1	Console input	A = Character from console device
2	Console output	E = Character to output on console
3	Reader input	A = Character from reader
4	Punch output	E = Character to output to punch
5	List output	E = Character to output to list
6	Direct control I/O	A = Character or status returned
		E = FFH for character input, or *character* for output
7	Get I/O byte	A = I/O byte returned
8	Set I/O byte	E = New I/O byte value
9	Print string	DE = String address
10	Read console buffer	DE = buffer address
11	Get console status	A = Returned status
12	Return version number	HL = Version number
13	Reset disk system	None
14	Select disk	E = Disk number
15	Open file	DE = FCB address
		A = Directory code
16	Close file	DE = FCB address
		A = Directory code
17	Search for first	DE = FCB address
		A = Directory code
18	Search for next	A = Directory code
19	Delete file	DE = FCB address
		A = Directory code
20	Read sequential	DE = FCB address
		A = Error code
21	Write sequential	DE = FCB address
		A = Directory code
22	Make file	DE = FCB address
		A = Directory code
23	Rename file	DE = FCB address
		A = Directory code

Table I.1: *CP/M 2.2 BDOS function list.*

CP/M versions 1.4 and 2.2. Each function is called by loading the C register with the function number, and other registers with data are needed. The BDOS then performs the function and may return a value in a register indicating success or failure.

Disk-File Access

Access to a file on disk is done through an FCB (File Control Block). An FCB is supplied for each file the user wishes to access. Figure I.2 shows the FCB and all fields within it. To open a file, the BDOS is called with the address of the FCB in the DE registers. The user need only fill in the file name as it appears in the disk directory. The "open file" function number is then loaded into the C register and the call is made to the BDOS. If the file name is found, the BDOS fills in the FCB with all necessary information to access the file. All subsequent file-access calls must have the FCB address in the DE registers before calling the BDOS.

DR	FNAME	EXT	e x	X	X	R C	Disk Block Allocation	C R	R_0	R_1	R_2
00	01 08	09 11	12			15	16 31	32		35	

DR	Drive Code 0 = Default disk drive 1 = Assume disk A 2 = Assume disk B 16 = Assume disk P
FNAME	Contains filename in uppercase ASCII, with bit 7 = 0.
EXT	Contains filetype in uppercase ASCII. Bit 7 in the first character indicates read only status. Bit 7 in the second character indicates system file status.
ex	Contains the current extent number.
RC	Record count for this extent.
Disk Block Allocation	Contains block mapping for the file.
CR	Current record to read or write (sequentially).
R_0, R_1, R_2	Optional random record number.

Figure I.2: *The file control block (FCB) in CP/M and MP/M.*

Disk space is allocated on a block-by-block basis. The minimum allocation is 1 K byte. On double-density disk, the minimum allocation is typically 2 K bytes. A block-allocation map is maintained for each file in the directory. Files may have up to 65,536 records of 128 bytes each, allowing up to 8 megabytes per file. Version 1.4 of CP/M allowed files of only 256 K bytes each. Figure I.3 shows CP/M disk-space allocations. The first two tracks contain the bootstrap loader and the CP/M system (if required). The directory follows and usually has room for 64 entries, although the BIOS disk-definition tables may be modified to allow for 128 or more entries. The remainder of the disk is available for user files.

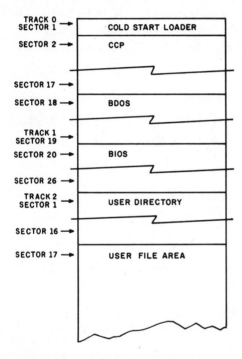

Figure I.3: *CP/M disk space allocation. (This is valid for single-density, 26-sector, soft-sectored, eight-inch diskettes.)*

The BIOS

The BDOS (and only the BDOS) makes calls to the BIOS, which interfaces with the actual hardware environment of the microcomputer. The BIOS is a collection of user-written (by whomever installed CP/M on the system in question) subroutines for primitive-character I/O and disk access. Disk functions include set DMA address, set track and sector, read sector, write sector, and so on. The skeleton of a typical BIOS is shown in listing I.1. A series of jump vectors is located at the head of the BIOS and points to all internal subroutines. The BDOS locates subroutines in the BIOS by calling the subroutine at the known location in the jump vector area. This way the placement of subroutines in the BIOS is completely up to the programmer. Assuming that a working version of CP/M is available for program development, the user-written BIOS may be loaded and overlaid on the existing copy of CP/M using the dynamic debugging tool (DDT) program supplied with CP/M. Once a custom BIOS has been written using the supplied 8080 assembler, it is placed in a memory map of the CP/M system and then the entire copy of CP/M is written back to a .COM (memory image) file. The resulting file can then be used to generate new CP/M systems on the system tracks (tracks one and two) of a disk.

When generating CP/M from the ground up, the system-alteration guide gives detailed instructions on how to read the distribution copy of the disk, patch it for temporary operation, and then write it back to disk. Once this is accomplished, CP/M may be loaded off disk and patched using the assembler and DDT programs.

Disk Definitions in CP/M Version 2.0

Certain BDOS disk-access functions in CP/M version 2.0 and higher have been moved to the BIOS for more user control. When the SELDISK function is called, it must return a pointer to the base address of a disk parameter header (DPH) for the selected drive. The DPH is 16 bytes long and contains five pointers. The first is called XLT and points to the logical-to-physical sector-translation vector. This allows user control of sector skewing or mapping (as described in Chapter 4).

The next four bytes are scratch-pad areas for the BDOS. The next pointer is called DIRBUF and points to a 128-byte scratch-pad area for directory operations in the BDOS. All disks use the same buffer, so only one is needed. The last three pointers are DPB, CSV, and ALV. The DPB is the disk parameter block, which defines the unique characteristics of a disk drive. The DPB contains 10 data values, including number of sectors per track (SPT), total storage capacity of the disk drive (DSM), and number of directory entries allowed (DRM). A macro definition library called DISKDEF is included on the distribution disk for CP/M 2.x. DISKDEF allows the user to define all the parameters for a disk with a few simple statements in the BIOS.

Sector Blocking and Deblocking

CP/M 2.x also has provisions for sector blocking and deblocking. If the disk controller allows for a sector size that is a multiple of 128 bytes, the user can add blocking and deblocking to greatly speed up disk access. Each BDOS call to the BIOS write function includes a value in the C register that indicates the type of write operation to be performed. A zero indicates a normal sector write, a one is a write to a directory sector, and a two is a write to the first sector of a new data block. The CP/M 2.x alteration guide includes some sample blocking and deblocking algorithms that may be incorporated into the user's BIOS.

```
CP/M RMAC ASSEM 1.1      #001    SAMPLE BIOS FOR CP/M 2.2
                         TITLE   'SAMPLE BIOS FOR CP/M 2.2'
                 ;
                 ;       A typical BIOS for a CP/M 2.2 System.
                 ;
                 ;       The disk interface portion of this BIOS has been
                 ;       deleted from the listing since it is highly
                 ;       controller dependent.
                 ;
                 ;       This listing is intended as an example only.
                 ;       By Mark Dahmke, 1981.
                 ;
                 ;"BIAS" IS ADDRESS OFFSET FROM 3400H
                 ;
0016 =           VERS:   EQU     22       ;CP/M VERSION NUMBER
0038 =           MSIZE:  EQU     56       ;CP/M MEMORY SIZE IN KILOBYTES
9000 =           BIAS:   EQU     (MSIZE-20)*1024
C400 =           CCP:    EQU     3400H+BIAS      ;BASE OF CCP
CC06 =           BDOSV:  EQU     CCP+806H        ;BASE OF BDOS
DA00 =           BIOS:   EQU     CCP+1600H       ;BASE OF BIOS
                 ;
                 ;
0030 =           SDATA   EQU     30H             ;SERIAL I/O DATA PORT
0035 =           SSTAT   EQU     SDATA + 5       ;SERIAL I/O STATUS PORT
                 ;
                 ;
0000 =           WBOOTV: EQU     0       ;VECTOR FOR WARM RESTART
0003 =           IOBYTE: EQU     3       ;ADDRESS OF I/O CONTROL BYTE
0005 =           BDOS:   EQU     5
                 ;
0001 =           RXRDY:  EQU     00000001B       ;RECEIVE DATA AVAILABLE BIT
0020 =           TXMTY:  EQU     00100000B       ;TRANSMIT BUFFER EMPTY BIT
                 ;
0007 =           BELL:   EQU     7       ;ASCII BELL CHARACTER
000D =           CR:     EQU     0DH     ;ASCII CARRIAGE RETURN
000A =           LF:     EQU     0AH     ;ASCII LINE FEED
                 ;
                 ;
DA00                     ORG     BIOS    ;ORIGIN OF THIS PROGRAM
                 ;
                 ;Jump vectors to subroutines.
                 ;
DA00 C3D3DA              JMP     BOOT    ;COLD START
DA03 C377DA              JMP     WBOOT   ;WARM START
DA06 C333DA              JMP     TTST    ;CONSOLE STATUS
DA09 C33CDA              JMP     TTYIN   ;CONSOLE CHARACTER IN
DA0C C350DA              JMP     TTYOUT  ;CONSOLE CHARACTER OUT
DA0F C350DA              JMP     TTYOUT  ;LIST CHARACTER OUT
DA12 C350DA              JMP     TTYOUT  ;PUNCH CHARACTER OUT
DA15 C33CDA              JMP     TTYIN   ;READER CHARACTER OUT
DA18 C37FDA              JMP     HOME    ;MOVE HEAD TO HOME POSITION
DA1B C37ADA              JMP     SELDSK  ;SELECT DISK
DA1E C37BDA              JMP     SETTRK  ;SET TRACK NUMBER
DA21 C37CDA              JMP     SETSEC  ;SET SECTOR NUMBER
DA24 C37EDA              JMP     SETDMA  ;SET DMA ADDRESS
DA27 C380DA              JMP     DREAD   ;READ DISK
DA2A C381DA              JMP     DWRITE  ;WRITE DISK
```

Listing I.1 cont.

```
CP/M RMAC ASSEM 1.1      #002     SAMPLE BIOS FOR CP/M 2.2
  DA2D C347DA            JMP      TTOST    ;RETURN LIST STATUS
  DA30 C37DDA            JMP      SECTRAN  ;SECTOR TRANSLATE
                  ;
                  ;BIOS SUBROUTINES
                  ;
                  ; I/O DRIVERS FOR THE 8250 UART CHIP
                  ;
  DA33 DB35     TTST:    IN       SSTAT
  DA35 E601              ANI      RXRDY
  DA37 C8                RZ
  DA38 3EFF              MVI      A,0FFH
  DA3A B7                ORA      A
  DA3B C9                RET
                  ;
  DA3C CD33DA   TTYIN:   CALL     TTST     ;GET PORT STATUS
  DA3F CA3CDA            JZ       TTYIN    ;LOOP UNTIL DATA IS READY
  DA42 DB30              IN       SDATA    ;READ THE DATA
  DA44 E67F              ANI      7FH      ;STRIP OFF THE PARITY BIT
  DA46 C9                RET
                  ;
  DA47 DB35     TTOST:   IN       SSTAT
  DA49 E620              ANI      TXMTY    ;IS TRANSMITTER BUFFER EMPTY?
  DA4B C8                RZ                ;IF NOT, RETURN.
  DA4C 3EFF              MVI      A,0FFH
  DA4E B7                ORA      A
  DA4F C9                RET
                  ;
  DA50 CD47DA   TTYOUT:  CALL     TTOST    ;TEST FOR OUTPUT STATUS
  DA53 79                MOV      A,C
  DA54 E67F              ANI      7FH
  DA56 D330              OUT      SDATA    ;OUTPUT THE CHARACTER.
  DA58 C9                RET
                  ;
                  ;        Output a message to the console.
                  ;        Message address is in HL-registers.
                  ;
                  PMSG:
  DA59 CD6ADA            CALL     CRLF     ;OUTPUT A CR, LF.
  DA5C C5       LOOP:    PUSH     B
  DA5D 4E                MOV      C,M      ;GET THE CHARACTER AT (HL).
  DA5E CD50DA            CALL     TTYOUT   ;SEND IT.
  DA61 23                INX      H
  DA62 79                MOV      A,C
  DA63 E680              ANI      80H      ;TEST TOP BIT FOR A '1'.
  DA65 C25CDA            JNZ      LOOP
  DA68 C1                POP      B
  DA69 C9                RET
                  ;
                  ;        Output a Carriage return and a line feed.
                  ;
                  CRLF:
  DA6A E5                PUSH     H
  DA6B 0E0D              MVI      C,CR
  DA6D CD50DA            CALL     TTYOUT   ;OUTPUT A CR
  DA70 0E0A              MVI      C,LF
  DA72 CD50DA            CALL     TTYOUT   ;OUTPUT A LF
```

Listing I.1 cont.

```
CP/M RMAC ASSEM 1.1      #003    SAMPLE BIOS FOR CP/M 2.2
DA75 E1                 POP     H
DA76 C9                 RET
                ;
                ;
                ;
                ;
                WBOOT:
                ;       Jumping to this routine causes the CP/M system to
                ;       reload itself.  Everything from the CCP up to but
                ;       not including the BIOS is reloaded from disk.
                ;
DA77 C300C4             JMP     CCP     ;Go To CP/M for further processing.
                ;
                SELDSK:
                ;       This routine causes a new disk drive to be selected
                ;       for further processing.
                ;       The disk number must be provided in the C-register
                ;       upon entry.  SELDSK must return the address of the
                ;       disk parameter header in the HL-registers.
                ;
DA7A C9                 RET
                ;
                ;
                SETTRK:
                ;       This routine causes the track number specified in
                ;       the BC-registers to be selected for further disk
                ;       access.
                ;
DA7B C9                 RET
                ;
                ;
                ;
                SETSEC:
                ;       This routine causes the sector number specified
                ;       in the BC-registers to be selected for further
                ;       disk accesses.
                ;
DA7C C9                 RET
                ;
                SECTRAN:
                ;       This routine translates a logical sector number
                ;       into a physical sector number.
                ;       A translate table is included later in this listing.
                ;
                ;
DA7D C9                 RET
                ;
                ;
                SETDMA:
                ;       This routine selects the memory address of the
                ;       128 byte sector buffer that will be used for
                ;       subsequent disk reads and writes.
                ;       The address is assumed to be in the BC-registers.
                ;
DA7E C9                 RET
                ;
```

Listing I.1 cont.

```
CP/M RMAC ASSEM 1.1      #004    SAMPLE BIOS FOR CP/M 2.2
                 ;
                 HOME:
                 ;       This routine returns the disk head of the currently
                 ;       selected disk to track 00.
                 ;
                 ;
DA7F C9                  RET
                 ;
                 ;
                 DREAD:
                 ;       This routine reads a sector specified by SETTRK
                 ;       and SETSEC into memory at the address specified
                 ;       by SETDMA.
                 ;
DA80 C9                  RET
                 ;
                 ;
                 DWRITE:
                 ;       This routine writes the sector specified by SETTRK
                 ;       and SETSEC from memory at the address specified
                 ;       by SETDMA.
                 ;
                 ;
DA81 C9                  RET
                 ;
                 ;       Parameters for drive 0
                 ;
DA82 00000000 DPBASE: DW     0,0
DA86 00000000         DW     0,0
DA8A EEDA0000         DW     DIRBF,0
DA8E ACDB6EDB         DW     CHK00,ALL00
                 ;
                 ;       Parameters for drive 1
                 ;
DA92 00000000         DW     0,0
DA96 00000000         DW     0,0
DA9A EEDA0000         DW     DIRBF,0
DA9E BCDB8DDB         DW     CHK01,ALL01
                 ;
                 ;
                 ;
                 ;
                 ;       The following is a parameter table for drive constants.
                 ;       These tables assume 8 inch single density disk drives.
                 ;
                 ;
DAA2 0000     PRMTBL: DB     0,0      ;DRIVE 0 STEP RATE, SELECT BYTES
DAA4 0000             DB     0,0      ;      1
DAA6 0000             DB     0,0      ;      2
DAA8 0000             DB     0,0      ;      3
                 ;
DAAA 1A00     DP8SO:  DW     26       ;SECTORS PER TRACK
DAAC 03               DB     3        ;BLOCK SHIFT FACTOR
DAAD 07               DB     7        ;BLOCK MASK
DAAE 00               DB     0        ;EXTENT MASK
DAAF F200             DW     242      ;BLOCKS PER DISKETTE
```

Listing I.1 cont.

```
CP/M RMAC ASSEM 1.1      #005    SAMPLE BIOS FOR CP/M 2.2
DAB1 3F00               DW      63      ;# DIRECTORY ENTRIES
DAB3 C0                 DB      192     ;ALLOC 0
DAB4 00                 DB      0       ;ALLOC 1
DAB5 1000               DW      16      ;DIR CHECK VECTOR SIZE
DAB7 0200               DW      2       ;SYSTEM TRACK OFFSET
DAB9 01070D1319T8S0:    DB      1,7,13,19,25
DABE 050B1117           DB      5,11,17,23
DAC2 03090F15           DB      3,9,15,21
DAC6 02080E141A         DB      2,8,14,20,26
DACB 060C1218           DB      6,12,18,24
DACF 040A1016           DB      4,10,16,22
                        ;
                        ;
                        BOOT:
                        ;       Boot is called when CP/M is cold started.
                        ;       Boot must initialize any interrupt structures,
                        ;       and must set up any initial variables or constants.
                        ;       When finished, Boot may issue a console message.
                        ;
                        ;
DAD3 21D9DA             LXI     H,LOGMSG
DAD6 CD59DA             CALL    PMSG            ;DISPLAY THE MESSAGE.
                        ;
                        ;
                        ;
DAD9 3536       LOGMSG: DB      MSIZE/10+'0',MSIZE MOD 10 + '0'
DADB 6B204350 2F        DB      'k CP/M version '
DAEA 322E32A0           DB      VERS/10+'0','.',VERS MOD 10+'0',80H+' '
                        ;
                        ;
                        ;SCRATCH RAM AREA FOR BDOS USE
                        ;
DAEE =          BEGDAT  EQU     $       ;BEGINNING OF DATA AREA
DAEE            DIRBF:  DS      128     ;SCRATCH DIRECTORY AREA
DB6E           ALL00:   DS      31      ;ALLOCATION VECTOR 0
DB8D           ALL01:   DS      31      ;ALLOCATION VECTOR 1
                        ;
DBAC           CHK00:   DS      16      ;CHECK VECTOR 0
DBBC           CHK01:   DS      16      ;CHECK VECTOR 1
                        ;
DBCC =          ENDDAT  EQU     $       ;END OF DATA AREA
00DE =          DATSIZ  EQU     $-BEGDAT;SIZE OF DATA AREA
                        ;
DBCC                    END
```

Listing I.1: *Sample BIOS for CP/M 2.2.*

The Console Command Processor (CCP)

When CP/M becomes active, it gives control to the CCP, which, like the CINT I described, is actually an application program loaded at the top of the TPA. When first entered, the CCP displays a prompt character, along with a letter of the alphabet from A to P. This letter indicates which disk drive is currently logged in for use. To change drives, the user simply enters the drive name and a colon (for example, B:). This causes the CCP to request the BDOS function call "select disk," with register E containing a number representing the requested drive (A = 1, B = 2, and so forth). The prompt would be returned as B>. The "greater than" symbol indicates that CP/M (actually the CCP) is ready to accept commands. There are five built-in commands: TYPE, DIR, REN, ERA, and SAVE. A number of transient commands are also provided: SYSGEN, PIP, ED, ASM, DUMP, LOAD, STAT, MOVCPM, SUBMIT, and DDT. These commands are actually .COM files or memory-image files. They all appear in the directory as files like STAT.COM. The COM extension means literally "command." When STAT is entered on the console, the CCP first checks for built-in commands and then searches the directory for a .COM file with the same name as the command. If this fails, an error message is issued. If successful, the CCP loads the file into memory at 0100H, which is the start of the TPA. If the load is successful, the CCP transfers control to whatever is at 0100H. After the program is loaded, there is no further need for the CCP, so it may be overwritten by the program in the TPA. When execution is terminated (by jumping to location 0000H), CP/M performs a warm start, which reloads the CCP from disk and returns control to it. The A> should reappear on the console.

The MP/M Multiuser Operating System

The multiprogramming monitor control program (MP/M) allows CP/M users to upgrade to a multiprogramming environment without having to switch to an incompatible operating system. MP/M is built on a multitasking nucleus. The nucleus provides numerous functions such as task (process in MP/M) dispatching, queue management, memory management, flag management, and system time-base management. MP/M has provisions for full prioritization of tasks. Each task can be given a priority from 0 to 255, where 0 is the highest priority. The highest-priority ready task gets control of the CPU until interrupted or until it calls the BDOS. Whenever the BDOS is called, the system clock generates an interrupt, or when any other interrupt occurs, task dispatching occurs. This means that the nucleus scans for the highest-priority task that is ready to execute and hands control to it. If tasks have the same priority, they are given equal amounts of CPU time.

Memory management is also handled by the nucleus. If one contiguous address space is available, the user can partition it into several segments, each of which can run a user program or system utility. If several banks of memory are available on the system, the nucleus will manage up to eight segments (up to 48 K bytes each).

Queues are provided to handle several important real-time functions in MP/M. They are used for communication between tasks, for synchronization of tasks, and for mutual exclusion. All queues are first-in, first-out (FIFO) in nature.

Flags give MP/M a logical interrupt structure independent of the machine environment's physical interrupt structure, which may be quite different. Thus events in a real-time environment may be flagged and brought to the attention of the nucleus.

Time-base management includes obvious functions like time of day, job scheduling by time of day and date, and task-delay functions.

MP/M System Organization

MP/M is organized like CP/M, but has more modules and more options. Figure I.4 shows the internal layout of MP/M. Starting at the top, SYSTEM.DAT is the system-data area that defines MP/M according to the user's wishes. SYSTEM.DAT is generated through the GENSYS program. CONSOLE.DAT contains the information used to manage each console device on the system. Each console requires 256 bytes of space in this area, so if four consoles are included, 1 K byte is required.

USERSYS.STK is optional and is needed only if the user wishes to run .COM files on the MP/M system. If only .PRL (page relocatable files) are executed on the system, there is no need for USERSYS.STK.

The XIOS is the extended input/output system and includes the CP/M BIOS. This segment is user written as in CP/M. Almost all the old CP/M entry points are the same, but several additional jump vectors are required for MP/M. The SELMEMORY entry point allows the user to select memory banks and to protect unselected memory if that capability is available on the system. POLLDEVICE allows MP/M to be run in a polled environment where there are no interrupts. The device to be polled is in the C register upon entry. STARTCLOCK is used when a task is delayed for a specified number of clock periods. STOPCLOCK stops the clock interrupts to avoid unnecessary timer interrupts if they are not needed. MAXCONSOLE returns the number of consoles the BIOS will support.

The BDOS contains the MP/M disk-file management functions, just as in CP/M. In systems with bank switching, the ODOS is included instead of BDOS. The BDOS also handles multiple consoles.

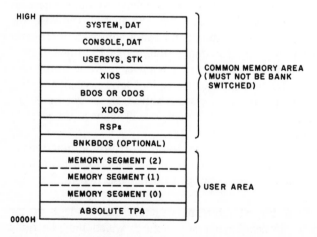

Figure I.4: *Internal layout of MP/M.*

The extended BDOS (XDOS) contains the priority-driven MP/M nucleus. The XDOS contains all of the management functions described above, such as time-base management, flag and memory management, and queue management. Table I.2 shows all XDOS functions available in MP/M.

Resident system processes (RSPs) (tasks) are either system provided or user written, or both. Each RSP is a task, just like any other, but is permanently resident in the MP/M operating system. MPMSTAT, SCHED, and SPOOL are provided on the distribution disk and may be added to the operating system at GENSYS time.

FUNCTION #	DESCRIPTION	REGISTERS (C Register = Function Number)
128	Absolute memory request	DE = Memory descriptor address
		A = Return code
129	Relocatable memory request	DE = Memory descriptor address
		A = Return code
130	Memory free	DE = Memory descriptor address
131	Poll device	E = Device number (as defined in the XIOS)
132	Flag wait	E = Flag number
		A = Return code
133	Flag set	E = Flag number
		A = Return code
134	Make queue	DE = QCB address
135	Open queue	DE = UQCB address
		A = Return code
136	Delete queue	DE = QCB address
		A = Return code
137	Read queue	DE = UQCB address
138	Conditional read queue	DE = UQCB address
		A = Return code
139	Write queue	DE = UQCB address
140	Conditional write queue	DE = UQCB address
		A = Return code
141	Delay	DE = Number of time units
142	Dispatch	None
143	Terminate process	D = Conditional memory free
		E = Terminate code
144	Create process	DE = Process descriptor address
145	Set process priority	E = Priority (0 - 255)
146	Attach console	None
147	Detach console	None
148	Set console	E = Console
149	Assign console	DE = APB address
		A = return code
150	Send CLI command	DE = CLICMD address
151	CALL resident system procedure	DE = CPB address
		HL = Return code
152	Parse filename	DE = PFCB address
		HL = Return code or FCB address
153	Get console number	A = Console number
154	System data address	Returns: HL = System data page address
155	Get time and date	DE = TOD address
156	Return process descriptor address	HL = PD address
157	Abort specified process	DE = APB address
		A = Return code

Table I.2: *XDOS functions available in MP/M.*

A user-written RSP might, for example, be a resident file-lister program or a disk-file hexadecimal dump routine. Having a common utility resident—saving the need to load and reload it into a memory segment (partition)—can save much time and helps keep user partitions free to run programs in. For example, I wrote an RSP to display all memory segments and any programs running in the segments. The RSP executed once a second, using the XDOS delay function to introduce the appropriate time constant and displayed its information in the unused upper corner of my 86 × 40 video memory board. The user might easily write an RSP that would show real-time processes or interrupts in action, or might set up an interactive electronic mail facility. The SPOOL RSP allows printed output from a disk file to be sent to a printer as a background task, allowing users to continue working at the console. The BNKBDOS must be included in any system that has multiple banks of memory. It is placed at the top of each bank and communicates with the BDOS.

The GENSYS Utility

GENSYS allows the user to generate an MP/M system that fits the user's hardware and operating environment. Listing I.2 shows GENSYS in operation. The entries are as follows: top page of memory, enter the hexadecimal page number of the highest memory in the system, in this case 64 K bytes.

```
GENSYS

MP/M 1.1 System Generation
===========================

Top page of memory = BF
Number of consoles = 2
Breakpoint RST #   = 6
Add system call user stacks (Y/N)? y
Z80 CPU (Y/N)? y
Bank switched memory (Y/N)? n
Memory segment bases, (ff terminates list)
  : 00
  : 40
  : ff
Select Resident System Processes: (Y/N)
MPMSTAT  ? y
DA       ? n
ABORT    ? y
SLVSP    ? n
SPOOL    ? y
NETWRKIF ? n
```

Listing I.2: *MP/M GENSYS example.*

Number of consoles may be less than or equal to the number defined in the XIOS. Breakpoint RST # is the RST instruction to be used by the DDT when software breakpoints are used in debugging. System call user stacks? If you plan to run .COM files, answer yes. If you are using a Z80 CPU, answer yes. This will improve performance, since the BDOS can then manage the alternate registers in the Z80. If you are using bank-switched memory (and have added the appropriate code to the XIOS), answer yes.

Each memory segment must be defined in terms of start address. In this case, the first segment starts at page 00 and is 50H pages long, or 20 K bytes long. The second segment starts at 50H and extends to page A0H, making it 20 K bytes long also. The third segment starts at A0H and is 11H pages long, or just over 4 K bytes. The FFH terminates the list. After A0H, the system determines how much memory is left between A0H and the bottom of the operating system, and will give it to the third segment.

GENSYS then searches the disk for all RSPs and asks if the user wants them included in the operating system. The user may answer yes or no for each one. When GENSYS is finished, it writes a file to disk called MPM.SYS, which contains the load module for the entire MP/M operating system that has been created. The program MPMLDR.COM may be entered from a CP/M system, which will load MP/M over CP/M and begin executing it. The MP/M loader is shown in listing I.3.

```
MPMLDR

MP/M 1.1 Loader
==================

Number of consoles =  2
Breakpoint RST #    =  6
Z80 CPU
Top of memory       =  BFFFH

Memory Segment Table:
SYSTEM   DAT  BF00H  0100H
CONSOLE  DAT  BD00H  0200H
USERSYS  STK  BC00H  0100H
XIOS     SPR  AB00H  1100H
BDOS     SPR  9700H  1400H
XDOS     SPR  7800H  1F00H
MPMSTAT  RSP  6B00H  0D00H
ABORT    RSP  6A00H  0100H
SPOOL    RSP  5D00H  0D00H
-----------------------------
Memseg   Usr  4000H  1D00H
Memseg   Usr  0000H  4000H

MP/M
```

Listing I.3: *An example of the MP/M loader.*

MP/M System Utilities

None of the CP/M commands such as DIR and ERA are resident on MP/M. That is, if the user enters DIR, MP/M loads DIR.PRL from disk and executes it in a memory segment. The available utilities are DIR, ERA, ERAQ, DSKRESET, CONSOLE, USER, TYPE, PIP, ED, ASM, SUBMIT, STAT, TOD, SPOOL, SCHED, ABORT, STOPSPLR, DUMP, LOAD, GENMOD, GENHEX, and PRLCOM. Most of these commands are directly from CP/M or are immediately obvious. DSKRESET is necessary in MP/M, since many users may be accessing the same disk all at once. When executed, DSKRESET checks to see if anyone is using the disk, and if so, denies the reset. GENMOD generates files of type .PRL from files of type .HEX. GENHEX creates a .HEX file from a .COM file, and PRLCOM converts a .PRL file to a .COM file. SPOOL allows a file to be printed in background mode, SCHED schedules programs by time of day, ABORT kills a program in a segment, STOPSPLR stops the spooler program, and TOD gives the current time of day, or allows the user to enter a new time-of-day value.

Console Functions

MP/M handles consoles differently from CP/M, simply because there may be more than one. Each console is initially owned by a terminal message process (TMP). The TMP issues the console prompt "nA>" where the n is the user number assigned to the console. As the command is typed in by the user, the TMP checks for control characters, just as in CP/M. When carriage return is typed, the TMP writes the entire command to the command line interpreter (CLI) queue.

The CLI parses the command line and first tries to find a queue with the same name as the command. If the name is found, CLI writes the command tail (the portion after the first word on the command line) to the queue of the same name and is finished. If a queue is not found, the CLI attempts to find a file of type .PRL on the requested disk drive. If found, it reads the header of the file to determine memory requirements, and makes a relocatable memory request to the XDOS. If the request is honored, the .PRL file is loaded into the requested memory segment and is executed.

If the CLI cannot find a .PRL file, it tries to find a .COM file. If that is found, CLI issues a request for an absolute transient program area (TPA) starting at 0000H in a memory bank. If successful, it will read the .COM file in and execute it.

The CLI also checks the command tail for up to two other file names and creates FCBs in the memory segment occupied by the program. It also creates a process descriptor (task-control table entry) for the program, and sets up a 20-level stack for it.

The Process Descriptor

The process descriptor is a 52-byte area set up for each process or task on the system. Figure I.5 shows a typical process descriptor. Processes that may be aborted from a console should be in uppercase letters. If one does not want the user to be able to abort the process, it should have at least one lowercase letter in its name.

```
PD:   DW    0                ;PD   Link field
      DB    0                ;Process status
      DB    255              ;Process priority (0-255)
      DB    STK + 38         ;Stack pointer initial value
      DB    'PROGNAME'       ;Process name (8 characters)
      DB    0                ;Assigned console device
      DB    0                ;Memory Segment
      DS    2                ;Scratch area
      DS    2                ;Process list thread
      DS    2                ;Disk DMA address
      DS    1                ;Default disk user code
      DS    2                ;system scratch byte
      DS    1                ;Search L (System use)
      DS    2                ;Search A (System use)
      DS    2                ;DRVACT (list of drives being used)
      DS    20               ;Registers (save area)
      DS    2                ;Scratch bytes

STK:  DS    38               ;Process stack area
      DW    PROG$START$ADDR            ;entry point of process
```

Figure I.5: *MP/M process descriptor.*

Queue Data Structures

MP/M queues are used for intertask communication, task synchronization, and mutual exclusion. Two major types of queues are allowed: circular and linked. A circular queue accommodates message lengths of zero to two bytes, whereas linked queues may have message lengths of three or more bytes. The structure of a circular queue is shown in figure I.6.

```
CIRQUE:   DS    2          ;Queue link field
          DB    'Circque   ;Queue name (8 characters)
          DW    2          ;message length
          DW    20         ;number of messages
          DS    2          ;DQ process head
          DS    2          ;NQ process head
          DS    2          ;pointer to next message in
          DS    2          ;pointer to next message out
          DS    2          ;number of messages in queue
BUFFER:   DS    40         ;size is equal to message length
                           ;times number of messages
```

Figure I.6: *Circular queue with 20 messages, two bytes each.*

A linked queue is similar, but has a series of buffers and links between them. Figure I.7 shows a linked queue.

```
LINKQUE:    DS    2              ;Queue link field
            DB    'Linkque       ;Queue name ( 8 characters )
            DW    60             ;message length
            DW    5              ;number of messages
            DS    2              ;DQ process head
            DS    2              ;NQ process head
            DS    2              ;message head
            DS    2              ;message tail
            DS    2              ;buffer head
BUFFER:     DS    2              ;message #1 link
            DS    60             ;message #1 data
            DS    2              ;message #2 link
            DS    60             ;message #2 data
            DS    2              ;message #3 link
            DS    60             ;message #3 data
            DS    2              ;message #4 link
            DS    60             ;message #4 data
            DS    2              ;message #5 link
            DS    60             ;message #5 data
```

Figure I.7: *Linked queue with five messages, 60 bytes each.*

Queues may be established by either the operating system or the user, depending on the application. That is, the user can make his own queues. XDOS function calls are provided for creating, reading, and writing messages to queues, and even for conditional reading and writing of queues. The mutual-exclusion queue is treated specially by MP/M. Any queue that has MX as the first two letters of the name may be used to obtain exclusive control of a resource such as a printer or dial-up modem. Since these devices are obviously not shareable, the operating system has to have some way of controlling them. MX queues provide this mechanism. When a process requires control of a device, it must read the MX queue for the device. The MX queue contains a two-byte value that is a pointer to the process descriptor of the process that owns the mutual-exclusion message. The user is then responsible for reading the message, saving it, and replacing it in the MX queue when finished with it. Then some other process may read it.

Appendix II:
The UNIX Operating System

UNIX was developed at Bell Laboratories as a programmer's tool, an operating system that would provide a useful environment for programming research. The UNIX environment differs in many respects from those I have discussed in this book. UNIX offers some features that are almost never seen on larger systems: a hierarchical file system supporting demountable volumes; compatible device and interprocess I/O; asynchronous process creation; over 100 programs and subsystems, including a dozen high-level languages; and a system command language that is user selectable. The final feature in this list—portability—is the most valuable.

Until recently, UNIX was not available to the average computer user and was certainly not available to the microcomputer user. Since a number of UNIX-compatible 16-bit systems have appeared on the market, I felt it necessary to include a description of UNIX structure and facilities.

The UNIX kernel is the nucleus of the operating system. As in CP/M, the user is not allowed to tamper with that portion of the operating system. The kernel supports process control, the I/O system, and the file system. The UNIX shell is very similar to the CCP in CP/M, or the CINT in the hypothetical machine I describe in this book. Like the CCP, the UNIX shell is just another user program, having no special authority in the system environment. It can be overlaid if extra space is needed.

The Kernel

A user program is executed in an environment called the user process. Like the situation with CP/M, when the UNIX program requires system services, it calls the operating system as a subroutine. Processes are created by a system primitive called fork. Fork creates a child process that is a copy of the original, or parent, process. A process may execute another program. The user process remains, but after issuing the execute function, it runs a different program. Thus a compiler may execute a second pass, which overlays the old program in memory.

Processes may be synchronized by having them wait for events. A process may wait for a child process to terminate. A process may also wait for any event. For example, if the process requests additional main memory, it may have to wait for that amount of memory to be released by another process.

Like the situation with MP/M, multitasking is available. Each process has a priority. Disk events have higher priority than character I/O events. User process priorities are assigned on the basis of an algorithm that compares the ratio of compute time to real time used by the process. Since system processes always have higher priority than user processes, they get control first until they are all serviced.

The I/O System

Like the hypothetical operating system I described, the UNIX I/O system is broken into block and character I/O. Block I/O is set up as a group of randomly addressed secondary-memory segments of 512 bytes each. Blocks are addressed from zero to the size of the device. Block I/O devices are accessed through buffer software that coordinates access to a series of memory buffers.

Character I/O devices are all devices that are not treated as block devices. This includes the typical serial terminal, paper-tape reader, and line printer. Characters are generally queued up in a producer/consumer arrangement. As characters are placed in the queue, the device driver pulls them off, one by one, and sends them to the destination device.

The File System

In the UNIX scheme of things, files are simply a unidimensional array of bytes. No other structure is required by the system, although some structures may be required by application programs such as compilers or text editors. The file system breaks a disk into four regions. The first block is unused, and may contain a boot-load procedure. The second block is called the superblock. It contains information about the size of a disk and the boundaries of the other two regions. The next region is called the i-list. It contains file definitions for all files on the disk. Each file is represented by an i-node, which is 64 bytes long. After the i-list is the actual file storage area on the disk.

This file-directory structure is extended by adding hierarchial directory capability. This is done by allowing a special type of file called a directory. A directory is treated as a normal file, except that only the operating system is allowed to write it. With this structure, any number of directories can be chained together. This organization allows files that are logically related to be placed in separate and distinct directories for convenience.

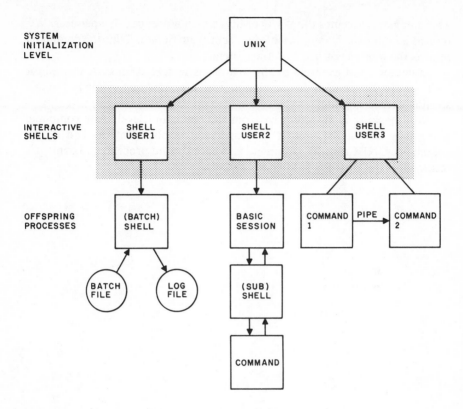

Figure II.1: *Tree-structured hierarchies in the UNIX system.*

The Shell

The shell is the user interface with the UNIX system. It provides a command-level language that is quite powerful. A large number of primitive utilities are provided on the system, making many programming and data-manipulation functions simple. The command format for the shell is quite simple. A command is a sequence of words separated by spaces or tabs. File names may be qualified all the way to the root of the directory by preceding the name with a "/." If no slash is found, the file name is assumed to start at the current- or default-directory level for that user. Each slash points to a hierarchial directory. Thus /name1/name2/name3 points to directory name1, which points to directory name2, which points to name3.

Commands may also be strung together with a vertical bar. This uses a UNIX facility called a pipe. A pipe acts like a file connecting two processes. The first process writes a file that the second one reads in, and so on. An example of this uses some system utilities for displaying the number of users on the system.

who | wc

This command executes the WHO utility, which writes one line per user. WC returns a count of the number of lines sent from WHO. Thus the command returns the number of users on the system.

Another good example of this feature is in text editing. A text editor could be invoked, and upon completion, the formatted text would be fed to a spelling-check program.

Multitasking is also allowed from the command level. Any command string may be entered, and if an ampersand is placed at the end of the command, UNIX runs the command as a background process, and control is returned to the shell for further commands.

Appendix III:
Structured Programming and Structural Flowcharts*

Gregg Williams, Editor
BYTE
POB 372
Hancock NH 03449

Structured programming—that phrase, unfamiliar to me and, I assume, to most people several years ago—is now endowed with such magical powers that most books on programming include it somewhere in their titles.

But what is structured programming? Most of us feel that it is probably good for us, like getting regular exercise or brushing our teeth after each meal. You may also think it's too complicated (not true), that it slows down programming (wrong, it usually speeds it up), or that it cannot be done unless your computer runs a language like Pascal or ALGOL (wrong again).

Simply put, structured programming is a set of techniques that makes programs easier to write, easier to understand, easier to fix, and easier to change. These techniques are simple and general and can be adapted to any computer language that has a *goto* statement—that includes BASIC, assembly language, FORTRAN, and COBOL. The purpose of this article is to show you a new form of notation that will help you write structured programs. But first, let's review structured programming.

The Elements of Structured Programming

A structured program is like a set of notes written in outline form. The headings accompanied by Roman numerals—I, II, III, and so on—provide the overall organization. Each Roman-numerical topic is broken into several component topics (A, B, and C, for example), and each of these is subdivided further (1, 2, 3, ...) and further (a, b, c, ...) as needed. Table 1 shows a problem and its solution written in this outline form.

---

*Reprinted from BYTE, March 1981.

Problem: Given a numeric array V with N elements, find the largest element, MAXV, and its index, MAXINDEX. These variables are related as follows:

- 1 < MAXINDEX < N
- MAXV = V (MAXINDEX)
- MAXV is the largest value in V(1), V(2),...V(N).

Table 1: *A problem and its solution in outline form. The common outline form used for summarizing a body of material can also be used to give structure to the emerging design of a program.*

Solution:
I. Set problem up:
  A. Set MAXVAL = -9×10^{20}
  B. Set MAXINDEX = 0
  C. Set INDEX = 1
II. Find largest element:
  A. Set up a loop that increments the variable INDEX from the beginning to the end of the array V.
  For each value of INDEX:
    1. Compare the current array value (V (INDEX)) to MAXVAL:
      a. if MAXVAL is equal or larger, do nothing;
      b. if MAXVAL is smaller, replace MAXVAL with the current array value and MAXINDEX with the current index (the value of INDEX).
III. Print the largest element (MAXVAL) and its index (MAXINDEX).

The above example demonstrates a process known as *decomposition*: breaking a task (problem) into its subtasks. This process represents the *most* important concept in structured programming, i.e., that a problem can be solved by repeatedly breaking it into subproblems, until *every* subproblem can be solved. If you plan this decomposition before you try to write it out in the narrow, precise, and time-consuming syntax of the target language (i.e., the programming language you use to solve the problem), you will have a better chance of getting your program right the first time.

But how do you decide which way to break the problem into subproblems? Common sense helps. Ask yourself, "What sequence of actions and decisions would I have to make if I were doing this without a computer?"

The rest of the answer comes from the literature of structured programming. It has been mathematically proven that *any* program can be written using three basic patterns, called *programming constructs* (or simply *constructs*): sequence, *if...then...else*, and *while...do*. The first construct, sequence, gives you the basic capability of breaking a task into a set of subtasks that accomplish the main task when executed sequentially.

The second construct, *if...then...else*, performs one of two subtasks, depending on the truth or falsity of a stated condition. An everyday example of this construct is given in the following sentence: "If it is raining outside, I will take my umbrella with me; if it is not, I will leave the umbrella at home."

The third and least familiar construct, *while...do*, is actually a generalized DO loop that repeats a set of actions (called the *body* of the loop) while a stated condition is true. You use this construct when making iced tea from a mix: "As long as (while) the mix is not completely dissolved, I will continue to stir it."

If you combine lines of code in the three ways described above, the resulting program is said to be *structured*. In most languages (BASIC, for example) you will still use *goto* statements, but they will be *restricted* to carry your program to specific points, i.e., the beginnings and ends of tasks or subtasks. Each module (subtask) in a structured program has a property known as "one-in, one-out"; that is, there is only one entrance and one exit from these modules, and no module will ever jump into the middle of another one. Instead of being like a plate of spaghetti, a program is more like a string of pearls (with each pearl containing another, smaller string of pearls, and so on); each module has a definite and unchanging position on the string. When such regularity can be counted on, existing modules can be changed or deleted, and entirely new modules can be added without problems caused by unexpected module interaction.

That is the theory of structured programming—now for putting it into practice. Figures 1 through 3 show the three constructs (sequence, *if...then...else*, and *while...do*) in standard flowchart form and as BASIC code. (For a more detailed look at writing structured programs in BASIC, see "Applied Structured Programming," listed in the references. This article appears in an anthology that contains several other good articles on program decomposition—sometimes called *top-down design* or *programming by stepwise refinement*—and structured programming.)

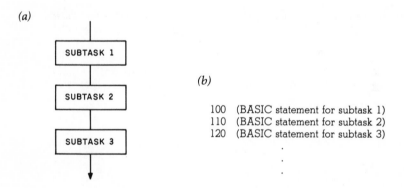

(a)

(b)

```
100   (BASIC statement for subtask 1)
110   (BASIC statement for subtask 2)
120   (BASIC statement for subtask 3)
         .
         .
         .
```

Figure III.1 *Sequence as a control structure. Figure 1a shows how a linear sequence of subtasks is drawn using conventional flowchart notation. Figure 1b shows the equivalent sequence as a series of BASIC lines.*

(a)

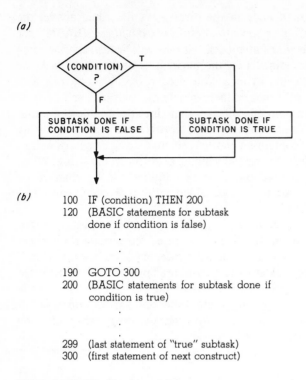

(b)
```
100   IF (condition) THEN 200
120   (BASIC statements for subtask
      done if condition is false)
        .
        .
        .
190   GOTO 300
200   (BASIC statements for subtask done if
      condition is true)
        .
        .
        .
299   (last statement of "true" subtask)
300   (first statement of next construct)
```

Figure III.2: *The* if...then...else *construct as a control structure. Figure 2a shows the conventional notation for this construct, and figure 2b shows the BASIC equivalent.*

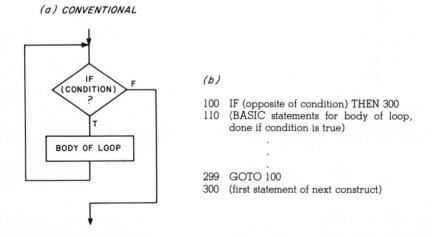

(a) CONVENTIONAL

(b)
```
100   IF (opposite of condition) THEN 300
110   (BASIC statements for body of loop,
      done if condition is true)
        .
        .
        .
299   GOTO 100
300   (first statement of next construct)
```

Figure III.3: *The* while...do *loop as a control structure. Figure 3a shows the* while...do *loop in conventional flowchart notation. Figure 3b shows the equivalent loop in BASIC code.*

The Origins of a New Notation

When I got my first job as a commercial programmer, I realized that I was going to have to write longer programs than I had previously written. This prompted me to adapt structured programming techniques to my work in BASIC, COBOL, and RPG II. (As it turned out, my longest program was a 35-page COBOL program that grew to 75 pages without going out of control. I could not have done this without the rigorous use of structured programming techniques.)

As my programs grew larger, I became dissatisfied with the methods I used to plan my programs. Conventional flowcharts obscured the structure of my programs. Nassi-Schneiderman charts and Warnier-Orr diagrams were unsatisfactory for other reasons.

The best solution offered in structured programming texts was *structured pseudocode*, an informally written Pascal-like "program" that uses terse English phrases to describe the program. Listing 1 shows the structured pseudocode for the program outlined in table 1b. I used structured pseudocode extensively to outline programs but found that the details of the resulting pseudocode often obscured the overall design of the program.

In retrospect, I can see that I wanted a design notation that could do the following:

- Completely describe the algorithm to be programmed.
- Provide overview and detailed documentation that was easy to read.
- Not need to be redrawn every time a change was made in the flowchart.
- Use a minimum of unfamiliar notation.
- Be visually pleasing.

This *structured flowchart* notation, which I developed over a period of several years, meets these criteria.

```
Program FINDMAX:
Initialize system variables (MAXV = −9 × 10²⁰, MAXINDEX = 0, INDEX = 1)
While INDEX ≤ N
    find value of current array element ( CURRV = V (INDEX) );
    if current array element (CURRV) > maximum element so far (MAXV)
        new maximum element = current element
        new maximum index = current index ( MAXINDEX = INDEX )
    endif
    increment INDEX by 1
endwhile
print MAXV, MAXINDEX
(end of program)
```

Listing III.1: *A structured pseudocode solution of the FINDMAX problem given in the text and in table 1. Structured pseudocode is a terse, informal, Pascal-like program that helps the user design a program before writing it in a formal programming language.*

Basic Constructs in Structured Flowcharting

According to the tenets of structured programming, any program can be expressed as a combination of four basic building blocks. These are sequence, *if...then...else, while...do,* and decomposition. (The first three constructs, described in conventional flowcharts in figures 1a through 3a, are given in structured flowcharts in figures 4a, 4b, and 4c, respectively.)

The sequence construct (figure 4a) is identical for both conventional and structured flowcharts; however, a later construct, decomposition, will distinguish the structured-flowchart sequence construct from its conventional counterpart.

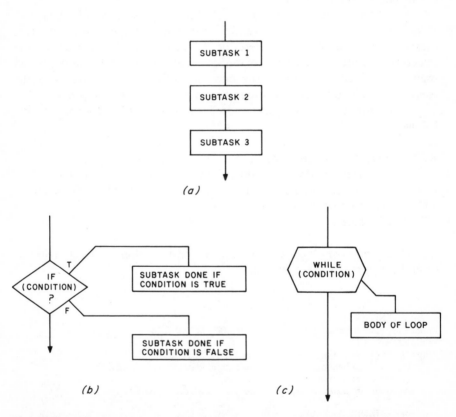

Figure III.4: *The basic structured flowchart notations. Figure 4a shows the structured flowchart notation for a sequence of tasks; it is equivalent to the flowchart of figure 1a. Figure 4b shows the structured flowchart notation for the* if...then...else *construct (equivalent to figure 2a); note that it is the placement of the letters T and F (for* true *and* false*) that determines the conditions under which a given subtask is performed. Figure 4c shows the structured flowchart notation for the* while...do *construct (equivalent to figure 3a); the diagonal line leading down indicates that the condition (in the hexagon) is performed* before *the body of the loop.*

The *if...then...else* construct is fairly straightforward in the conventional flowchart (figure 2a). In the structured-flowchart version (figure 4b), the boxes to be performed are to the right of the decision diamond, with the understanding that only one of the two boxes will be performed based on the value of the condition in the diamond. If the "else" side of the construct is not needed, the box labeled F is eliminated. In this case, if the condition does not evaluate to *true*, no action is performed, and control continues with the next construct following the decision diamond.

The notation for the *while...do* construct is not as easily derived. The conventional flowchart cannot directly express this kind of loop; it must use a decision diamond and an external loop (figure 3a). The structured flowchart version (figure 4c) introduces a new symbol, a hexagon. (Actually, the hexagon is used to denote one of several kinds of loop structures; the word *while* makes this a *while...do* loop.) The box connected below and to the right of the hexagon is performed as long as the condition listed in the hexagon is true. The condition is performed first (denoted by the position of the hexagon being spatially *above* the box being performed); this allows the possibility of the body of the loop being performed zero times if the condition is initially false.

The fourth and pivotal construct of this programming notation, decomposition, can best be stated as a rule: *any box representing a task can be broken into multiple boxes that represent the necessary subtasks*. The subtasks may be rectangular boxes that represent simple tasks, or they may be any other valid structured flowchart construct (*if...then...else, while...do*, etc.). They are written top to bottom in the order of performance, with the line denoting program flow entering each subtask box from its top and exiting from the bottom.

Figure 5 illustrates the above construct. Task X is composed of five subtasks performed in numeric sequence. Tasks 1, 2, and 5 are simple subtasks. Subtask 3 is an *if...then...else* construct that allows either subtask 3a or subtask 3b to be performed. Subtask 4 is performed as long as the condition within the hexagon ($B > Y$) is true. Of course, any subtask box may be further divided into its component subtasks.

Since any box can be broken into component subtasks, you can now see how this notation is used to design a program. The boxes in the leftmost column give the overall design of the program; boxes are then expanded to the right as each box (task) is divided into boxes representing the appropriate combination of subtasks. As a result, you can scan any one of several of the leftmost columns of boxes for an overview of varying depths of the program design, or you can study the implementation of any major or minor subtask by concentrating on only the boxes and control structures growing to the right of the given subtask.

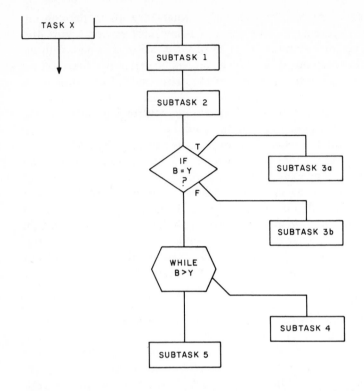

Figure III.5: *Example of the subdivision of a task. A central rule of structured flowchart is that any box can be broken into multiple boxes that represent the necessary subtasks. Here, task X is broken into five subtasks executed in top-to-bottom order. Subtasks 1, 2, and 5 are simple subtasks. Subtask 3 is an* if...then...else *construct. Subtask 4 is a* while...do *loop.*

An Example

The following example will illustrate the process of developing a program using structured flowcharts. Using the example of table 1a, suppose you are given an array of N numbers, V(1), V(2),...,V(N), and have to find the index value MAXINDEX such that the largest value in the V array is MAXV = V(MAXINDEX). The entire structured flowchart for this problem is given in figure 6.

Cover the right three-fourths of the flowchart so that only the subtasks numbered 1, 2, and 3 are visible. This is what the "first pass" of the flowcharting effort should look like. Subtask 1 is the initialization of the problem. Subtask 2 is the determination of MAXINDEX and MAXV. Subtask 3 is the printing of these two values. Since the task in subtask 3 is simple enough to be directly accomplished in the target language (for example, BASIC), it need not be subdivided.

Subtasks 1 and 2 are developed concurrently. Subtask 2 is basically a loop that examines V(1), V(2),...,V(N) in turn, keeping the appropriate values for MAXV and MAXINDEX for the I elements encountered thus far. The values of MAXV, MAXINDEX, and INDEX must be set (as is done in subtasks 1.1, 1.2, and 1.3). Note that this loop could have been done more easily using a DO loop; other optimizations could also have been made, but this example is given for the purposes of illustration only.

The main work for each element is done as subtask 2.1.2: if the current V element being examined (i.e.: CURRV) is greater than the maximum V element so far, MAXV and MAXINDEX are set to the current array and index values, respectively. These subtasks, numbered 2.1.2.1 and 2.1.2.2, are performed only when the relationship given in the diamond of 2.1.2 is true.

Once the structured flowchart has reached the level of detail shown in figure 6, most of the design considerations have been conceived and perfected; it is then a simple task to translate the program into BASIC (see listing 2) or any other general-purpose computer language. The benefits are more pronounced when used with a larger program. If a structured flowchart is subdivided to the right until each box represents a task that can be directly coded in the target language, you will catch most of the "oops, I forgot to..." insertions and changes that programmers generally think of *after* they have started coding the program.

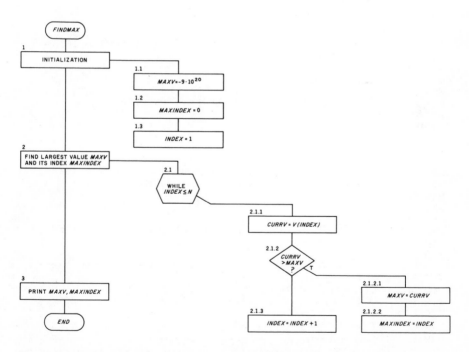

Figure III.6: *Structured flowchart for program FINDMAX. Given an array V with N elements, the problem is to find the largest element, MAXV, and its index within the V array, MAXINDEX. The numbers above each box give the sequence and level of that box in relation to the entire problem. For example, box 1 can be broken into three subtask boxes: 1.1, 1.2, and 1.3.*

```
100 :
110 REM                      PROGRAM FINDMAX
120 :
130 REM     THIS PROGRAM TAKES AN ARRAY OF NUMBERS, V, AND
140 REM    FINDS THE LARGEST ELEMENT, MAXV, AND ITS INDEX,
150 REM    MAXINDEX, SUCH THAT:
160 REM                  MAXV = V (MAXINDEX)
170 :
180 REM     (FOR THE PURPOSES OF ILLUSTRATION, WE WILL ASSUME
190 REM    THAT THE DATA IS ALREADY IN THE ARRAY V.)
200 :
210 :
220 REM ================= MAIN PROGRAM =====================
230 :
240 DIM V(12)
250 GOSUB 800: REM    --NOT PART OF ALGORITHM IN FIGURE 6; THIS
260 REM                    SUBROUTINE ENTERS DATA INTO ARRAY V
270 :
280 REM ---------- BOX 1: INITIALIZATION ROUTINE ---------------
290 :
300 MAXV = -9 * 10[20
310 MINDEX = 0
320 INDEX = 1
330 :
340 REM ---------- BOX 2: FIND LARGEST VALUE ----------------
350 :
360 REM -- (BEGINNING OF WHILE...DO LOOP)
370 IF INDEX > N THEN 520
380     CURRV = V (INDEX)
390 :
400     IF CURRV < MAXV THEN 440
410         MAXV = CURRV: REM -- (THIS PART EXECUTED IF FALSE)
420         MINDEX = INDEX
430 :
440     INDEX = INDEX + 1
450 :
460 REM -- (JUMP TO BEGINNING OF WHILE...DO LOOP)
470 GOTO 370
480 :
490 :
500 REM ----------- BOX 3: PRINT FINAL VALUES ----------------
510 :
520 PRINT:  PRINT "THE LARGEST VALUE IN THE  V  ARRAY IS:"
530 PRINT "            V("; MINDEX ; ") = "; MAXV
540 PRINT
550 :
560 END
570 REM ============= END OF MAIN PROGRAM ==================
760 :
770 :
780 REM ----------- SUBROUTINE TO FILL V ARRAY ---------------
790 :
800 DATA 12: REM -- (NUMBER OF ITEMS TO BE READ IN)
810 DATA 1, 15, -28, 3.24, -17.92, 0, 5, 1, 0, 21.4, -205, 17
820 READ N
830 FOR I=1 TO N: READ V(I): NEXT I
840 RETURN
```

Listing III.2: *A BASIC implementation of the FINDMAX problem from table 1. In this program, the variable MAXINDEX has been shortened to MINDEX to distinguish it from the variable MAXV. This program is written in TRS-80 Model I Level II BASIC, and it will run on other computers that use Microsoft BASIC.*

Other Control Structures

Although the three constructs discussed so far are sufficient for writing any program, it is not always convenient to use only these constructs. Other control structures can be devised for the convenience of the programmer. For example, boxes 1.3, 2.1, and 2.1.3 in figure 6 can be replaced by a control structure that is available in most programming languages—a *DO loop* that varies INDEX from 1 to N. An example of the notation I have devised for this is given in figure 7a; the body of the loop is performed according to the parameters given in the hexagon.

Another well-known control structure is the *repeat...until* loop, shown in figure 7b. The position of the body of the loop, above and to the right of its associated hexagon, is meant to signify that the body of the loop is performed *before* the condition is tested. Although the meaning of this notation does not implicitly follow from its form, it was chosen for its simplicity and consistency with the notation already developed.

Other constructs come to mind: a *case* structure, an unconditional *goto*, and two controlled *gotos*—the *restart* (restart the innermost containing loop) and the *exit* (go to the first task after the innermost containing loop). Although I have used some of these constructs for quite some time, they are not presented here because I am not yet satisfied with the notations I have developed for them. In any case, structured flowcharts are meant to be a personal notation—you should add to and modify these constructs to fit your needs.

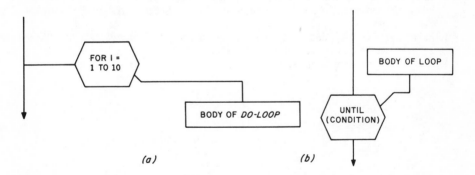

(a) (b)

Figure III.7 *Structured flowchart notation for a* do-loop *and a* repeat...until *loop. In the do-loop, figure III.7a, the hexagon contains all pertinent information defining the loop, and in the form most comfortable to the user. In the* repeat...until *loop, figure III.7b, the notation is interpreted as showing the body of the loop being executed before the condition is tested. In both cases, the box representing the body of the loop can be expanded to the right, into its component subtasks.*

Conclusions

I have found structured flowcharts helpful in designing programs. The notation is obviously intended for weakly structured languages (like BASIC), as its utility decreases when the structure of the target language increases.

The notation is, at the moment, informal, and it should stay that way. It should be extended and modified in whatever way seems useful to you. In particular, you should use additional notation for special features of the target language (e.g.: global and local variables, use of a stack of intermediate computation) when applicable. If the structured flowchart is to be read by another person, however, you should define all the structures used in terms of their equivalent unstructured (conventional) flowcharts.

If the final structured flowchart is to be redrawn, you should do so with clarity in mind. Place only those boxes that help explain the overall design with the main flowchart; leave the implementation details to subordinate flowcharts.

I hope you will find this notation useful. I would appreciate your suggestions, criticisms, and comments. ■

References

1. Page-Jones, Meillir. *The Practical Guide to Structured Systems Design*. New York: Yourdon Press, 1980.
2. Ross, D. T., Goodenough, J. B., and Irvine, C. A. "Software Engineering: Process, Principles, and Goals." *Computer*. Institute of Electrical and Electronics Engineers (IEEE), May 1975. Also *Tutorial on Software Design Techniques*, 3rd ed. P. Freeman and A. I. Wasserman, eds. Long Beach, CA: IEEE Computer Society, 1980.
3. Williams, G. "Applied Structured Programming." *Program Design*, Blaise Liffick, ed. Peterborough, NH: BYTE Books, 1978.
4. *Classics in Software Engineering*, E. N. Yourdon, ed. New York: Yourdon Press, 1979.

Structured Programming: A Qualification

About a year ago, I thought that structured programming was the ultimate tool in the analysis, design, and implementation of a computer program. I had read several books on the subject, browsed through a great many more, and successfully applied the techniques to real-world problems. Many books spoke of structured design, but I saw the concept as simply the same structured-programming tools applied to the earlier process of program design—that is, of transforming a situation to be solved into a set of programs that will accomplish the task. I was more wrong than right.

Through my experience with a particular programming project, I suddenly recognized a major point that I had formerly not comprehended: structured programming does not encompass the entire process of programming. The process of programming begins with some sort of description or specification of the program to be written. With small programs (the kind we spend most of our lives writing), this is usually enough. But as the problem gets bigger (and perhaps more ill-defined), more and more crucial decisions must be made before you divide the problem into programs.

I also learned that certain design decisions within a given program are overlooked by the main ideas of structured programming. Structured programming is a literal-minded discipline that deals exclusively with the orderly disassembly of a problem into the series of program statements that solves it. It does this while assuming several givens: the overall algorithm to be used (e.g., bubble sort of heapsort), the data structures used (e.g., linked lists, arrays, or binary trees), and implementation details (e.g., sequential or random-access files the packing of one or two characters per byte). These details, which may have a tremendous effect on the quality of the program (in such aspects as size, speed, readability, and maintainability), are factors that are evaluated and weighed in the design process.

The purpose of these paragraphs is twofold: first, to affirm that the techniques described in this article can make a significant imporovement in your skills as a programmer and that they are sufficient for many programs; and, second, to emphasize that the quality of a program can often be greatly improved by attention to the design decisions that are made in the early stages of analyzing the program design. I am including a list of particularly helpful books and articles in the references.

Appendix IV:
8080/Z80 Listing of Development-System Monitor

```
               ;
               ;
               ;          Z-80 MONITOR PROGRAM
               ;          FOR "MICROCOMPUTER OPERATING SYSTEMS"
               ;
               ;          MARK DAHMKE,   5/25/81
               ;
               ;          MACLIB   Z80
               ;
F000                      ORG      0F000H
               ;
               ;
               ;******************************************************************
               ;
               ;          THIS MONITOR IS GIVEN AS AN EXAMPLE OF TECHNIQUES
               ;          DISCUSSED IN CHAPTER 3.  NOTE THAT NO ATTEMPT HAS
               ;          BEEN MADE TO OPTIMIZE IT, SINCE IT IS MORE USEFUL
               ;          TO THE READER FOR EDUCATIONAL PURPOSES   WITHOUT
               ;          ANY CLEANUP.
               ;
               ;
               ;          IF YOU ARE GOING TO USE A VIDEO DISPLAY MEMORY
               ;          BOARD, ASSEMBLE WITH VDM = TRUE.  SET THE LINE
               ;          WIDTH AND NUMBER OF LINES TO THE SIZE OF THE VDM
               ;          BOARD.  IF USING A SERIAL TERMINAL, ASSEMBLE
               ;          WITH VDM = FALSE.  YOU MUST MAKE SURE THE EQUATES
               ;          FOR IPORT- AND OPORT- ARE SET UP FOR YOUR SERIAL
               ;          TERMINAL, AS WELL AS THE INITIALIZATION CODE AT
               ;          "DEVICE$INIT".  IF A LINE PRINTER IS AVAILABLE,
               ;          ASSEMBLE WITH LPTR = TRUE, AND LPORT- EQUATES
               ;          FOR YOUR PRINTER PORT.
               ;
               ;          A MACRO ASSEMBLER IS NOT NECESSARY.  I HAVE ONLY
               ;          USED Z80 INSTRUCTIONS WHERE THEY CAN EASILY
               ;          BE SIMULATED WITH 8080 SUBROUTINE CALLS, AND
               ;          MACROS ARE EASILY DEALT WITH WHEN RETYPING THIS
               ;          LISTING.
               ;
               ;******************************************************************
               ;
               ;
               ;
FFFF =         TRUE:    EQU      0FFFFH
0000 =         FALSE:   EQU      NOT TRUE
               ;
               ;
FFFF =         LPTR:    EQU      TRUE           ;IS THERE A LINE PRINTER?
FFFF =         VDM:     EQU      TRUE           ;IS THERE A VIDEO DISPLAY
0000 =         SERIAL:  EQU      NOT VDM        ;(MEMORY MAPPED VIDEO BOARD)
                                               ;OR SERIAL TERMINAL?
                                               ;IF SERIAL TERMINAL,
                                               ;CHANGE TO FALSE.
               ;
               ;
               ;
```

Listing cont.

```
0001 =          RSTI    EQU     1                   ;RESTART INSTRUCTION
                                                    ;USED IN BREAKPOINT
                ;
                ;
                        IF      VDM                 ;IF VDM IS TRUE, SET UP VIDEO
                                                    ; PARAMETERS
A000 =          VDMRAM: EQU     0A000H              ;START OF VIDEO RAM AREA
0040 =          VIDW:   EQU     64                  ;NUMBER OF CHARACTERS WIDE
0010 =          VIDL:   EQU     16                  ;NUMBER OF LINES OF VIDW
                ;
                        ENDIF
                ;
                ;
FFFF =          JTBL:   EQU     TRUE                ;TRUE IF YOU WANT JUMP TABLE
                                                    ;DRIVEN, FALSE IF YOU WANT
                                                    ;COMPARE AND BRANCH.
                ;
                ;
                ;
0013 =          IPORTS: EQU     13H                 ;INPUT PORT STATUS
0001 =          IPORTM: EQU     00000001B           ;INPUT PORT STATUS MASK.
0010 =          IPORTD: EQU     10H                 ;INPUT PORT DATA
                ;
                        IF      NOT VDM             ;INCLUDE ONLY IF PORT OUTPUT.
                OPORTS: EQU     13H                 ;OUTPUT PORT STATUS
                OPORTM: EQU     00001000B           ;OUTPUT PORT STATUS MASK.
                OPORTD: EQU     11H                 ;OUTPUT PORT DATA
                        ENDIF
                ;
                        IF      LPTR                ;IF LINE PRINTER, INCLUDE THIS.
0013 =          LPORTS: EQU     13H                 ;LINE PRINTER PORT STATUS.
0002 =          LPORTM: EQU     00000010B           ;LINE PRINTER STATUS MASK.
0010 =          LPORTD: EQU     10H                 ;LINE PRINTER DATA OUTPUT PORT.
                        ENDIF
                ;
                ;
0000 =          BOTTOM$OF$RAM: EQU 0000H                       ;LOWER LIMIT OF RAM
0010 =          BADDR:  EQU     BOTTOM$OF$RAM + 10H   ;FIXED STORAGE AREA
0012 =          PTR:    EQU     BADDR + 2             ;TEMPORARY STORAGE AREA
0014 =          PTR1:   EQU     BADDR + 4
0016 =          PTR2:   EQU     BADDR + 6
0018 =          PTR3:   EQU     BADDR + 8
001A =          PTR4:   EQU     BADDR + 10
001C =          LPT:    EQU     BADDR + 12
001D =          COUNTER: EQU    BADDR + 13
                ;
                        IF      VDM
001E =          CURSOR: EQU     BADDR + 14          ;VDM CURSOR STORAGE AREA
0020 =          LINE:   EQU     BADDR + 16          ;VDM STORAGE AREA
                ;
                        ENDIF
                ;
                ;
                ;
000D =          CR:     EQU     0DH
000A =          LF:     EQU     0AH
```

Listing cont.

```
                    ;
                    ;
0008 =      COLS    EQU     8                   ;NUMBER OF COLUMNS TO DISPLAY IN
                                                ;"DUMP"
0008 =      LINES   EQU     8                   ;NUMBER OF LINES TO DISPLAY IN
                                                ;"DUMP"
                    ;
                    ;
            ENTRY   MACRO   ?CHAR,?ADDR
                    DB      ?CHAR
                    DW      ?ADDR
                    ENDM
                    ;
                    ;
            MSG     MACRO   ?ADDR
                    LXI     H,?ADDR
                    CALL    DISP
                    ENDM
                    ;
                    ;
            GETPTR  MACRO   ?MSG,?PTR
                    MSG     ?MSG
                    CALL    HEXIN
                    SHLD    ?PTR
                    CPI     '.'
                    JZ      PRMPT
                    ENDM
                    ;
                    ;
F000 C318F0 START:  JMP     COLD$START
F003 C349F0 WSTART: JMP     WARM$START          ;BYPASS ALL INITIALIZATION.
F006 C316FA CST:    JMP     CSTAT               ;KEYBOARD STATUS
F009 C31FFA CI:     JMP     CIN                 ;CONSOLE INPUT
F00C C33FFA CO:     JMP     COUT                ;CONSOLE OUTPUT
                    IF      NOT VDM
                    JMP     POUT                ;PRINTER OUTPUT ROUTINE.
                    ENDIF
                    ;
F00F C339FA CLRS:   JMP     CLRSCN
F012 C328FA UCI:    JMP     UCIN                ;UPPER CASE INPUT ROUTINE
F015 C31CF5         JMP     HEXO2               ;2 DIGIT HEX OUT ROUTINE
                    ;
                    ;
                    ;
            COLD$START:
                    ;
F018 210000 MEMCHK: LXI     H,BOTTOM$OF$RAM ;START AT BOTTOM OF MEMORY
F01B 7E     MEM1:   MOV     A,M                 ;GET A BYTE
F01C 2F             CMA                         ;COMPLIMENT IT
F01D 77             MOV     M,A                 ;PUT IT BACK
F01E BE             CMP     M                   ;NOW COMPARE WITH MEMORY
F01F 2F             CMA                         ;COMPLIMENT BACK TO ORIGINAL
F020 77             MOV     M,A                 ;AND REPLACE IN MEMORY
F021 C228F0         JNZ     FINISH              ;DONE. WE HAVE FOUND THE TOP
F024 24             INR     H                   ;IF SAME, INCREMENT TO NEXT PAGE
F025 C31BF0         JMP     MEM1                ;AND TRY AGAIN.
```

Listing cont.

```
                                           ;
F028 25          FINISH: DCR    H          ;WE HAVE ADDR OF THE PAGE
                                           ;JUST BEFORE THE LAST.
                 MEMINIT:
F029 F9                  SPHL               ;INITIALIZE THE STACK POINTER.
F02A 221000              SHLD   BADDR       ;SAVE BASE ADDRESS POINTER
                                           ;IN FIXED MEMORY.
F02D 3EC3                MVI    A,0C3H      ;MAKE A JUMP INSTRUCTION
F02F 320000              STA    BOTTOM$OF$RAM    ;WARM START VECTOR
F032 320800              STA    BOTTOM$OF$RAM + 8  ;FIRST RESTART VECTOR.
                 ;
F035 2149F0              LXI    H,WARM$START ;GET ADDR OF WARM START
                                           ;VECTOR
F038 220100              SHLD   BOTTOM$OF$RAM + 1  ;MAKE JUMP INSTRUCTION
                 ;
F03B 2196F3              LXI    H,BKPT$TRAP  ;GET ADDR OF BREAKPOINT
                                           ;ROUTINE
F03E 220900              SHLD   BOTTOM$OF$RAM + 9  ;MAKE JUMP INSTRUCTION
                                           ;AT RST 1
                 ;
                 DEVICE$INIT:
                 ;
                         IF     VDM
F041 CDOFF0              CALL   CLRS        ;CLEAR VIDEO SCREEN,
                                           ;IF VDM = TRUE
                         ENDIF
                 ;
                         IF     NOT VDM
                                           ;INSERT YOUR SERIAL
                                           ;DEVICE
                                           ;INITIALIZATION
                                           ;INSTRUCTIONS HERE.
                                           ;
                 OCTRL:  EQU    20H         ;UART CONTROL PORT
                 OCTC:   EQU    21H         ;COUNTER TIMER CIRCUIT
                 ;
                         MVI    A,0FH       ;INITIALIZE UART
                         OUT    OCTRL
                 ;
                         MVI    A,83H       ;INITIALIZE DATA RATE
                         OUT    OCTC
                 ;
                 ;
                         ENDIF
                 ;
F044 3E00                MVI    A,0
F046 321C00              STA    LPT         ;INITIALIZE PRINTER FLAG
                 ;
                 ;
                 ;
                 WARM$START:
                 ;
                         MSG    MENU        ;DISPLAY COMMAND MENU
F049+218BF5              LXI    H,MENU
F04C+CDFFF9              CALL   DISP
                 PRMPT:  MSG    PROMPT      ;DISPLAY PROMPT
```

Listing cont.

```
F04F+21C6F7          LXI     H,PROMPT
F052+CDFFF9          CALL    DISP
                                              ;MESSAGE AND CHARACTER.
F055 CD12F0          CALL    UCI               ;GET CHARACTER (UCI
                                              ;CONVERTS IT TO
                                              ;UPPER CASE)
F058 F5              PUSH    PSW
F059 4F              MOV     C,A
F05A CD0CF0          CALL    CO                ;ECHO CHARACTER
F05D CD0BFA          CALL    CRLF              ;GO TO NEW LINE
F060 F1              POP     PSW
                ;
                     IF      NOT JTBL          ;IF JUMP TABLE, SKIP
                                              ;THIS PART.
                     CPI     'G'
                     JZ      GO                ;EXECUTE AT ADDRESS
                     CPI     'D'               ;DISPLAY MEMORY
                     JZ      DUMP
                     CPI     'S'               ;EXAMINE AND
                                              ;MODIFY MEMORY
                     JZ      EXAMINE
                     CPI     'M'               ;BLOCK MOVE COMMAND?
                     JZ      MOVE$BLOCK
                     CPI     'B'               ;BOOT COMMAND?
                     JZ      BOOT
                     CPI     'I'               ;INPUT FROM PORT?
                     JZ      INPUT$PORT
                     CPI     'O'               ;OUTPUT TO PORT?
                     JZ      OUTPUT$PORT
                     CPI     'F'               ;FILL MEMORY?
                     JZ      FILL$MEM
                     CPI     'L'               ;SEARCH FOR STRING?
                     JZ      LOCATE$STRING
                     CPI     'T'               ;MEMORY TEST ?
                     JZ      MEM$TEST
                     CPI     'C'               ;COMPARE BLOCKS?
                     JZ      COMPARE$MEM
                     CPI     'P'               ;TURN ON/OFF PRINTER?
                     JZ      PRINTER$TOGGLE
                     CPI     'W'               ;DISPLAY MENU?
                     JZ      WARM$START
                     CPI     'V'               ;SET BREAKPOINT?
                     JZ      SET$BKPT
                     CPI     'U'               ;UNSET BREAKPOINT?
                     JZ      UNSET$BKPT
                     CPI     'R'               ;RESUME FROM BREAKPOINT?
                     JZ      RESUME$BKPT
                     CPI     'X'               ;EXAMINE REGISTERS?
                     JZ      DISP$REGS
                ;
                     JMP     PRMPT
                     ENDIF
                ;
                ;
                     IF      JTBL              ;IF USING A JUMP TABLE,
                                              ;INCLUDE THIS PORTION
```

Listing cont.

```
                          ;
F061 2183F0               LXI     H,JTABLE        ;GET ADDR OF THE TABLE
F064 4E         JTCONT: MOV       C,M             ;GET CHARACTER FROM TABLE ENTRY
                          ;
F065 0C                   INR     C
F066 0D                   DCR     C               ;USE THIS TRICK TO SET FLAGS
                                                  ;BASED ON C.
F067 CA7AF0               JZ      JTEND           ;END OF TABLE. TERMINATE.
                                                  ;
F06A B9                   CMP     C               ;COMPARE TO A-REG.
F06B C274F0               JNZ     NEXTJV          ;IF NOT SAME, MOVE TO NEXT ENTRY
F06E 23                   INX     H               ;IF HERE, WE HAVE IT.
F06F 5E                   MOV     E,M             ;GET FIRST BYTE
F070 23                   INX     H
F071 56                   MOV     D,M             ;AND SECOND BYTE OF ADDRESS
F072 EB                   XCHG
F073 E9                   PCHL                    ;AND JUMP TO IT.
                          ;
                          ;
F074 23         NEXTJV: INX       H
F075 23                   INX     H
F076 23                   INX     H               ;POINT TO NEXT ENTRY...
F077 C364F0               JMP     JTCONT          ;AND TRY AGAIN.
                          ;
                JTEND:  MSG       JTERR           ;IF HERE, IT WAS A BAD KEY.
F07A+21CBF7               LXI     H,JTERR
F07D+CDFFF9               CALL    DISP
F080 C349F0               JMP     WARM$START      ;ISSUE ERROR MESSAGE,
                                                  ;AND TRY AGAIN
                          ;
                          ;
                JTABLE: ENTRY     'G',GO
F083+47                   DB      'G'
F084+B9F0                 DW      GO
                          ENTRY   'D',DUMP
F086+44                   DB      'D'
F087+D3F0                 DW      DUMP
                          ENTRY   'S',EXAMINE
F089+53                   DB      'S'
F08A+44F1                 DW      EXAMINE
                          ENTRY   'M',MOVE$BLOCK
F08C+4D                   DB      'M'
F08D+C8F2                 DW      MOVE$BLOCK
                          ENTRY   'R',RESUME$BKPT
F08F+52                   DB      'R'
F090+6BF3                 DW      RESUME$BKPT
                          ENTRY   'B',BOOT
F092+42                   DB      'B'
F093+2CF4                 DW      BOOT
                          ENTRY   'I',INPUT$PORT
F095+49                   DB      'I'
F096+2FF2                 DW      INPUT$PORT
                          ENTRY   'O',OUTPUT$PORT
F098+4F                   DB      'O'
F099+4AF2                 DW      OUTPUT$PORT
                          ENTRY   'F',FILL$MEM
```

Listing cont.

```
F09B+46              DB      'F'
F09C+77F2            DW      FILL$MEM
                     ENTRY   'T',MEM$TEST
F09E+54              DB      'T'
F09F+D1F3            DW      MEM$TEST
                     ENTRY   'C',COMPARE$MEM
F0A1+43              DB      'C'
F0A2+88F4            DW      COMPARE$MEM
                     ENTRY   'V',SET$BKPT
F0A4+56              DB      'V'
F0A5+33F3            DW      SET$BKPT
                     ENTRY   'L',LOCATE$STRING
F0A7+4C              DB      'L'
F0A8+8AF1            DW      LOCATE$STRING
                     ENTRY   'U',UNSET$BKPT
F0AA+55              DB      'U'
F0AB+5CF3            DW      UNSET$BKPT
                     ENTRY   'P',PRINTER$TOGGLE
F0AD+50              DB      'P'
F0AE+16F3            DW      PRINTER$TOGGLE
                     ENTRY   'W',WARM$START
F0B0+57              DB      'W'
F0B1+49F0            DW      WARM$START
                     ENTRY   'X',DISP$REGS
F0B3+58              DB      'X'
F0B4+2FF4            DW      DISP$REGS
                     ENTRY   0,0
F0B6+00              DB      0
F0B7+0000            DW      0
              ;
              ;
                     ENDIF
              ;
              ;      GO --   ENTER A HEX NUMBER TO JUMP TO.
              ;
              GO:    MSG     NUM         ;PUT OUT MESSAGE
F0B9+216AF5          LXI     H,NUM
F0BC+CDFFF9          CALL    DISP
F0BF CDF1F4          CALL    HEXIN
F0C2 FE2E            CPI     '.'         ;IF '.', THEN ABORT
F0C4 CA4FF0          JZ      PRMPT
F0C7 221200          SHLD    PTR
F0CA 2A1000          LHLD    BADDR       ;GET BASE ADDRESS
F0CD 25              DCR     H
F0CE F9              SPHL                ;SET UP USER STACK POINTER.
F0CF 2A1200          LHLD    PTR         ;RELOAD EXECUTION ADDRESS
F0D2 E9              PCHL                ;EXECUTE ADDRESS IN HL-REG.
              ;
              ;
              DUMP:  MSG     NUM
F0D3+216AF5          LXI     H,NUM
F0D6+CDFFF9          CALL    DISP
F0D9 CDF1F4          CALL    HEXIN
F0DC 221200          SHLD    PTR
F0DF FE2E            CPI     '.'
F0E1 CA4FF0          JZ      PRMPT
```

Listing cont.

```
F0E4 CD0BFA    L1:      CALL    CRLF
F0E7 1E08               MVI     E,COLS    ;SET NUMBER OF COLUMNS OF HEX BYTES
F0E9 1608      LIN:     MVI     D,LINES   ;SET NUMBER OF LINES TO
                                          ;DISPLAY PER PASS.
F0EB CD21F5             CALL    HEXOUT    ;OUTPUT THE ADDRESS
F0EE CD44F5    COL:     CALL    SPACE
F0F1 2A1200             LHLD    PTR       ;GET ADDR AGAIN
F0F4 66                 MOV     H,M
F0F5 CD1CF5             CALL    HEXO2     ;OUTPUT THE VALUE
F0F8 2A1200             LHLD    PTR
F0FB 23                 INX     H         ;INCR POINTER
F0FC 221200             SHLD    PTR
F0FF 15                 DCR     D
F100 C2EEF0             JNZ     COL
F103 CD44F5             CALL    SPACE
F106 1608               MVI     D,COLS
F108 01F8FF             LXI     B,-COLS
F10B 2A1200             LHLD    PTR
F10E 09                 DAD     B         ;POINT AT START OF LINE AGAIN
F10F 4E       CH1:      MOV     C,M
F110 79                 MOV     A,C
F111 FE80               CPI     80H
F113 D21BF1             JNC     COL2
F116 FE20               CPI     ' '
F118 D21DF1             JNC     COL3
F11B 0E2E     COL2:     MVI     C,'.'
F11D CD0CF0   COL3:     CALL    CO
F120 23                 INX     H
F121 15                 DCR     D         ;DCR COUNTER
F122 C20FF1             JNZ     CH1
F125 CD0BFA             CALL    CRLF
F128 1D                 DCR     E
F129 C2E9F0             JNZ     LIN
F12C CD12F0             CALL    UCI
F12F FE20               CPI     ' '
F131 CAE4F0             JZ      L1        ;GO AGAIN
F134 FE2E               CPI     '.'
F136 CA4FF0             JZ      PRMPT     ;QUIT
F139 FE0D               CPI     CR
F13B CA4FF0             JZ      PRMPT     ;QUIT
F13E CD0BFA             CALL    CRLF
F141 C34FF0             JMP     PRMPT
              ;
              EXAMINE: GETPTR EXPRMP,PTR        ;EXAMINE AND MODIFY MEMORY
F144+214CF5             LXI     H,EXPRMP
F147+CDFFF9             CALL    DISP
F14A+CDF1F4             CALL    HEXIN
F14D+221200             SHLD    PTR
F150+FE2E               CPI     '.'
F152+CA4FF0             JZ      PRMPT
F155 CD0BFA   EXAM1:    CALL    CRLF
F158 CD44F5             CALL    SPACE
F15B CD21F5             CALL    HEXOUT    ;DISPLAY THE ADDRESS
F15E CD44F5             CALL    SPACE
F161 2A1200             LHLD    PTR
F164 66                 MOV     H,M
```

Listing cont.

```
F165 CD1CF5              CALL    HEX02
F168 CD44F5              CALL    SPACE
F16B CDF1F4              CALL    HEXIN    ;GET THE BYTE
F16E FE2E                CPI     '.'
F170 CA4FF0              JZ      PRMPT    ;QUIT
F173 FE0D                CPI     CR
F175 CA84F1              JZ      EX2
F178 7D                  MOV     A,L
F179 2A1200              LHLD    PTR
F17C 77                  MOV     M,A      ;STORE THE BYTE
F17D 23         EX3:     INX     H
F17E 221200              SHLD    PTR
F181 C355F1              JMP     EXAM1    ;GO AGAIN.
F184 2A1200     EX2:     LHLD    PTR
F187 C37DF1              JMP     EX3
                ;
                ;
                LOCATE$STRING:
                         GETPTR  SADDR$MSG,PTR   ;GET FIRST HEX NUMBER
F18A+2111F8              LXI     H,SADDR$MSG
F18D+CDFFF9              CALL    DISP
F190+CDF1F4              CALL    HEXIN
F193+221200              SHLD    PTR
F196+FE2E                CPI     '.'
F198+CA4FF0              JZ      PRMPT
                                          ;WHICH IS START ADDRESS
                                          ;TO SEARCH
                         GETPTR  EADDR$MSG,PTR1  ;GET END ADDRESS NUMBER
F19B+2129F8              LXI     H,EADDR$MSG
F19E+CDFFF9              CALL    DISP
F1A1+CDF1F4              CALL    HEXIN
F1A4+221400              SHLD    PTR1
F1A7+FE2E                CPI     '.'
F1A9+CA4FF0              JZ      PRMPT
                                          ;END OF SEARCH ADDRESS
                         MSG     BSTR$MSG
F1AC+213FF8              LXI     H,BSTR$MSG
F1AF+CDFFF9              CALL    DISP
F1B2 2A1000              LHLD    BADDR
F1B5 114000              LXI     D,40H            ;SET UP OFFSET
F1B8 19                  DAD     D
F1B9 221600              SHLD    PTR2             ;POINTER TO STRING AREA
F1BC 221800              SHLD    PTR3             ;POINTER TO CURRENT CHAR
                                                  ;WITHIN STRING
F1BF 3E00                MVI     A,0
F1C1 321A00              STA     PTR4             ;INIT COUNTER
                GETBYTES:
F1C4 CDF1F4              CALL    HEXIN            ;GET FIRST BYTE
F1C7 FE2E                CPI     '.'
F1C9 CA4FF0              JZ      PRMPT            ;IF PERIOD, ABORT.
F1CC FE2C                CPI     ','
F1CE CAE4F1              JZ      COMPARE          ;IF COMMA, DO SEARCH.
                ;
F1D1 7D                  MOV     A,L              ;GET THE BYTE JUST ENTERED
F1D2 2A1800              LHLD    PTR3             ;AND GET POINTER TO STORAGE AREA
F1D5 77                  MOV     M,A              ;SAVE IT.
```

Listing cont.

```
F1D6 23                INX    H              ;POINT TO NEXT BYTE LOCATION
F1D7 221800            SHLD   PTR3           ;AND UPDATE THE POINTER.
                ;
F1DA 3A1A00            LDA    PTR4           ;LOAD COUNTER VALUE.
F1DD 3C                INR    A
F1DE 321A00            STA    PTR4           ;INCREMENT, AND STORE AWAY AGAIN
F1E1 C3C4F1            JMP    GETBYTES       ;GET ANOTHER BYTE IN THE STRING.
                ;
            COMPARE:
F1E4 2A1200            LHLD   PTR
                       LDED   PTR2           ;LOAD ADDRESS OF STRING
F1E7+ED5B              DB     0EDH,5BH
F1E9+1600              DW     PTR2
                                             ;TO LOOK FOR.
F1EB 3A1A00            LDA    PTR4           ;GET COUNTER
F1EE 47                MOV    B,A            ;TO B-REG.
F1EF CD27F2            CALL   COMPSTR        ;COMPARE THE STRINGS,
                                             ;OF LENGTH (B).
F1F2 A7                ANA    A              ;ON RETURN, MAKE
                                             ;SURE FLAGS ARE SET.
F1F3 CA15F2            JZ     FOUND$STR      ;IF ZERO, WE HAVE FOUND A MATCH.
F1F6 2A1200            LHLD   PTR
                       LDED   PTR1
F1F9+ED5B              DB     0EDH,5BH
F1FB+1400              DW     PTR1
                       DSBC   D              ;PTR-PTR1
F1FD+ED52              DB     0EDH,D*8+42H
F1FF C20BF2            JNZ    CONT           ;IF NOT THE SAME, CONTINUE
                       MSG    NOTFOUND
F202+21DFF7            LXI    H,NOTFOUND
F205+CDFFF9            CALL   DISP
F208 C34FF0            JMP    PRMPT          ;DONE.
                ;
F20B 2A1200  CONT:     LHLD   PTR
F20E 23                INX    H
F20F 221200            SHLD   PTR
F212 C3E7F1            JMP    COMPARE + 3    ;CONTINUE THE SEARCH.
                ;
            FOUND$STR:
                       MSG    FOUND          ;ISSUE MESSAGE.
F215+21F5F7            LXI    H,FOUND
F218+CDFFF9            CALL   DISP
F21B 2A1200            LHLD   PTR            ;GET ADDRESS OF LOCATED STRING
F21E CD21F5            CALL   HEXOUT         ;AND OUTPUT IT.
F221 CD0BFA            CALL   CRLF
F224 CA4FF0            JZ     PRMPT          ;DONE.
                ;
            COMPSTR:                    *    ;COMPARE TWO STRINGS.
                                             ;HL = SOURCE STRING
                                             ;DE = COMPARE STRING
                                             ;B = LENGTH OF STRING (0-255)
F227 1A                LDAX   D
F228 96                SUB    M              ;A-M
F229 C0                RNZ                   ;RETURN IF NOT EQUAL
F22A 13                INX    D
F22B 23                INX    H
```

Listing cont.

```
                         DJNZ    COMPSTR
F22C+10F9                DB      10H,COMPSTR-$-1
F22E C9                  RET
                ;
                ;


                INPUT$PORT:
                         MSG     PORT$MSG        ;ISSUE PROMPT MSG
F22F+21C0F8              LXI     H,PORT$MSG
F232+CDFFF9              CALL    DISP
F235 CDF1F4              CALL    HEXIN           ;GET THE PORT ADDRESS
F238 FE2E                CPI     '.'             ;CHECK FOR ABORT.
F23A CA4FF0              JZ      PRMPT
F23D 4D                  MOV     C,L             ;GET PORT NUMBER
                         INP     A               ;Z80 INPUT INSTRUCTION
F23E+ED78                DB      0EDH,A*8+40H
F240 67                  MOV     H,A             ;MOVE THE RESULTANT NUMBER TO H
F241 CD1CF5              CALL    HEXO2           ;TO DISPLAY IT.
F244 CD0BFA              CALL    CRLF

F247 C34FF0              JMP     PRMPT           ;END.
                ;
                OUTPUT$PORT:
                         MSG     PORT$MSG
F24A+21C0F8              LXI     H,PORT$MSG
F24D+CDFFF9              CALL    DISP
F250 CDF1F4              CALL    HEXIN
F253 FE2E                CPI     '.'
F255 CA4FF0              JZ      PRMPT           ;IF PERIOD, ABORT.
F258 7D                  MOV     A,L             ;GET PORT NUMBER IN A-REG.
F259 321200              STA     PTR             ;AND SAVE IT.
                         MSG     BYTE$MSG
F25C+21D1F8              LXI     H,BYTE$MSG
F25F+CDFFF9              CALL    DISP
F262 CDF1F4              CALL    HEXIN
F265 FE2E                CPI     '.'
F267 CA4FF0              JZ      PRMPT
F26A 3A1200              LDA     PTR             ;RESTORE THE PORT NUMBER
F26D 4F                  MOV     C,A
F26E 7D                  MOV     A,L             ;PUT VALUE IN A, PORT IN C
                         OUTP    A               ;AND SEND IT.
F26F+ED79                DB      0EDH,A*8+41H
F271 CD0BFA              CALL    CRLF
F274 C34FF0              JMP     PRMPT           ;DONE.
                ;
                FILL$MEM:
                         GETPTR  SADDR$MSG,PTR   ;GET START ADDR
F277+2111F8              LXI     H,SADDR$MSG
F27A+CDFFF9              CALL    DISP
F27D+CDF1F4              CALL    HEXIN
F280+221200              SHLD    PTR
F283+FE2E                CPI     '.'
F285+CA4FF0              JZ      PRMPT
                         GETPTR  EADDR$MSG,PTR1  ;AND END ADDR
F288+2129F8              LXI     H,EADDR$MSG
F28B+CDFFF9              CALL    DISP
```

Listing cont.

```
F28E+CDF1F4            CALL    HEXIN
F291+221400            SHLD    PTR1
F294+FE2E              CPI     '.'
F296+CA4FF0            JZ      PRMPT
                       GETPTR  FCHAR$MSG,PTR2   ;AND FILL CHARACTER (BYTE)
F299+21E4F8            LXI     H,FCHAR$MSG
F29C+CDFFF9            CALL    DISP
F29F+CDF1F4            CALL    HEXIN
F2A2+221600            SHLD    PTR2
F2A5+FE2E              CPI     '.'
F2A7+CA4FF0            JZ      PRMPT
              ;
                       LDED    PTR              ;GET START ADDR
F2AA+ED5B              DB      0EDH,5BH
F2AC+1200              DW      PTR
F2AE 2A1400            LHLD    PTR1             ;AND END ADDR
                       DSBC    DE               ;END-START = LENGTH
F2B1+ED52              DB      0EDH,DE*8+42H
              ;
F2B3 E5                PUSH    H
F2B4 C1                POP     B                ;MOVE LENGTH TO BC
              ;
F2B5 211600            LXI     H,PTR2           ;POINT TO FILL CHAR
                       LDED    PTR              ;DESTINATION
F2B8+ED5B              DB      0EDH,5BH
F2BA+1200              DW      PTR
              FILL:    LDI
F2BC+EDA0              DB      0EDH,0A0H
F2BE 2B                DCX     H                ;MAKE SURE WE ARE STILL
                                                ;POINTING AT
                                                ;FILL CHAR
F2BF EABCF2            JPE     FILL             ;LOOP UNTIL DONE
              ;
F2C2 CD0BFA            CALL    CRLF
F2C5 C34FF0            JMP     PRMPT            ;DONE.
              ;
              MOVE$BLOCK:
                       GETPTR  SADDR$MSG,PTR    ;GET SOURCE ADDR
F2C8+2111F8            LXI     H,SADDR$MSG
F2CB+CDFFF9            CALL    DISP
F2CE+CDF1F4            CALL    HEXIN
F2D1+221200            SHLD    PTR
F2D4+FE2E              CPI     '.'
F2D6+CA4FF0            JZ      PRMPT
                       GETPTR  EADDR$MSG,PTR1   ;AND END ADDR (OF SOURCE)
F2D9+2129F8            LXI     H,EADDR$MSG
F2DC+CDFFF9            CALL    DISP
F2DF+CDF1F4            CALL    HEXIN
F2E2+221400            SHLD    PTR1
F2E5+FE2E              CPI     '.'
F2E7+CA4FF0            JZ      PRMPT
                       GETPTR  DADDR$MSG,PTR2   ;AND DESTINATION ADDR OF BLOCK.
F2EA+21F7F8            LXI     H,DADDR$MSG
F2ED+CDFFF9            CALL    DISP
F2F0+CDF1F4            CALL    HEXIN
F2F3+221600            SHLD    PTR2
```

Listing cont.

```
F2F6+FE2E              CPI     '.'
F2F8+CA4FF0            JZ      PRMPT
                ;
F2FB 2A1400            LHLD    PTR1            ;END ADDR
                       LDED    PTR             ;START ADR
F2FE+ED5B              DB      0EDH,5BH
F300+1200              DW      PTR
                       DSBC    DE              ;LENGTH
F302+ED52              DB      0EDH,DE*8+42H
F304 23                INX     H               ;LENGTH + 1
F305 E5                PUSH    H
F306 C1                POP     B               ;MOVE LENGTH TO BC
                ;
F307 2A1200            LHLD    PTR             ;SOURCE
                       LDED    PTR2            ;DEST
F30A+ED5B              DB      0EDH,5BH
F30C+1600              DW      PTR2
                       LDIR                    ;DO BLOCK MOVE
F30E+EDB0              DB      0EDH,0B0H
                ;
F310 CD0BFA            CALL    CRLF
F313 C34FF0            JMP     PRMPT           ;DONE.
                ;
                ;
                PRINTER$TOGGLE:
F316 3A1C00            LDA     LPT             ;CHECK TO SEE IF PRINTER
                                               ;IS ENABLED.
F319 2F                CMA                     ;IF ON, TURN OFF.
                                               ;IF OFF, TURN ON.
F31A 321C00            STA     LPT             ;AND SAVE NEW FLAG.
                ;
F31D A7                ANA     A
F31E CA2AF3            JZ      PRTR$OFF
                       MSG     PRTR$ON$MSG     ;MESSAGE IF ACTIVE.
F321+210FF9            LXI     H,PRTR$ON$MSG
F324+CDFFF9            CALL    DISP
F327 C34FF0            JMP     PRMPT
                ;
                PRTR$OFF:
                       MSG     PRTR$OFF$MSG    ;MESSAGE IF INACTIVE.
F32A+212BF9            LXI     H,PRTR$OFF$MSG
F32D+CDFFF9            CALL    DISP
F330 C34FF0            JMP     PRMPT
                ;
                ;
                SET$BKPT:
                       GETPTR  BKPT$MSG,PTR    ;GET ADDRESS TO
F333+219EF9            LXI     H,BKPT$MSG
F336+CDFFF9            CALL    DISP
F339+CDF1F4            CALL    HEXIN
F33C+221200            SHLD    PTR
F33F+FE2E              CPI     '.'
F341+CA4FF0            JZ      PRMPT
                                               ;PUT BREAKPOINT AT.
F344 7E                MOV     A,M             ;GET THE BYTE AT THAT ADDR
F345 2A1000            LHLD    BADDR
```

Listing cont.

```
                        LDED    PTR             ;GET ADDRESS TO PUT BKPT IN.
F348+ED5B               DB      0EDH,5BH
F34A+1200               DW      PTR
F34C 73                 MOV     M,E
F34D 23                 INX     H
F34E 72                 MOV     M,D             ;SAVE THE PTR
F34F 23                 INX     H
F350 77                 MOV     M,A             ;AND THE OLD CONTENTS
                                                ;OF THE BYTE
F351 2A1200             LHLD    PTR             ;GET ADDRESS AGAIN
F354 36CF               MVI     M,(RSTI*8 + 0C7H) ;MAKE THE RESTART INSTRUCTION.
            ;
F356 CD0BFA             CALL    CRLF
F359 C34FF0             JMP     PRMPT           ;DONE
            ;
            ;
            UNSET$BKPT:
F35C 2A1000             LHLD    BADDR           ;GET ADDRESS OF THE BREAKPOINT
F35F E5                 PUSH    H
F360 D1                 POP     D               ;COPY ADDR INTO DE
            ;
F361 23                 INX     H
F362 23                 INX     H               ;GET OLD DATA BYTE
F363 7E                 MOV     A,M             ;INTO A-REG
F364 12                 STAX    D               ;AND STORE IT INTO BKPT ADDRESS
            ;
            ;
F365 CD0BFA             CALL    CRLF
F368 C34FF0             JMP     PRMPT           ;DONE.
            ;
            ;
            RESUME$BKPT:                        ;RESUME FROM A BREAKPOINT.
F36B 2A1000             LHLD    BADDR
F36E 112000             LXI     D,20H           ;GET OFFSET INTO SAVE AREA
F371 19                 DAD     D
F372 F9                 SPHL                    ;SET UP THE STACK POINTER.
            ;
F373 F1                 POP     PSW
F374 C1                 POP     B
F375 D1                 POP     D
F376 E1                 POP     H
            ;
                        EXAF
F377+08                 DB      08H
                        EXX                     ;SWAP WITH ALTERNATE REGISTERS.
F378+D9                 DB      0D9H
            ;
F379 E1                 POP     H
F37A 221600             SHLD    PTR2            ;GET PC (UNUSED)
F37D E1                 POP     H
F37E 221400             SHLD    PTR1            ;GET OLD SP
                        POPIX
F381+DDE1               DB      0DDH,0E1H
                        POPIY
F383+FDE1               DB      0FDH,0E1H
F385 F1                 POP     PSW
```

Listing cont.

```
F386 C1              POP      B
F387 D1              POP      D
F388 E1              POP      H
                     EXX
F389+D9              DB       0D9H
                     EXAF                    ;SWAP REGISTERS AGAIN.
F38A+08              DB       08H
              ;
F38B 221200          SHLD     PTR            ;SAVE CURRENT HL
F38E 2A1400          LHLD     PTR1           ;GET SP
F391 F9              SPHL                    ;RESTORE USER'S STACK POINTER
              ;
F392 2A1200          LHLD     PTR            ;RESTORE USER'S HL
              ;
F395 C9              RET                     ;RETURN FROM THE RESTART
                                             ;INSTRUCTION
                                             ;AT THE BREAKPOINT.  USER'S PC
                                             ;IS RELOADED FROM THE
                                             ;STACK AS IN A NORMAL
                                             ;SUBROUTINE RETURN.

              ;
              ;
              BKPT$TRAP:
F396 221200          SHLD     PTR            ;SAVE HL FIRST
              ;
F399 210000          LXI      H,0
F39C 39              DAD      SP             ;GET THE USER'S  STACK POINTER
              ;
F39D 221400          SHLD     PTR1           ;SAVE IT.
F3A0 E1              POP      H
F3A1 E5              PUSH     H              ;GET A COPY OF THE
                                             ;PROGRAM COUNTER.
F3A2 221600          SHLD     PTR2           ;AND SAVE IT
              ;
F3A5 113800          LXI      D,38H
F3A8 2A1000          LHLD     BADDR
F3AB 19              DAD      D              ;GET OFFSET INTO SAVE AREA (TOP)
              ;
F3AC F9              SPHL                    ;SET UP DUMMY STACK POINTER AT
                                             ;TOP OF REGISTER SAVE AREA.
                                             ;WE ARE GOING TO
                                             ;USE THE STACK TO

                                             ;SAVE SOME EFFORT.
                                             ;NOTE: THIS IS NOT
                                             ;RECOMMENDED IF YOUR
                                             ;SYSTEM USES INTERRUPTS!!!
              ;
                     EXX
F3AD+D9              DB       0D9H
                     EXAF                    ;GET ALTERNATE REGISTERS
F3AE+08              DB       08H
F3AF E5              PUSH     H
F3B0 D5              PUSH     D
F3B1 C5              PUSH     B
F3B2 F5              PUSH     PSW
```

Listing cont.

```
                        PUSHIX
F3B3+DDE5               DB      0DDH,0E5H
                        PUSHIY
F3B5+FDE5               DB      0FDH,0E5H
            ;
F3B7 2A1400             LHLD    PTR1            ;GET OLD STACK POINTER
F3BA E5                 PUSH    H
            ;
                        EXX
F3BB+D9                 DB      0D9H
                        EXAF
F3BC+08                 DB      08H
F3BD 2A1600             LHLD    PTR2            ;GET OLD PROGRAM COUNTER
F3C0 E5                 PUSH    H
            ;
F3C1 2A1200             LHLD    PTR             ;AND GET OLD HL
F3C4 E5                 PUSH    H
F3C5 D5                 PUSH    D
F3C6 C5                 PUSH    B
F3C7 F5                 PUSH    PSW
            ;
F3C8 311000             LXI     SP,BADDR        ;RESET THE STACK POINTER FOR
                                                ;USE BY THE MONITOR.
F3CB CD0BFA             CALL    CRLF
F3CE C34FF0             JMP     PRMPT           ;RETURN TO THE MONITOR.
            ;
            ;
            MEM$TEST:                           ;RUN A MEMORY TEST.
                        GETPTR  SADDR$MSG,PTR
F3D1+2111F8             LXI     H,SADDR$MSG
F3D4+CDFFF9             CALL    DISP
F3D7+CDF1F4             CALL    HEXIN
F3DA+221200             SHLD    PTR
F3DD+FE2E               CPI     '.'
F3DF+CA4FF0             JZ      PRMPT
                        GETPTR  EADDR$MSG,PTR1  ;GET START AND END ADDRESSES.
F3E2+2129F8             LXI     H,EADDR$MSG
F3E5+CDFFF9             CALL    DISP
F3E8+CDF1F4             CALL    HEXIN
F3EB+221400             SHLD    PTR1
F3EE+FE2E               CPI     '.'
F3F0+CA4FF0             JZ      PRMPT
            ;
            ;
            MEM$ITER:
F3F3 2A1200             LHLD    PTR
                        LDED    PTR1            ;LOAD START AND END ADDRESSES.
F3F6+ED5B               DB      0EDH,5BH
F3F8+1400               DW      PTR1
            ;
            MEM$LOOP:
F3FA 7E                 MOV     A,M             ;GET A BYTE.
F3FB 2F                 CMA                     ;REVERSE EACH BIT
F3FC 77                 MOV     M,A             ;AND SAVE IT.
F3FD 46                 MOV     B,M             ;GET IT AGAIN
F3FE B8                 CMP     B               ;COMPARE A-REG WITH B-REG
```

Listing cont.

```
F3FF C212F4          JNZ     MEM$ERROR          ;IF NOT THE SAME,
                                                ;THERE IS AN ERROR
                ;
F402 2F              CMA
F403 77              MOV     M,A                ;PUT IT BACK AS IT WAS FOUND.
                ;
F404 23              INX     H
F405 E5              PUSH    H
F406 D5              PUSH    D
F407 EB              XCHG
                     DSBC    D
F408+ED52            DB      OEDH,D*8+42H
F40A D1              POP     D
F40B E1              POP     H
F40C CA23F4          JZ      MEM$DONE           ;DONE WITH THIS LOOP.




                ;
F40F C3FAF3          JMP     MEM$LOOP           ;IF NOT DONE, GO FOR NEXT LOOP.
                                        ;
            MEM$ERROR:
F412 E5              PUSH    H
                     MSG     MEM$ERR$MSG        ;PRINT ERROR MSG
F413+2148F9          LXI     H,MEM$ERR$MSG
F416+CDFFF9          CALL    DISP
F419 E1              POP     H
F41A CD21F5          CALL    HEXOUT             ;DISPLAY BAD ADDRESS
                ;
F41D CD0BFA          CALL    CRLF
F420 C34FF0          JMP     PRMPT
                ;
            MEM$DONE:
F423 CD16FA          CALL    CSTAT              ;LOOK FOR KEYBOARD INPUT.
F426 C24FF0          JNZ     PRMPT              ;DONE.
                ;
F429 C3F3F3          JMP     MEM$ITER           ;DO IT AGAIN.
                ;
                ;
            BOOT:                               ;INSERT TAPE OR DISK BOOT LOADER
                                                ;HERE.
F42C C349F0          JMP     WARM$START
                ;
                ;
            DISP$REGS:                          ;DISPLAY CPU REGISTERS
                                                ;(AFTER A BREAKPOINT).
                ;
                     MSG     REGS$1             ;DISPLAY FIRST HEADER LINE.
F42F+215BF9          LXI     H,REGS$1
F432+CDFFF9          CALL    DISP
                ;
F435 112000          LXI     D,20H
```

Listing cont.

```
F438 2A1000              LHLD    BADDR           ;GET SAVE AREA ADDR
F43B 19                  DAD     D
F43C EB                  XCHG                    ;ADDRESS IN DE.
F43D 3E08                MVI     A,8
F43F 321D00              STA     COUNTER         ;SET UP COUNTER.
             DISP$NEXT:
F442 CD81F4              CALL    GET$PAIR        ;GET A PAIR OF BYTES
                                                 ;FROM (DE) INTO HL.
             ;
F445 CD21F5              CALL    HEXOUT
F448 CD44F5              CALL    SPACE           ;OUTPUT A SPACE CHAR
             ;
F44B 3A1D00              LDA     COUNTER
F44E 3D                  DCR     A
F44F 321D00              STA     COUNTER
F452 C242F4              JNZ     DISP$NEXT       ;IF NOT ZERO, CONTINUE
F455 3E04                MVI     A,4
F457 321D00              STA     COUNTER
                         MSG     REGS$2          ;SECOND LINE OF
F45A+2186F9              LXI     H,REGS$2
F45D+CDFFF9              CALL    DISP
                                                 ;REGISTER DISPLAY
             ;
F460 2A1000              LHLD    BADDR
F463 113000              LXI     D,30H
F466 19                  DAD     D
F467 EB                  XCHG                    ;START ADDR  OF SECOND GROUP
             DISP$2:
F468 CD81F4              CALL    GET$PAIR        ;GET NEXT SET OF BYTES
F46B CD21F5              CALL    HEXOUT
F46E CD44F5              CALL    SPACE
F471 3A1D00              LDA     COUNTER
F474 3D                  DCR     A
F475 321D00              STA     COUNTER
F478 C268F4              JNZ     DISP$2          ;IF NOT DONE, CONTINUE
             ;
F47B CD0BFA              CALL    CRLF
F47E C34FF0              JMP     PRMPT           ;DONE.
             ;
             GET$PAIR:
F481 1A                  LDAX    D
F482 6F                  MOV     L,A
F483 13                  INX     D
F484 1A                  LDAX    D
F485 67                  MOV     H,A             ;GET FIRST AND SECOND BYTES
F486 13                  INX     D
F487 C9                  RET
             ;
             ;
             COMPARE$MEM:
                         GETPTR  SADDR$MSG,PTR   ;GET START ADDRESS
F488+2111F8              LXI     H,SADDR$MSG
F48B+CDFFF9              CALL    DISP
F48E+CDF1F4              CALL    HEXIN
F491+221200              SHLD    PTR
F494+FE2E                CPI     '.'
```

Listing cont.

```
F496+CA4FF0           JZ      PRMPT
                      GETPTR  EADDR$MSG,PTR1   ;GET END ADDRESS
F499+2129F8           LXI     H,EADDR$MSG
F49C+CDFFF9           CALL    DISP
F49F+CDF1F4           CALL    HEXIN
F4A2+221400           SHLD    PTR1
F4A5+FE2E             CPI     '.'
F4A7+CA4FF0           JZ      PRMPT
                      GETPTR  CADDR$MSG,PTR2   ;ADDRESS TO COMPARE TO.
F4AA+21BBF9           LXI     H,CADDR$MSG
F4AD+CDFFF9           CALL    DISP
F4B0+CDF1F4           CALL    HEXIN
F4B3+221600           SHLD    PTR2
F4B6+FE2E             CPI     '.'
F4B8+CA4FF0           JZ      PRMPT
                   ;
F4BB 2A1200           LHLD    PTR
                      LDED    PTR2
F4BE+ED5B             DB      0EDH,5BH
F4C0+1600             DW      PTR2
                      LBCD    PTR1             ;END OF BLOCK 1
F4C2+ED4B             DB      0EDH,4BH
F4C4+1400             DW      PTR1
                   ;
                   COMP$ITER:
F4C6 1A               LDAX    D
F4C7 BE               CMP     M                ;COMPARE BYTE 1 WITH  BYTE 2
F4C8 C2E0F4           JNZ     COMP$ERR         ;NOT THE SAME.
F4CB 23               INX     H
F4CC 13               INX     D
                   ;
F4CD 78               MOV     A,B
F4CE BC               CMP     H                ;COMPARE B WITH H.
F4CF C2C6F4           JNZ     COMP$ITER        ;IF NOT EQU, CONTINUE
                   ;
F4D2 79               MOV     A,C
F4D3 BD               CMP     L                ;COMPARE C WITH L.
F4D4 C2C6F4           JNZ     COMP$ITER
                   ;
                      MSG     COMP$EQU         ;IF HERE, COMPARE WAS SUCCESSFUL
F4D7+21E5F9           LXI     H,COMP$EQU
F4DA+CDFFF9           CALL    DISP
F4DD C34FF0           JMP     PRMPT            ;DONE.
                   ;
                   COMP$ERR:
F4E0 E5               PUSH    H
                      MSG     MEM$ERR$MSG      ;AN ERROR WAS FOUND.
F4E1+2148F9           LXI     H,MEM$ERR$MSG
F4E4+CDFFF9           CALL    DISP
F4E7 E1               POP     H
F4E8 CD21F5           CALL    HEXOUT           ;DISPLAY ADDRESS OF ERROR
F4EB CD0BFA           CALL    CRLF
F4EE C34FF0           JMP     PRMPT
                   ;
                   ;
                   ;
```

Listing cont.

```
                     ;
F544 C5        SPACE:  PUSH    B
F545 0E20              MVI     C,' '
F547 CD0CF0            CALL    CO
F54A C1                POP     B
F54B C9                RET
               ;
               ;
               ;
F54C 5553452053EXPRMP: DB      'USE SPACE BAR TO MODIFY MEMORY'
F56A 0D0A0A    NUM:    DB      CR,LF,LF
F56D 454E544552       DB      'ENTER A 4 DIGIT HEX ADDRESS: ',0
               ;
F58B 0D0A5A3830MENU    DB      CR,LF,'Z80 MONITOR'
F598 0D0A464F52       DB      CR,LF,'FOR "MICROCOMPUTER OPERATING SYSTEMS"'
F5BF 0D0A0A4259       DB      CR,LF,LF,'BY MARK DAHMKE, 5/25/81'
F5D9 0A               DB      LF
F5DA 0D0A202042       DB      CR,LF,'  B - BOOT FROM TAPE OR DISK.'
F5F9 0D0A202043       DB      CR,LF,'  C - COMPARE MEMORY BLOCKS.'
F617 0D0A202044       DB      CR,LF,'  D - DUMP MEMORY TO CONSOLE.'
F636 0D0A202046       DB      CR,LF,'  F - FILL MEMORY WITH A CONSTANT.'
F65A 0D0A202047       DB      CR,LF,'  G - GO (EXECUTE).'
F66F 0D0A202049       DB      CR,LF,'  I - INPUT FROM A PORT.'
F689 0D0A20204C       DB      CR,LF,'  L - LOCATE A STRING IN MEMORY.'
F6AB 0D0A20204D       DB      CR,LF,'  M - MOVE A BLOCK OF MEMORY.'
F6CA 0D0A20204F       DB      CR,LF,'  O - OUTPUT TO A PORT.'
                      IF      LPTR
F6E3 0D0A202050       DB      CR,LF,'  P - PRINTER ECHO TOGGLE.'
                      ENDIF
F6FF 0D0A202052       DB      CR,LF,'  R - RESUME FROM A BREAKPOINT.'
F720 0D0A202053       DB      CR,LF,'  S - EXAMINE/MODIFY MEMORY.'
F73E 0D0A202054       DB      CR,LF,'  T - TEST MEMORY.'
F752 0D0A202055       DB      CR,LF,'  U - UNSET BREAKPOINT.'
F76B 0D0A202056       DB      CR,LF,'  V - SET BREAKPOINT.'
F782 0D0A202057       DB      CR,LF,'  W - WARM START (DISPLAY THIS MENU).'
F7A9 0D0A202058       DB      CR,LF,'  X - EXAMINE REGISTERS.'
F7C3 0D0A00           DB      CR,LF,0
F7C6 0D0A3F2000PROMPT: DB      CR,LF,'? ',0
               ;
F7CB 0D0A4E4F20JTERR:  DB      CR,LF,'NO SUCH COMMAND',CR,LF,0
               ;
               NOTFOUND:
F7DF 0D0A535452       DB      CR,LF,'STRING NOT FOUND.',CR,LF,0
               ;
               FOUND:
F7F5 0D0A535452       DB      CR,LF,'STRING FOUND AT ADDRESS: ',0
               ;
               SADDR$MSG:
F811 0D0A454E54       DB      CR,LF,'ENTER START ADDRESS: ',0
               ;
               EADDR$MSG:
F829 0D0A454E54       DB      CR,LF,'ENTER END ADDRESS: ',0
               ;
               BSTR$MSG:
F83F 0D0A454E54       DB      CR,LF,'ENTER THE SEARCH STRING,'
```

Listing cont.

```
                    ;
F4F1 210000  HEXIN:  LXI    H,0
F4F4 CD12F5  HEX:    CALL   GET          ;GET AND ECHO CHARACTER.
F4F7 FE30            CPI    '0'
F4F9 D8              RC
F4FA FE3A            CPI    ':'
F4FC DA07F5          JC     HEXSH
F4FF FE41            CPI    'A'
F501 D8              RC
F502 FE47            CPI    'G'
F504 D0              RNC
F505 C609            ADI    9
F507 E60F    HEXSH:  ANI    15
F509 29              DAD    H
F50A 29              DAD    H
F50B 29              DAD    H
F50C 29              DAD    H
F50D B5              ORA    L
F50E 6F              MOV    L,A
F50F C3F4F4          JMP    HEX          ;GET NEXT CHAR.
                    ;
F512 CD12F0  GET:    CALL   UCI          ;GET CHAR
F515 F5              PUSH   PSW
F516 4F              MOV    C,A
F517 CD0CF0          CALL   CO
F51A F1              POP    PSW
F51B C9              RET
                    ;
F51C 0E02    HEXO2:  MVI    C,2
F51E C323F5          JMP    HEXO
                    ;
F521 0E04    HEXOUT: MVI    C,4
F523 AF      HEXO:   XRA    A
F524 29              DAD    H
F525 17              RAL
F526 29              DAD    H
F527 17              RAL
F528 29              DAD    H
F529 17              RAL
F52A 29              DAD    H
F52B 17              RAL
F52C FE0A            CPI    10
F52E DA33F5          JC     XOTA
F531 C607            ADI    7
F533 C630    XOTA:   ADI    '0'
F535 CD3DF5          CALL   PUT          ;OUTPUT CHARACTER.
F538 0D              DCR    C
F539 C223F5          JNZ    HEXO
F53C C9              RET
                    ;
F53D C5      PUT:    PUSH   B
F53E 4F              MOV    C,A
F53F CD0CF0          CALL   CO
F542 C1              POP    B
F543 C9              RET
                    ;
```

Listing cont.

```
F859 0D0A494E20      DB      CR,LF,'IN HEX. HIT SPACE BAR OR <CR>'
F878 0D0A414654      DB      CR,LF,'AFTER EACH BYTE, AND TERMINATE'
F898 0D0A535452      DB      CR,LF,'STRING ENTRY WITH A COMMA.'
F8B4 0D0A0A5354      DB      CR,LF,LF,'STRING: ',0
                ;
            PORT$MSG:
F8C0 0D0A504F52      DB      CR,LF,'PORT ADDRESS: ',0
                ;
            BYTE$MSG:
F8D1 0D0A425954      DB      CR,LF,'BYTE TO OUTPUT: ',0
                ;
            FCHAR$MSG:
F8E4 0D0A46494C      DB      CR,LF,'FILL CHARACTER: ',0
                ;
            DADDR$MSG:
F8F7 0D0A444553      DB      CR,LF,'DESTINATION ADDRESS: ',0
                ;
            PRTR$ON$MSG:
F90F 0D0A505249      DB      CR,LF,'PRINTER ECHO IS ENABLED',CR,LF,0
                ;
            PRTR$OFF$MSG:
F92B 0D0A505249      DB      CR,LF,'PRINTER ECHO IS DISABLED',CR,LF,0
                ;
            MEM$ERR$MSG:
F948 0D0A455252      DB      CR,LF,'ERROR FOUND AT: ',0
                ;
F95B 0D0A204146REGS$1: DB    CR,LF,' AF    BC    DE    HL    PC    SP    IX    IY'
F983 0D0A00          DB      CR,LF,0
                ;
F986 0D0A414627REGS$2: DB    CR,LF,'AF''  BC''  DE''  HL'' '
F99B 0D0A00          DB      CR,LF,0
                ;
            BKPT$MSG:
F99E 0D0A454E54      DB      CR,LF,'ENTER BREAKPOINT ADDRESS: ',0
                ;
            CADDR$MSG:
F9BB 0D0A454E54      DB      CR,LF,'ENTER ADDRESS OF BLOCK TO BE COMPARED: '
F9E4 00              DB      0
                ;
            COMP$EQU:
F9E5 0D0A424C4F      DB      CR,LF,'BLOCKS ARE IDENTICAL.'
F9FC 0D0A00          DB      CR,LF,0
                ;
                ;
                ;
                ;      DISP -- DISPLAYS A STRING OF CHARACTERS ON THE CONSOLE
                ;             DEVICE.  ON ENTRY, HL = STRING ADDRESS, WITH
                ;             STRING TERMINATED BY A 00H BYTE.
                ;
                ;
F9FF 7E         DISP:  MOV    A,M
FA00 FE00              CPI    0
FA02 C8                RZ
FA03 4F                MOV    C,A
FA04 CD0CF0            CALL   CO
FA07 23                INX    H
```

Listing cont.

```
FA08 C3FFF9              JMP     DISP
                  ;
                  ;
                  ;
                  ;          CRLF - OUTPUTS A CARRIAGE RETURN,
                  ;                 LINE FEED TO THE CONSOLE.
                  ;
                  ;
FA0B 0E0D        CRLF:   MVI     C,CR
FA0D CD0CF0              CALL    CO
FA10 0E0A               MVI     C,LF
FA12 CD0CF0             CALL    CO
FA15 C9                 RET
                  ;
                  ;
                  ;          CSTAT -- THIS ROUTINE IS CP/M COMPATIBLE.
                  ;
                  ;                   CSTAT WILL RETURN AN FFH IF A CHARACTER
                  ;                   IS AVAILABLE, AND A 00H IF ONE IS NOT.
                  ;
                  ;
FA16 DB13        CSTAT:  IN      IPORTS          ;INPUT FROM KEYBOARD PORT
FA18 2F                 CMA                     ;COMPLIMENT ALL BITS.
FA19 E601               ANI     IPORTM          ;MASK OFF ALL OTHER BITS
FA1B C8                 RZ                      ;RETURN IF NOT READY.
FA1C 3EFF               MVI     A,0FFH
FA1E C9                 RET                     ;RETURN FFH IF A
                                                ;CHARACTER IS READY.
                  ;
                  ;          CIN -- THIS ROUTINE IS COMPATIBLE WITH CP/M.
                  ;
                  ;
                  ;
FA1F CD16FA      CIN:    CALL    CSTAT           ;CHECK THE PORT STATUS.
FA22 CA1FFA              JZ      CIN
FA25 DB10               IN      IPORTD          ;READ THE CHARACTER.
FA27 C9                 RET
                  ;
                  ;
                  ;          UCIN -- UPPER CASE INPUT -- GETS AN INPUT CHARACTER,
                  ;                  AND CONVERTS ALL ALPHA CHARACTERS TO UPPER CASE.
                  ;
                  ;
                  ;
                  ;
FA28 CD1FFA      UCIN:   CALL    CIN
FA2B FE61               CPI     61H             ;IS CHAR LT LC A?
FA2D DA37FA             JC      UCS
FA30 FE7B               CPI     7BH             ;IS CHAR LT LC Z?
FA32 D237FA             JNC     UCS
FA35 D620               SUI     20H             ;MAKE IT UPPER CASE
FA37 A7          UCS:   ANA     A               ;SET FLAGS
FA38 C9                 RET
                  ;
                  ;
                        IF      NOT VDM
```

Listing cont.

```
                ;
        COUT:   CALL    COSTAT      ;READ STATUS BIT FOR OUTPUT PORT
                JZ      COUT        ;NOT READY?  LOOP UNTIL READY.
                MOV     A,C
                OUT     OPORTD      ;OUTPUT THE CHARACTER.
                ;
                IF      LPTR        ;IF LINE PRINTER INCLUDED,
                LDA     LPT         ;LOOK AT LINE PRINTER FLAG.
                ANA     A           ;SET FLAGS BASED ON A-REGISTER.
                RZ                  ;RETURRN, IF PRINTER TURNED OFF.
                CALL    POUT        ;PRINT THE CHARACTER.
                ENDIF
                RET                 ;FINISHED.
                ;
                ;
        COSTAT: IN      OPORTS
                ANI     OPORTM      ;MASK OFF BITS.
                RZ
                MVI     A,OFFH
                RET                 ;RETURN OFFH IF READY.
                ;
                ;
                ENDIF
                ;
        CLRSCN:                     ;CLEAR SCREEN
FA39 0E0C       MVI     C,CTLL
FA3B CD0CF0     CALL    CO          ;OUTPUT TO CONSOLE.
FA3E C9         RET
                ;
                ;
                ;
                ;
                ;
                IF      VDM
                ;
                ;
                ;
                ;       C O  (CONSOLE OUTPUT SUBROUTINE)
                ;
                ;       EMULATES AN ADDRESSABLE CURSOR -
                ;       SMART TERMINAL.
                ;
                ;
                ;COMMANDS:
                ;       CR - RET CURSOR TO START OF LINE
                ;       LF - LINE FEED (SAME AS NORMAL)
                ;       ESC    - LOAD CURSOR ADDR (LINE,COL)
                ;       CTL-L - CLEAR SCREEN - HOME UP
                ;       CTL-O - CLEAR TO END OF LINE
                ;       CTL-B - BACKSPACE CURSOR
                ;
                ;
                ;
001B =  ESC:    EQU     1BH
000C =  CTLL:   EQU     0CH
000F =  CTLO:   EQU     0FH
```

Listing cont.

```
0002 =          CTLB:   EQU     02H
                ;
                ;
00A0 =          VIDT:   EQU     ((VDMRAM AND 0FF00H) SHR 8 )
0040 =          NMCHRS: EQU     VIDW
000F =          NMLINS: EQU     VIDL - 1        ; EQUALS LINES - 1
00A5 =          VDMTOP: EQU     ((VDMRAM + (VIDW*VIDL)) SHR 8) + 1
                ;
                SAVE    MACRO
                        PUSH    PSW
                        PUSH    B
                        PUSH    D
                        PUSH    H
                        ENDM
                ;
                RESTR   MACRO
                        POP     H
                        POP     D
                        POP     B
                        POP     PSW
                        ENDM
                ;
                CMPBIT  MACRO
                        PUSH    PSW
                        MOV     A,M
                        XRI     80H
                        MOV     M,A
                        POP     PSW
                        ENDM
                ;
                ;
                COUT:
                        IF      LPTR    ;IF LINE PRINTER INCLUDED,
FA3F CD4CFA             CALL    VDMOUT  ;DISPLAY THE CHARACTER
FA42 3A1C00             LDA     LPT
FA45 A7                 ANA     A
FA46 C8                 RZ              ;RETURN IF NO ECHO.
FA47 79                 MOV     A,C
FA48 CD4BFB             CALL    POUT
FA4B C9                 RET
                        ENDIF
                ;
                ;
                VDMOUT: SAVE
FA4C+F5                 PUSH    PSW
FA4D+C5                 PUSH    B
FA4E+D5                 PUSH    D
FA4F+E5                 PUSH    H
FA50 79                 MOV     A,C
                ;
FA51 2A1E00             LHLD    CURSOR
                        CMPBIT
FA54+F5                 PUSH    PSW
FA55+7E                 MOV     A,M
FA56+EE80               XRI     80H
FA58+77                 MOV     M,A
```

Listing cont.

```
FA59+F1                    POP     PSW
FA5A FE0C                  CPI     CTLL      ;CLEAR SCREEN
FA5C CA8DFA                JZ      CLR
FA5F FE0F                  CPI     CTLO      ;CLEAR TO END OF LINE
FA61 CAABFA                JZ      CLREL
FA64 FE1B                  CPI     ESC       ;MOVE CURSOR
FA66 CAC9FA                JZ      LCURS
FA69 FE0D                  CPI     CR        ;CARRIAGE RETURN
FA6B CAFEFA                JZ      CRET
FA6E FE0A                  CPI     LF        ;LINE FEED
FA70 CA0DFB                JZ      LFEED
FA73 FE02                  CPI     CTLB      ;BACKSPACE
FA75 CAEBFA                JZ      BKSP
FA78 FE03                  CPI     CTLB+1
FA7A CAEBFA                JZ      BKSP
FA7D 77                    MOV     M,A
FA7E 23                    INX     H
              SAVE$CURS:
FA7F 221E00                SHLD    CURSOR
                           CMPBIT            ;COMPLEMENT BIT TO MAKE A NEW CURSOR.
FA82+F5                    PUSH    PSW
FA83+7E                    MOV     A,M
FA84+EE80                  XRI     80H
FA86+77                    MOV     M,A
FA87+F1                    POP     PSW
              RTRN:        RESTR
FA88+E1                    POP     H
FA89+D1                    POP     D
FA8A+C1                    POP     B
FA8B+F1                    POP     PSW
FA8C C9                    RET
              ;
              ;
FA8D 2100A0   CLR:         LXI     H,VDMRAM         ;CLEAR SCREEN.
FA90 3620     CLRS1:       MVI     M,' '
FA92 23                    INX     H
FA93 7C                    MOV     A,H
FA94 FEA5                  CPI     VDMTOP           ;CHECK FOR TOP OF VIDEO RAM
FA96 C290FA                JNZ     CLRS1
FA99 2100A0                LXI     H,VDMRAM
FA9C 221E00                SHLD    CURSOR
FA9F 222000                SHLD    LINE
                           CMPBIT
FAA2+F5                    PUSH    PSW
FAA3+7E                    MOV     A,M
FAA4+EE80                  XRI     80H
FAA6+77                    MOV     M,A
FAA7+F1                    POP     PSW
FAA8 C388FA                JMP     RTRN
              ;
              ;
FAAB C5       CLREL:       PUSH    B                ;CLEAR LINE.
FAAC E5                    PUSH    H
FAAD 2A2000                LHLD    LINE
FAB0 3E40                  MVI     A,NMCHRS
FAB2 85                    ADD     L
```

Listing cont.

```
FAB3 E1                   POP    H
FAB4 0620                 MVI    B,' '
FAB6 70        CLRL1:     MOV    M,B
FAB7 23                   INX    H
FAB8 BD                   CMP    L
FAB9 C2B6FA               JNZ    CLRL1
FABC C1                   POP    B
FABD 2A1E00               LHLD   CURSOR
                          CMPBIT
FAC0+F5                   PUSH   PSW
FAC1+7E                   MOV    A,M
FAC2+EE80                 XRI    80H
FAC4+77                   MOV    M,A
FAC5+F1                   POP    PSW
FAC6 C388FA               JMP    RTRN
               ;
               ;
               ;
FAC9 C5        LCURS:     PUSH   B            ;MOVE CURSOR.
FACA D5                   PUSH   D
FACB 2100A0               LXI    H,VDMRAM
FACE 114000               LXI    D,NMCHRS
FAD1 79                   MOV    A,C
FAD2 A7                   ANA    A
FAD3 CADEFA               JZ     LCUR2
FAD6 FAE6FA               JM     LCUR3
FAD9 19        LCUR1:     DAD    D
FADA 0D                   DCR    C
FADB C2D9FA               JNZ    LCUR1
FADE 222000    LCUR2:     SHLD   LINE
FAE1 58                   MOV    E,B
FAE2 19                   DAD    D
FAE3 221E00               SHLD   CURSOR
                          STBIT
FAE6 D1        LCUR3:     POP    D
FAE7 C1                   POP    B
FAE8 C37FFA               JMP    SAVE$CURS
               ;
               BKSP:      CMPBIT              ;BACKSPACE CURSOR.
FAEB+F5                   PUSH   PSW
FAEC+7E                   MOV    A,M
FAED+EE80                 XRI    80H
FAEF+77                   MOV    M,A
FAF0+F1                   POP    PSW
FAF1 2B                   DCX    H
                          CMPBIT
FAF2+F5                   PUSH   PSW
FAF3+7E                   MOV    A,M
FAF4+EE80                 XRI    80H
FAF6+77                   MOV    M,A
FAF7+F1                   POP    PSW
FAF8 221E00               SHLD   CURSOR
FAFB C388FA               JMP    RTRN
               ;
               ;
FAFE 2A2000    CRET:      LHLD   LINE         ;CARRIAGE RETURN.
```

Listing cont.

```
FB01 221E00            SHLD    CURSOR
                       CMPBIT
FB04+F5                PUSH    PSW
FB05+7E                MOV     A,M
FB06+EE80              XRI     80H
FB08+77                MOV     M,A
FB09+F1                POP     PSW
FB0A C388FA            JMP     RTRN
              ;
              LFEED:                                  ;LINE FEED.
FB0D 7C                MOV     A,H
FB0E 11C0A3            LXI     D,VDMRAM + (NMCHRS*NMLINS)
FB11 BA                CMP     D
FB12 C22BFB            JNZ     LFD2
FB15 7D                MOV     A,L
FB16 BB                CMP     E
FB17 FA2BFB            JM      LFD2
FB1A 2140A0            LXI     H,VDMRAM + NMCHRS
FB1D 1100A0            LXI     D,VDMRAM
FB20 010004            LXI     B,NMCHRS*(NMLINS+1)
                       LDIR                           ;Z-80 BLOCK MOVE INSTR.
FB23+EDB0              DB      0EDH,0B0H
FB25 2A1E00            LHLD    CURSOR
FB28 C3ABFA            JMP     CLREL
              ;
FB2B 114000   LFD2:    LXI     D,NMCHRS
FB2E 19                DAD     D
FB2F 221E00            SHLD    CURSOR
                       CMPBIT
FB32+F5                PUSH    PSW
FB33+7E                MOV     A,M
FB34+EE80              XRI     80H
FB36+77                MOV     M,A
FB37+F1                POP     PSW
FB38 2A2000            LHLD    LINE
FB3B 19                DAD     D
FB3C 222000            SHLD    LINE
FB3F C388FA            JMP     RTRN
              ;
                       ENDIF
              ;
              ;
              ;
                       IF      LPTR                   ;IF LINE PRINTER
              ;
              ;
FB42 DB13     POSTAT:  IN      LPORTS                 ;GET LINE PRINTER STATUS
FB44 2F                CMA
FB45 E602              ANI     LPORTM                 ;MASK OFF BITS
FB47 C8                RZ                             ;RETURN IF NOT READY.
FB48 3EFF              MVI     A,0FFH
FB4A C9                RET                            ;RETURN 0FFH IF READY.
              ;
FB4B CD42FB   POUT:    CALL    POSTAT                 ;CHECK PRINTER STATUS
FB4E CA4BFB            JZ      POUT
FB51 79                MOV     A,C
```

Listing cont.

```
FB52 D310              OUT    LPORTD                    ;OUTPUT THE CHARACTER.
FB54 C9                RET
             ;
             ;
                       ENDIF
             ;
             ;
             ;
FB55                   END
```

0010 BADDR	0000 BC	F99E BKPTMSG	F396 BKPTTRAP	FAEB BKSP
F42C BOOT	0000 BOTTOMOFRAM		F83F BSTRMSG	F8D1 BYTEMSG
F9BB CADDRMSG	F10F CH1	F009 CI	FA1F CIN	FA8D CLR
FAAB CLREL	FAB6 CLRL1	F00F CLRS	FA90 CLRS1	FA39 CLRSCN
F00C CO	F0EE COL	F11B COL2	F11D COL3	F018 COLDSTART
0008 COLS	F1E4 COMPARE	F488 COMPAREMEM	F9E5 COMPEQU	F4E0 COMPERR
F4C6 COMPITER	F227 COMPSTR	F20B CONT	001D COUNTER	FA3F COUT
000D CR	FAFE CRET	FA0B CRLF	F006 CST	FA16 CSTAT
0002 CTLB	000C CTLL	000F CTLO	001E CURSOR	F8F7 DADDRMSG
0002 DE	F041 DEVICEINIT	F9FF DISP	F468 DISP2	F442 DISPNEXT
F42F DISPREGS	F0D3 DUMP	F829 EADDRMSG	001B ESC	F184 EX2
F17D EX3	F155 EXAM1	F144 EXAMINE	F54C EXPRMP	0000 FALSE
F8E4 FCHARMSG	F2BC FILL	F277 FILLMEM	F028 FINISH	F7F5 FOUND
F215 FOUNDSTR	F512 GET	F1C4 GETBYTES	F481 GETPAIR	F0B9 GO
F4F4 HEX	F4F1 HEXIN	F523 HEXO	F51C HEXO2	F521 HEXOUT
F507 HEXSH	0004 HL	F22F INPUTPORT	0010 IPORTD	0001 IPORTM
0013 IPORTS	0004 IX	0004 IY	F083 JTABLE	FFFF JTBL
F064 JTCONT	F07A JTEND	F7CB JTERR	F0E4 L1	FAD9 LCUR1
FADE LCUR2	FAE6 LCUR3	FAC9 LCURS	000A LF	FB2B LFD2
FB0D LFEED	F0E9 LIN	0020 LINE	0008 LINES	
F18A LOCATESTRING		0010 LPORTD	0002 LPORTM	0013 LPORTS
001C LPT	FFFF LPTR	F01B MEM1	F018 MEMCHK	F423 MEMDONE
F948 MEMERRMSG	F412 MEMERROR	F029 MEMINIT	F3F3 MEMITER	F3FA MEMLOOP
F3D1 MEMTEST	F58B MENU	F2C8 MOVEBLOCK	F074 NEXTJV	0040 NMCHRS
000F NMLINS	F7DF NOTFOUND	F56A NUM	F24A OUTPUTPORT	F8C0 PORTMSG
FB42 POSTAT	FB4B POUT	F316 PRINTERTOGGLE		F04F PRMPT
F7C6 PROMPT	F32A PRTROFF	F92B PRTROFFMSG	F90F PRTRONMSG	0012 PTR
0014 PTR1	0016 PTR2	0018 PTR3	001A PTR4	F53D PUT
F95B REGS1	F986 REGS2	F36B RESUMEBKPT	0001 RSTI	FA88 RTRN
F811 SADDRMSG	FA7F SAVECURS	0000 SERIAL	F333 SETBKPT	F544 SPACE
F000 START	FAE6 STBIT	FFFF TRUE	F012 UCI	FA28 UCIN
FA37 UCS	F35C UNSETBKPT	FFFF VDM	FA4C VDMOUT	A000 VDMRAM
00A5 VDMTOP	0010 VIDL	00A0 VIDT	0040 VIDW	F049 WARMSTART
F003 WSTART	F533 XOTA			

Appendix V:
Reference Card

Programmer's Reference Card

Microcomputer Operating Systems, Appendix V
©Mark Dahmke, 1982

16 Hex	8 Octal	10 Decimal	2 Binary	ASCII	Ctrl. Char.	EBCDIC	8080	Z80	6502	
00	000	000	00000000	NUL		NUL	NOP	NOP	BRK	IMP
01	001	001	00000001	SOH	A	SOH	LXI B,NN	LD BC,NN	ORA	,X
02	002	002	00000010	STX	B	STX	STAX B	LD (BC),A		
03	003	003	00000011	ETX	C	ETX	INX B	INC BC		
04	004	004	00000100	EOT	D	PF	INR B	INC B		
05	005	005	00000101	ENQ	E	HT	DCR B	DEC B	ORA	ZPG
06	006	006	00000110	ACK	F	LC	MVI B,N	LD B,N	ASL	ZPG
07	007	007	00000111	BEL	G	DEL	RLC	RLCA		
08	010	008	00001000	BS	H			EX AF,AF'	PHP	IMP
09	011	009	00001001	HT	I		DAD B	ADD HL,BC	ORA	IMM
0A	012	010	00001010	LF	J	SMM	LDAX B	LD A,(BC)	ASL	A
0B	013	011	00001011	VT	K	VT	DCX B	DEC BC		
0C	014	012	00001100	FF	L	FF	INR C	INC C		
0D	015	013	00001101	CR	M	CR	DCR C	DEC C	ORA	ABS
0E	016	014	00001110	SO	N	SO	MVI C,N	LD C,N	ASL	ABS
0F	017	015	00001111	SI	O	SI	RRC	RRCA		
10	020	016	00010000	DLE	P	DLE		DJNZ disp	BPL	REL
11	021	017	00010001	DC1	Q	DC1	LXI D,NN	LD DE,NN	ORA	,Y
12	022	018	00010010	DC2	R	DC2	STAX D	LD (DE),A		
13	023	019	00010011	DC3	S	TM	INX D	INC DE		
14	024	020	00010100	DC4	T	RES	INR D	INC D		
15	025	021	00010101	NAK	U	NL	DCR D	DEC D	ORA	ZPG,X
16	026	022	00010110	SYN	V	BS	MVI D,N	LD D,N	ASL	ZPG,X
17	027	023	00010111	ETB	W	IL	RAL	RLA		
18	030	024	00011000	CAN	X	CAN	JR disp		CLC	IMP
19	031	025	00011001	EM	Y	EM	DAD D	ADD HL,DE	ORA	ABS,Y
1A	032	026	00011010	SUB	Z	CC	LDAX D	LD A,(DE)		
1B	033	027	00011011	ESC	[	CU1	DCX D	DEC DE		
1C	034	028	00011100	FS	\	IFS	INR E	INC E		
1D	035	029	00011101	GS	]	IGS	DCR E	DEC E	ORA	ABS,X
1E	036	030	00011110	RS	↑	IRS	MVI E,N	LD E,N	ASL	ABS,X
1F	037	031	00011111	US		IUS	RAR	RRA		
20	040	032	00100000	space		DS	JR NZ,disp		JSR	ABS
21	041	033	00100001	!		SOS	LXI H,NN	LD HL,NN	AND	,X
22	042	034	00100010	"		FS	SHLD NN	LD (NN),HL		
23	043	035	00100011	#			INX H	INC HL		
24	044	036	00100100	$		BYP	INR H	INC H	BIT	ZPG
25	045	037	00100101	%		LF	DCR H	DEC H	AND	ZPG,X
26	046	038	00100110	&		ETB	MVI H,N	LD H,N	ROL	ZPG
27	047	039	00100111	'		ESC	DAA	DAA		
28	050	040	00101000	(				JR Z,disp	PLP	IMP
29	051	041	00101001	)			DAD H	ADD HL,HL	AND	IMM
2A	052	042	00101010	*		SM	LHLD NN	LD HL,(NN)	ROL	A
2B	053	043	00101011	+		CU2	DCX H	DEC HL		
2C	054	044	00101100	,			INR L	INC L	BIT	ABS
2D	055	045	00101101	-		ENQ	DCR L	DEC L	AND	ABS
2E	056	046	00101110	.		ACK	MVI L,N	LD L,N	ROL	ABS
2F	057	047	00101111	/		BEL	CMA	CPL		
30	060	048	00110000	0				JR NC,disp	BMI	REL
31	061	049	00110001	1			LXI SP,NN	LD SP,NN	AND	,Y
32	062	050	00110010	2		SYN	STA NN	LD (NN),A		
33	063	051	00110011	3			INX SP	INC SP		

16 Hex	8 Octal	10 Decimal	2 Binary	ASCII	Ctrl. Char.	EBCDIC	8080	Z80	6502	
34	064	052	00110100	4		PN	INR M	INC M		
35	065	053	00110101	5		RS	DCR M	DEC M	AND	ZPG,X
36	066	054	00110110	6		UC	MVI M,	LD (HL),N	ROL	ZPG,X
37	067	055	00110111	7		EOT	STC	SCF		
38	070	056	00111000	8				JR C,disp	SEC	IMP
39	071	057	00111001	9			DAD SP	ADD HL,SP	AND	ABS,Y
3A	072	058	00111010	:			LDA NN	LD A,(NN)		
3B	073	059	00111011	;		CU3	DCX SP	DEC SP		
3C	074	060	00111100	<		DC4	INR A	INC A		
3D	075	061	00111101	=		NAK	DCR A	DEC A	AND	ABS,X
3E	076	062	00111110	>			MVI A,N	LD A,N	ROL	ABS,X
3F	077	063	00111111	?		SUB	CMC	CCF		
40	100	064	01000000	@		space	MOV B,B	LD B,B	RTI	IMP
41	101	065	01000001	A			MOV B,C	LD B,C	EOR	,X
42	102	066	01000010	B			MOV B,D	LD B,D		
43	103	067	01000011	C			MOV B,E	LD B,E		
44	104	068	01000100	D			MOV B,H	LD B,H		
45	105	069	01000101	E			MOV B,L	LD B,L	EOR	ZPG
46	106	070	01000110	F			MOV B,M	LD B,(HL)	LSR	ZPG
47	107	071	01000111	G			MOV B,A	LD B,A		
48	110	072	01001000	H			MOV C,B	LD C,B	PHA	IMP
49	111	073	01001001	I			MOV C,C	LD C,C	EOR	IMM
4A	112	074	01001010	J			MOV C,D	LD C,D	LSR	A
4B	113	075	01001011	K			MOV C,E	LD C,E		
4C	114	076	01001100	L		<	MOV C,H	LD C,H	JMP	ABS
4D	115	077	01001101	M		(	MOV C,L	LD C,L	EOR	ABS
4E	116	078	01001110	N		+	MOV C,M	LD C,(HL)	LST	ABS
4F	117	079	01001111	O		|	MOV C,A	LD C,A		
50	120	080	01010000	P		&	MOV D,B	LD D,B	BVC	REL
51	121	081	01010001	Q			MOV D,C	LD D,C	EOR	,Y
52	122	082	01010010	R			MOV D,D	LD D,D		
53	123	083	01010011	S			MOV D,E	LD D,E		
54	124	084	01010100	T			MOV D,H	LD D,H		
55	125	085	01010101	U			MOV D,L	LD D,L	EOR	ZPG,X
56	126	086	01010110	V			MOV D,M	LD D,(HL)	LSR	ZPG,X
57	127	087	01010111	W			MOV D,A	LD D,A		
58	130	088	01011000	X			MOV E,B	LD E,B	CLI	IMP
59	131	089	01011001	Y			MOV E,C	LD E,C	EOR	ABS,Y
5A	132	090	01011010	Z		!	MOV E,D	LD E,D		
5B	133	091	01011011	[		$	MOV E,E	LD E,E		
5C	134	092	01011100	\		*	MOV E,H	LD E,H		
5D	135	093	01011101	]		)	MOV E,L	LD E,L	EOR	ABS,X
5E	136	094	01011110	↑		;	MOV E,M	LD E,(HL)	LSR	ABS,X
5F	137	095	01011111	_		≈	MOV E,A	LD E,A		
60	140	096	01100000	`		—	MOV H,B	LD H,B	RTS	IMP
61	141	097	01100001	a		/	MOV H,C	LD H,C	ADC	,X
62	142	098	01100010	b			MOV H,D	LD H,D		
63	143	099	01100011	c			MOV H,E	LD H,E		
64	144	100	01100100	d			MOV H,H	LD H,H		
65	145	101	01100101	e			MOV H,L	LD H,L	ADC	ZPG
66	146	102	01100110	f			MOV H,M	LD H,(HL)		
67	147	103	01100111	g			MOV H,A	LD H,A		
68	150	104	01101000	h			MOV L,B	LD L,B	PLA	IMP
69	151	105	01101001	i			MOV L,C	LD L,C	ADC	IMM
6A	152	106	01101010	j			MOV L,D	LD L,D		
6B	153	107	01101011	k		,	MOV L,E	LD L,E		
6C	154	108	01101100	l		%	MOV L,H	LD L,H	JMP	IMM
6D	155	109	01101101	m			MOV L,L	LD L,L	ADC	ABS
6E	156	110	01101110	n		>	MOV L,M	LD L,(HL)		
6F	157	111	01101111	o		?	MOV L,A	LD L,A		
70	160	112	01110000	p			MOV M,B	LD (HL),B	BVS	REL
71	161	113	01110001	q			MOV M,C	LD (HL),C	ADC	,Y
72	162	114	01110010	r			MOV M,D	LD (HL),D		
73	163	115	01110011	s			MOV M,E	LD (HL),E		
74	164	116	01110100	t			MOV M,H	LD (HL),H		
75	165	117	01110101	u			MOV M,L	LD (HL),L	ADC	ZPG,X
76	166	118	01110110	v			HLT	HALT		
77	167	119	01110111	w			MOV M,A	LD (HL),A		
78	170	120	01111000	x			MOV A,B	LD A,B	SEI	IMP
79	171	121	01111001	y			MOV A,C	LD A,C	ADC	ABS,Y
7A	172	122	01111010	z		:	MOV A,D	LD A,D		
7B	173	123	01111011	{		#	MOV A,E	LD A,E		

16 Hex	8 Octal	10 Decimal	2 Binary	ASCII	Ctrl. Char.	EBCDIC	8080	Z80	6502	
7C	174	124	01111100	|		@	MOV A,H	LD A,H		
7D	175	125	01111101	}		'	MOV A,L	LD A,L	ADC	ABS,X
7E	176	126	01111110	≈		=	MOV A,M	LD A,(HL)		
7F	177	127	01111111	DEL		"	MOV A,A	LD A,A		
80	200	128	10000000				ADD B	ADD A,B		
81	201	129	10000001			a	ADD C	ADD A,C	STA	,X
82	202	130	10000010			b	ADD D	ADD A,D		
83	203	131	10000011			c	ADD E	ADD A,E		
84	204	132	10000100			d	ADD H	ADD A,H	STY	ZPG
85	205	133	10000101			e	ADD L	ADD A,L	STA	ZPG
86	206	134	10000110			f	ADD M	ADD A,(HL)	STX	ZPG
87	207	135	10000111			g	ADD A	ADD A,A		
88	210	136	10001000			h	ADC B	ADC A,B	DEY	IMP
89	211	137	10001001			i	ADC C	ADC A,C		
8A	212	138	10001010				ADC D	ADC A,D	TXA	IMP
8B	213	139	10001011				ADC E	ADC A,E		
8C	214	140	10001100				ADC H	ADC A,H	STY	ABS
8D	215	141	10001101				ADC L	ADC A,L	STA	ABS
8E	216	142	10001110				ADC M	ADC A,(HL)	STX	ABS
8F	217	143	10001111				ADC A	ADC A,A		
90	220	144	10010000				SUB B	SUB A,B	BCC	REL
91	221	145	10010001			j	SUB C	SUB A,C	STA	,Y
92	222	146	10010010			k	SUB D	SUB A,D		
93	223	147	10010011			l	SUB E	SUB A,E		
94	224	148	10010100			m	SUB H	SUB A,H	STY	ZPG,X
95	225	149	10010101			n	SUB L	SUB A,L	STA	ZPG,X
96	226	150	10010110			o	SUB M	SUB A,(HL)	STX	ZPG,Y
97	227	151	10010111			p	SUB A	SUB A,A		
98	230	152	10011000			q	SBB B	SBC A,B	TYA	IMP
99	231	153	10011001			r	SBB C	SBC A,C	STA	ABS,Y
9A	232	154	10011010				SBB D	SBC A,D	TXS	IMP
9B	233	155	10011011				SBB E	SBC A,E		
9C	234	156	10011100				SBB H	SBC A,H		
9D	235	157	10011101				SBB L	SBC A,L	STA	ABS,X
9E	236	158	10011110				SBB M	SBC A,(HL)		
9F	237	159	10011111				SBB A	SBC A,A		
A0	240	160	10100000				ANA B	AND A,B	LDY	IMM
A1	241	161	10100001				ANA C	AND A,C	LDA	,X
A2	242	162	10100010			s	ANA D	AND A,D	LDX	IMM
A3	243	163	10100011			t	ANA E	AND A,E		
A4	244	164	10100100			u	ANA H	AND A,H	LDY	ZPG
A5	245	165	10100101			v	ANA L	AND A,L	LDA	ZPG
A6	246	166	10100110			w	ANA M	AND A,(HL)	LDX	ZPG
A7	247	167	10100111			x	ANA A	AND A,A		
A8	250	168	10101000			y	XRA B	XOR A,B	TAY	IMP
A9	251	169	10101001			z	XRA C	XOR A,C	LDA	IMM
AA	252	170	10101010				XRA D	XOR A,D	TAX	IMP
AB	253	171	10101011				XRA E	XOR A,E		
AC	254	172	10101100				XRA H	XOR A,H	LDY	ABS
AD	255	173	10101101				XRA L	XOR A,L	LDA	ABS
AE	256	174	10101110				XRA M	XOR A,(HL)	LDX	ABS
AF	257	175	10101111				XRA A	XOR A,A		
B0	260	176	10110000				ORA B	OR A,B	BCS	REL
B1	261	177	10110001				ORA C	OR A,C	LDA	,Y
B2	262	178	10110010				ORA D	OR A,D		
B3	263	179	10110011				ORA E	OR A,E		
B4	264	180	10110100				ORA H	OR A,H	LDY	ZPG,X
B5	265	181	10110101				ORA L	OR A,L	LDA	ZPG,X
B6	026	182	10110110				ORA M	OR A,(HL)	LDX	ZPG,Y
B7	267	183	10110111				ORA A	OR A,A		
B8	270	184	10111000				CMP B	CP A,B	CLV	IMP
B9	271	185	10111001				CMP C	CP A,C	LDA	ABS,Y
BA	272	186	10111010				CMP D	CP A,D	TSX	ABS,X
BB	273	187	10111011				CMP E	CP A,E		
BC	274	188	10111100				CMP H	CP A,H	LDY	ABS,X
BD	275	189	10111101				CMP L	CP A,L	LDA	ABS,X
BE	276	190	10111110				CMP M	CP A,(HL)	LDX	ABS,Y
BF	277	191	10111111				CMP A	CP A,A		
C0	300	192	11000000			{	RNZ	RET NZ	CPY	IMM
C1	301	193	11000001			A	POP B	POP BC	CMP	,X
C2	302	194	11000010			B	JNZ NN	JP NZ,NN		
C3	303	195	11000011			C	JMP NN	JP NN		

16 Hex	8 Octal	10 Decimal	2 Binary	ASCII	Ctrl. Char.	EBCDIC	8080	Z80	6502	
C4	304	196	11000100			D	CNZ NN	CALL NZ,NN	CPY	ZPG
C5	305	197	11000101			E	PUSH B	PUSH BC	CMP	ZPG
C6	306	198	11000110			F	ADI N	ADD A,N	DEC	ZPG
C7	307	199	11000111			G	RST 0	RST 0		
C8	300	200	11001000			H	RZ	RET NZ	INY	IMP
C9	311	201	11001001			I	RET	RET	CMP	IMM
CA	312	202	11001010				JZ NN	JP Z,NN	DEX	IMP
CB	313	203	11001011					See CB Group		
CC	314	204	11001100				CZ NN	CALL Z,NN	CPY	ABS
CD	315	205	11001101				CALL NN	CALL NN	CMP	ABS
CE	316	206	11001110				ACI N	ADC A,N	DEC	ABS
CF	317	207	11001111				RST 1	RST 1		
D0	320	208	11010000			}	RNC	RET NC	BNE	REL
D1	321	209	11010001			J	POP D	POP DE	CMP	,Y
D2	322	210	11010010			K	JNC NN	JP NC,NN		
D3	323	211	11010011			L	OUT N	OUT (N),A		
D4	324	212	11010100			M	CNC NN	CALL NC,NN		
D5	325	213	11010101			N	PUSH D	PUSH DE	CMP	ZPG,X
D6	326	214	11010110			O	SUI N	SUB A,N	DEC	ZPG,X
D7	327	215	11010111			P	RST 2	RST 2		
D8	330	216	11011000			Q	RC	RET C	CLD	IMP
D9	331	217	11011001			R			CMP	ABS,Y
DA	332	218	11011010				JC NN	JP C,NN		
DB	333	219	11011011				IN N	IN A,(N)		
DC	334	220	11011100				CC NN	CALL C,NN		
DD	335	221	11011101					See DD Grp	CMP	ABS,X
DE	336	222	11011110				SBI N	SBC A,N	DEC	ABS,X
DF	337	223	11011111				RST 3	RST 3		
E0	340	224	11100000				RPO	RET PO	CPX	IMM
E1	341	225	11100001				POP H	POP HL	SBC	,X
E2	342	226	11100010			S	JPO NN	JP PO,NN		
E3	343	227	11100011			T	XTHL	EX (SP),HL		
E4	344	228	11100100			U	CPO NN	CALL PO,NN	CPX	ZPG
E5	345	229	11100101			V	PUSH H	PUSH HL	SBC	ZPG
E6	346	230	11100110			W	ANI N	AND A,N	INC	ZPG
E7	347	231	11100111			X	RST 4	RST 4		
E8	350	232	11101000			Y	RPE	RET PE	INX	IMP
E9	351	233	11101001			Z	PCHL	JP (HL)	SBC	IMM
EA	352	234	11101010				JPE NN	JP PE,NN	NOP	IMP
EB	353	235	11101011				XCHG	EX DE,HL		
EC	354	236	11101100				CPE NN	CALL PE,NN	CPX	ABS
ED	355	237	11101101					See ED Group	SBC	ABS
EE	356	238	11101110				XRI	XOR A,N	INC	ABS
EF	357	239	11101111				RST 5	RST 5		
F0	360	240	11110000			0	RP	RET P	BEQ	REL
F1	361	241	11110001			1	POP PSW	POP AF	SBC	,Y
F2	362	242	11110010			2	JP NN	JP P,NN		
F3	363	243	11110011			3	DI	DI		
F4	364	244	11110100			4	CP NN	CALL P,NN		
F5	365	245	11110101			5	PUSH PSW	PUSH AF	SBC	ZPG,X
F6	366	246	11110110			6	ORI N	OR A,N	INC	ZPG,X
F7	367	247	11110111			7	RST 6	RST 6		
F8	370	248	11111000			8	RM	RET M	SED	IMP
F9	371	249	11111001			9	SPHL	LD SP,HL	SBC	ABS,Y
FA	372	250	11111010				JM NN	JP M,NN		
FB	373	251	11111011				EI	EI		
FC	374	252	11111100				CM NN	CALL M,NN		
FD	375	253	11111101					See FD Group	SBC	ABS,X
FE	376	254	11111110				CPI N	CP A,N	INC	ABS,X
FF	377	255	11111111				RST 7	RST 7		

Z80: CB Group (first byte is always CB):

Second byte	Instruction
00000xxx	RLC reg
00001xxx	RRC reg
00010xxx	RL reg
00011xxx	RR reg
00100xxx	SLA reg
00101xxx	SRA reg
00111xxx	SRL reg
01bbbxxx	BIT b,reg
10bbbxxx	RES b,reg
11bbbxxx	SET b,reg

Z80: CB Subgroup (First byte is FD or DD. Second byte is CB.):

Third Byte	Fourth Byte	Instruction
disp	06H	RLC (IX + disp)
disp	16H	RL (IX + disp)
disp	0EH	RRC (IX + disp)
disp	1EH	RR (IX + disp)
disp	26H	SLA (IX + disp)
disp	2EH	SRA (IX + disp)
disp	3EH	SRL (IX + disp)
disp	01bbb110	BIT b,(IX + disp)
disp	10bbb110	RES b,(IX + disp)
disp	11bbb110	SET b,(IX + disp)

Z80: DD/FD Group (First instruction is DD when using register IX, or FD when register is IY. IX is used here.)

Second Byte	Third and Fourth Byte	Instruction
21H	addr	LD IX,addr
22H	addr	LD (addr),IX
23H		INC IX
00xx1001		ADD IX,rp
2AH	addr	LD IX,addr
2BH		DEC IX
34H	disp	INC (IX + disp)
35H	disp	DEC (IX + disp)
36H	disp data	LD (IX + disp),data
01110sss	disp	LD (IX + disp),reg
01ddd110	disp	LD reg,(IX + disp)
86H	disp	ADD (IX + disp)
8EH	disp	ADC (IX + disp)
96H	disp	SUB (IX + disp)
9EH	disp	SBC (IX + disp)
A6H	disp	AND (IX + disp)
AEH	disp	XOR (IX + disp)
B6H	disp	OR (IX + disp)
BEH	disp	CP (IX + disp)
CBH		→subgroup CB
E1H		POP IX
E3H		EX (SP),IX
E5H		PUSH IX
E9H		JP (IX)
F9H		LD SP,IX

Z80: ED Group (first byte is always ED):

Second Byte	Third and Fourth Bytes	Instruction
01xx1010		ADC HL,rp
01ddd000		IN reg,(C)
01sss001		OUT reg,(C)
01xx0010		SBC HL,rp
43H	addr	LD (addr),BC
44H		NEG
45H		RETN
46H		IM0
47H		LD I,A
01xx1011	addr	LD rp,(addr)
53H	addr	LD (addr),DE
73H	addr	LD (addr),HL
4DH		RETI
4FH		LD R,A
56H		IM1
57H		LD A,I
5EH		IM2
5FH		LD A,R
67H		RRD
6FH		RLD
A0H		LDI
A1H		CPI
A2H		INI
A3H		OUTI
A8H		LLD
A9H		CPD
AAH		IND
ABH		OUTD
B0H		LDIR
B1H		CPIR
B2H		INIR
B3H		OTIR
B8H		LDDR
BAH		INDR
BBH		OUTDR

8080 Registers

A	PSW	A = Accumulator
		PSW = Program Status Word
B	C	⎫
D	E	⎬ register pairs
H	L	⎭

SP = Stack Pointer   (16 bits)
PC = Program Counter (16 bits)

Z80 Registers

The Z80 has all 8080 registers, plus the following:
IX, IY (16 bit index registers)
IV (8 bits) Interrupt Vector Register.
R (8 bits) Memory Refresh Register.

The Z80 has an alternate set of registers called: AF', BC', DE', HL'.

Note that the 8080 PSW is referred to as F.

Z80 Register Conventions

sss ddd xxx	reg	xx	rp	y	rp	yy	rp
000	B	00	BC	0	IX	00	BC
001	C	01	DE	1	IY	01	DE
010	D	10	HL			10	IX (IY)
011	E	11	SP			11	SP
100	H						
101	L						
110	M						
111	A						

8080 and Z80 Instruction set conventions:

N	8-bit immediate operand.
NN	16-bit immediate operand. The first immediate byte is the LSB, the second is the MSB.
disp	8-bit displacement value for relative addressing.

6502 Instruction set conventions:

ABS	absolute.
ABS,X	indexed absolute using x register.
A	accumulator.
ABS,Y	indexed absolute using y register.
,X	indexed indirect using x register.
,Y	indexed indirect using y register.
IMM	immediate.
IMP	implied.
REL	relative.
ZPG	zero page.
ZPG,X	indexed zero page using x register.
ZPG,Y	indexed zero page using y register.

Program Status Words

8080	PSW	Z80	PSW	6502	PSW
Bit 0	Carry	Bit 0	Carry	Bit 0	Carry Status
Bit 1	1	Bit 1	Subtract	Bit 1	Zero status
Bit 2	Parity	Bit 2	Parity/Overflow	Bit 2	Interrupt Disable
Bit 3	0	Bit 3	0	Bit 3	Decimal Mode
Bit 4	Auxy Carry	Bit 4	Aux Carry	Bit 4	Break status
Bit 5	0	Bit 5	0	Bit 5	0
Bit 6	Zero	Bit 6	Zero	Bit 6	Overflow
Bit 7	Sign	Bit 7	Sign	Bit 7	Sign

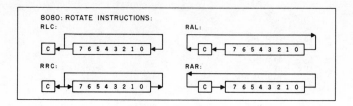

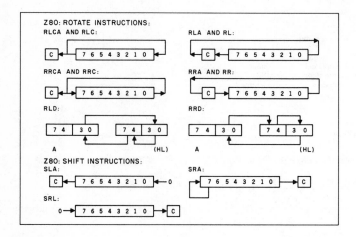

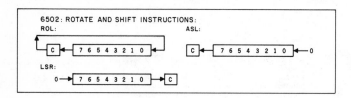

References

1. *An Introduction to CP/M Features and Facilities*. Pacific Grove, CA: Digital Research, 1978.
2. Barden, William. *The Z-80 Microcomputer Handbook*. Indianapolis: Howard W. Sams, 1978.
3. Booth, Grayce M. *The Distributed System Environment*. New York: McGraw-Hill, 1981.
4. Bowen, B. A., and Buhr, R. J. A. *The Logical Design of Multiple-Microprocessor Systems*. Englewood Cliffs, NJ: Prentice-Hall, 1980.
5. *CP/M Assembler User's Guide*. Pacific Grove, CA: Digital Research, 1978.
6. *CP/M Dynamic Debugging Tool (DDT) User's Guide*, Pacific Grove, CA: Digital Research, 1978.
7. *CP/M 2.2 System Alteration Guide*, Pacific Grove, CA: Digital Research, 1979.
8. *CP/M 2.2 User's Guide*. Pacific Grove, CA: Digital Research, 1979.
9. Davis, Williams. *Operating Systems*. Reading, MA: Addison-Wesley, 1977.
10. Hsiao, David. *Systems Programming*. Reading, MA: Addison-Wesley, 1975.
11. Lorin, Harold. *Aspects of Distributed Systems*. New York: Wiley, 1980.
12. *MP/M User's Guide*. Pacific Grove, CA: Digital Research, 1980.
13. Osborne, Adam, and Kane, Jerry. *An Introduction to Microprocessors,* Vol. 2. Berkeley: Osborne Associates, 1978.
14. Osborne, Adam, and Kane, Jerry. *An Introduction to Microprocessors*, Vol. 3. Berkeley: Osborne Associates, 1978.
15. Dahmke, Mark. "Introduction to Multiprogramming," *BYTE*, Sept. 1979.
    "Introduction to Multiprocessing," *Programming Techniques*, Vol. 4. Peterborough, NH: BYTE Books, 1979.
16. Tannenbaum, Andrew. *Structured Computer Organization*. Englewood Cliffs, NJ: Prentice-Hall, 1976.
17. *The Bell System Technical Journal*. Vol. 57, No. 6, Part 2, July-August, 1978.
18. Weitzman, Cay. *Distributed Micro/Minicomputer Systems*. Englewood Cliffs, NJ: Prentice-Hall, 1980.
19. Zaks, Rodney. *The CP/M Handbook*. Berkeley: Sybex, 1980.
20. Williams, Gregg. "Structured Programming & Structural Flowcharts," *BYTE*, March 1981.

Glossary

Accumulator   A register internal to the CPU that holds results of arithmetic operations.

Address bus   The portion of the system bus that carries the address of the memory or I/O port to be accessed.

Address space   The address space of a computer is a function of the addressing range. If a microcomputer has a 16-bit address range, the address space may be up to 64 K bytes in length.

ALU   Arithmetic-logic unit. The portion of the central processor that performs all arithmetic and logic operations on data in the registers of the microprocessor.

AP   See application program.

APA   See application program area.

Application program   Any user-written software that is run on a microcomputer, using the services of the nucleus.

Application program area   That portion of main memory set aside to run user-written programs.

APSP   Application program stack pointer. The stored value of the stack pointer for the designated task. Each task has its own APSP. Whenever the task is reactivated, the APSP is loaded into the stack pointer.

ASCII   American Standard Code for Information Interchange. A standard code for representing alphabetic, numeric, and special characters on a computer.

ASCII control character   A group of nonprintable ASCII character such as carriage return or line feed, used to control a peripheral device or send messages from one machine to another, such as STX (Start of Text), or ESC (Escape).

Assembler   A program that reads in mnemonic instructions written for the machine level of a computer and converts them to the operation codes that the computer can execute directly.

Asynchronous data transmission   A form of data transmission whereby each byte may be sent at any time, with no special timing between bytes, but with strict timing within the byte. Used mostly for low-data-rate applications such as dial-up terminals.

Background activity   Another name for low-priority programs running on a multiprogramming system. Since these programs have low priorities, they are said to execute in the "background."

Bank switching   A technique allowing computers with small address spaces (64 K bytes) to extend their addressing range in multiples of the address-space size. For example, this would allow each user or program to have its own address space, while not knowing of the existence of other users.

Batch programming   A method of executing programs whereby each is read into the system in order, and they are executed sequentially—as opposed to a time-sharing or multiprogramming system, whereby multiple users have concurrent access to the system.

BDOS   Basic disk operating system. The CP/M nucleus.

BIO   See byte-oriented input/output.

BIOS   Basic input/output system. The CP/M equivalent of the BIO in my hypothetical operating system.

Bit   A single binary digit, which may be either 1 or 0.

Boot-load   The action of loading the operating system or monitor into the computer after cold-start power-up. Normally the boot-load program is stored in programmable read-only memory so that it is present in the system on power-up.

Buffer   A block of memory set aside to hold.

Byte   A unit of data, usually 8 bits. Also a magazine about computers.

Byte-oriented input/output (BIO)   This portion handles all byte- or character-oriented input/output operations for the nucleus.

CCP   Console command processor. The CP/M command-interpreter program.

Character string   A sequence of data bytes that represent characters in ASCII or EBCDIC or some other code.

Circular queue   A queue that has a fixed number of entries that are reused circularly.

Cold start   The act of starting up a computer after power-on. The computer has no programs in memory and must be loaded from scratch.

.COM   In the CP/M operating system, a .COM file is an object or binary file containing an executable program .COM refers to a "command" file or one that can be executed by typing only the first part of the file name.

Compiler   A program that accepts as input a series of high-level commands and converts them to machine-level instructions that the computer can execute.

Console   The input device used to enter commands to the operating system. It may be anything from a teletype to a video display terminal.

Console interpreter (CINT)   The command line parser and interpreter that executes system commands. This is an application program like any other. It has no special privileges.

Control block   A data structure set up to keep track of information related to a task in a multiprogramming environment.

Control table   A data structure that contains information about a group of tasks or about physical I/O devices.

Control character   ASCII or EBCDIC characters used to control the input of data (e.g., carriage return, line feed, XON).

Controller   A hardware circuit that controls access to a peripheral device such as a disk drive.

CP/M   Control Program for Microcomputers. An operating system written and distributed by Digital Research. Runs on 8080 or Z80 compatible microprocessors. CP/M-86 will operate on the 8086 and 8088 16-bit microcomputers.

CPU   Central processor unit. That portion of the computer that controls all operations of the ALU and the interface between the computer and the outside world.

Cross assembler   A program that assembles machine instructions for a computer with a different instruction set than the one the cross assembler is running on. The output of the cross assembler is then downloaded to the target computer.

CTI   Current-task indicator. A single byte value that contains the number of currently active task.

Daisy chain   See ring network.

Data bus   The portion of the system bus that carries the data that is to be read or written to the main memory or I/O ports.

Debugger   A program that assist the user in testing and tracing errors in an application program.

Development system   A more powerful microcomputer system that may have either tape or disk storage, a moderate amount of main memory, and several peripheral interfaces. This type of system is used to develop new software for specialized applications.

Device assignments   Logical-to-physical assignments that allow peripheral devices to be traded as needed for an application without having to be physically disconnected and reconnected.

Device-assignment table See *SDT*.

Direct memory access (DMA) An action performed by a peripheral device that allows it to gain direct access to the main memory of the microcomputer. When the peripheral initiates direct memory access, the microprocessor is forced to stop all bus activity while the peripheral occupies the bus. This method allows extremely high data-transfer rates, at the expense of the microprocessor.

Disk file A logical grouping of information on a disk. A file may contain text, a program, or any other information in any representation.

Disk formatting A procedure that writes blank sectors of data to a disk, initializing it for later use.

Disk initialization See disk formatting.

Disk- (or block-oriented) input/output (DIO) This portion handles all block-oriented input and output for the nucleus.

Distributed network A loosely coupled network of computers that communicate over some form of data-communications link either asynchronously or synchronously. Each system has its own resources, but sharing of central resources may take place on the network.

DO loop A programming construct whereby a group of instructions can be repeated under certain conditions.

DOS Disk operating system. An operating system based primarily on disk-storage capabilities.

Downloading A way of transferring programs or data from a large computer system to a microcomputer. This allows program development or data acquisition to take place on the large computer whereas program execution may take place on the microcomputer.

EBCDIC Extended Binary-Coded Decimal Interchange Code. Another common code for representing alphanumeric and special characters on a computer.

EPROM Erasable programmable read-only memory. Similar to PROM, but can be erased when held under a shortwave ultraviolet light.

Evaluation system Any of a number of simple microcomputer systems that have a minimal amount of main memory, and few peripherals. It is generally used to evaluate a particular microprocessor for possible use in a product or full-scale microcomputer system.

Extent A dummy file control block used to extend the size of a disk file.

External storage Memory that is not directly accessible to the microcomputer, such as disk or tape storage.

FCB File control block. A block of data used to represent hold the name and physical attributes of a disk file. Usually stored on disk in a directory of files, but is copied to memory when the file is in use.

Floppy disk A flexible disk made of mylar with a magnetic coating. Disks are made in two normal sizes: 8 inches and 5.25 inches. A typical 8-inch disk can hold 250,000 bytes of information in single-density mode, 500,000 in double-density mode, and 1,000,000 bytes in double-density double-sided mode, depending on the type of disk controller and disk drives used.

Floppy-disk controller The hardware or circuit board used to interface the floppy-disk drive to the microcomputer bus.

Foreground activity Activity taking place at a higher priority in a multiprogramming system.

Full Duplex A form of serial data transmission in which two data links are running side by side, one in each direction.

Half Duplex A form of serial data transmission in which only one data link is used, so each computer must take turns talking and listening.

Hard disk A type of disk made from a rigid piece of metal that can store from 5 million bytes up to about 50 million bytes, and has a much faster access time.

Hardware   The physical circuitry that makes up the computer. This can include the central processor, the arithmetic unit, the main memory, disk drives, and so on.

.HEX   In either CP/M or MP/M, a .HEX file contains an executable program in hex-intel format. The LOAD program can be used to convert it to a .COM file.

Hexadecimal   A number system based on 16. The digits are represented as 0, 1, 2, 3, 4, 5, 6, 7, 8, 9, A, B, C, D, E, F.

Hex-Intel format   A standard format for storing binary information on paper tape, disk, or magnetic tape.

Instruction register   The internal CPU register that holds the current machine instruction to be executed.

Interpreter   A program that accepts as input a series of high-level commands and executes them as it goes, rather than saving them as machine instructions.

Interrupt   An external signal that causes the microprocessor to stop what it was doing and execute a series of instructions called the *interrupt handler*. An interrupt may be generated by a disk when an action is completed, or by an incoming character at a serial port. The use of interrupts allows the microprocessor to handle events as they come, rather than having to repeatedly "poll" or search for incoming data.

I/O   Input/output.

IPL   Initial program load. See *boot-load*.

Jump vector   A jump or branch instruction that transfers control to a specific subroutine or function.

Kansas City standard   A cassette-tape protocol designed in the early days of microcomputers for data transferral.

Linked queue   A queue that has a series of pointers that point to the actual data areas.

Loosely coupled   Refers to a multiprocessing system in which the central processors are connected loosely and cannot communicate rapidly.

Machine independence   A software-design philosophy allowing programs written on one type of computer to be run without changes on another type of computer.

Mass storage   Storage external to the microcomputer such as disk or tape. Generally this term is used in reference to hard-disk technology.

Memory   Any of several forms of storage, including RAM, PROM, disk, tape, or any magnetic media.

Memory dump   A list of a block of main memory, showing the data in hexadecimal or other notation, and the ASCII character representation of the data.

Microprocessor   A miniature computer contained on a single integrated circuit.

Monitor   A program similar to an operating system, but not as complex. A monitor allows the user of a small system to write simple programs, debug programs, and test the capabilities of the microprocessor in question.

Multiprocessor   A computer system that consists of multiple central processors that can access part or all of the aggregate resources of the system.

Multiprogramming operating system   An operating system that executes multiple programs concurrently.

MX queue   In MP/M, an MX queue is a mutual-exclusion queue that can be used to control serially reusable resources such as a printer.

NUC   See *nucleus*.

Nucleus   That part of an operating system that is the center of all control and resource-management activities. Whenever the application program requires service performed by a program or the operating system, but are waiting in line for a particular resource.

Operating system   Any program or group of related programs whose purpose is to act as intermediary between the hardware and the user. The operating system's main job is to manage resources such as disk drives, printers, and other peripherals, freeing the programmer from having to rewrite commonly used functions for each application. In this way, the operating system provides a uniform, consistent means for all user-written software to access the same machine resources.

Parallel interface A peripheral interface to the CPU by way of the system bus that sends or receives data in parallel from another computer or device.

Partition A memory segment in a multiprogramming system that an application program can be loaded in.

Peripheral Any device external to the CPU, such as input or output devices, disk drives, or tape drives.

Pointer A storage location or register that contains a memory address that may point to a specific location in memory.

Priority The active status given a program in a multiprogramming system. The priority of a program determines how much CPU time (how many time slices) it will get.

Priority scheduling A method of task dispatching that is based on a priority scheme. Each program is given a priority and is executed on the basis of what other programs have higher priorities.

.PRL In the MP/M operating system, a .PRL file is a page-relocatable file that like a .COM file can be executed, but in this case may be relocated to any page boundary. This is necessary when the system has multiple partitions.

Process descriptor In the MP/M operating system, the process descriptor keeps track of all parameters of a task or process. It is similar to the TCT in this book.

Program A sequence of machine instructions that the microprocessor reads and interprets to carry out arithmetic data movement and transfer of control functions.

Program counter The internal CPU register that holds the address of the current machine instruction.

PROM Programmable read-only memory. An integrated circuit that stores data when programmed with high-voltage pulses and cannot be erased.

Queue A data structure used by MP/M to keep track of functions that must be performed by a program or the operating system, but are waiting in line for a particular resource.

RAM Random-access memory. Memory that can be randomly accessed as necessary to retrieve data. This is the type used for the main memory of most computers.

Random allocation A software function whereby sectors are randomly allocated to files as needed, as opposed to *sequential allocation.*

Register pair On the 8080 or Z80, a pair of registers such as HL, BC, DE may be treated as one 16-bit register instead of two 8-bit registers for certain operations.

Resident console commands Commands that are built into the console command interpreter (CINT in this book), as opposed to transient commands, which must be loaded from disk to be executed. Generally, the only commands made resident are the most frequently used (and least destructive) of the system-level commands.

Ring network A distributed network with one connection from each slave to the next, making a continuous loop.

ROM Read-only memory. A kind of memory circuit that can only be programmed at the factory.

Scrolling The act of moving the displayed text lines of a video display up one line, to simulate the action of a teleprinter. Usually scrolling is done on receipt of a linefeed character.

SDT System device table. In this book, the SDT keeps track of all devices available to the system.

Secondary extents The space allocated to disk files when the first directory entry becomes full. Each directory entry in a randomly allocated disk-file system contains a list of sectors or blocks allocated to the file. When the directory entry is full, a second or third entry must be started. These secondary entries do not show up when the directory is listed.

Sector A sector is the smallest unit of blocked storage on a disk. Each sector on a single-density 8-inch disk holds 128 bytes of data.

Sector allocation A software function whereby sectors are kept track of in a sector "pool" and are allocated as needed to files on a disk.

Sector mapping   A method of improving disk-access time by skewing or shifting sector addresses around the disk. If the operating system reads a sector and then attempts to read the next sequential sector, the disk will generally have rotated out of position and will have to complete one revolution before it is in position again. Sector skewing involves a logical-to-physical mapping of sectors so they are offset around the disk, allowing the operating system time to process each sector before reading the next one. This saves a great deal of time because the computer need not wait through a whole revolution for each sector access.

Sector skew   See sector mapping.

Sequential allocation   A software function whereby sectors are sequentially allocated to disk files, rather than randomly allocated.

Serial interface   A peripheral interface to the CPU by way of the system bus that sends and receives data serially from another computer or terminal.

Simulator   A program that simulates the actions of the central processor, allowing a program to be stepped through, instruction by instruction, to determine where errors are occurring.

Slave   A computer with enough memory to run an operating system that is tied into a distributed network.

Slave processor   A computer, which may or may not be as powerful or as fast as the master or system processor, that is used to perform simple but time-consuming tasks for the master, freeing it to do other things.

Software   The program or machine instructions that the central processor interprets to perform arithmetic and data-movement functions on the hardware.

SRR   System resource request. The entry point of the nucleus in my examples. To request services of the nucleus, the application program must call this routine.

Stack   A data structure used in most microcomputers to save registers, CPU status flags, and the program counter. When a subroutine is called, the return address is "pushed" onto the stack.

Stack pointer   A CPU register that contains the address of the next available stack entry.

Star network   A distributed network with one connection from the master to each slave processor.

Subroutine   A program that can be called from another program. When the subroutine is completed, control is returned to the calling program.

Subroutine library   A collection of frequently referenced subroutines that can be loaded with an application program.

Synchronous data transmission   A form of data transmission whereby each byte is sent in a strict sequence, with strict timing between the bytes. This form is especially useful at high data rates, because it is more resistent to these errors.

System bus   The group of parallel data, address, and control lines that connect the CPU to the rest of the computer system.

System environment   The hardware and software organization of a microcomputer system.

System generation (SYSGEN)   A procedure that allows the user to customize the characteristics of an operating system to match the hardware available and the potential software application programs that will be run under the operating system.

System utilities   Programs that assist the user in performing certain housekeeping functions on the system.

Task   Any program that runs on a computer may be considered a task, but usually the term is reserved for programs running on multiprogramming systems.

TCT   Task control table. The table (in the hypothetical operating system in this book) that contains entries for each task executing in a multiprogramming system.

Terminal emulation   A program that when run on a microcomputer system with a video display will emulate a dumb terminal, allowing the user to access another computer system. The purpose is to allow access to other computers without having to reconnect cables or rearrange the system.

Tightly coupled Refers to a multiprocessing system in which the processors can share main memory or disk memory and can communicate at a fairly high rate.

Time-sharing A form of multiprogramming, oriented to multiple users at console devices.

Time-slice The period of time allocated to each program or task in a multiprogramming system.

TIOB Task I/O block. In this book, the TIOB keeps track of device allocations for each task.

Transient console commands Commands that are not part of the CINT. These commands are generally low-usage utilities such as a disk-format routine, a device-assignment utility, a disk-copy program, and so on. It is also wise to make all destructive commands transient.

Transient program A program that is used only briefly or only once in a great while. A program that is not resident in the operating system.

UART Universal asynchronous receiver/transmitter. An integrated circuit that contains all circuitry required to send and receive serial data.

Uploading A way of transferring programs or data from a microcomputer system to a host or time-sharing system. The data being transmitted is sent by means of a serial data link, (usually telephone) to another computer system.

USART Universal synchronous-asynchronous receiver/transmitter. An integrated circuit that contains all circuitry required to send and receive serial data either synchronously or asynchronously.

Video display A display device using a cathode ray tube (CRT) as the display mechanism. Used to display character and graphic information.

VDT Video display terminal. A terminal that uses a video display rather than a printer to display incoming text.

Virtual memory Main memory that is simulated on disk, allowing the address space of a machine to exceed the physical main memory available. "Pages" of memory (usually 4 K bytes) are swapped in and out of real main memory as needed.

Wait state A machine cycle inserted into the normal operation of the microprocessor when it becomes necessary to slow down and wait for a slow memory of I/O device.

Warm start The act of restarting a computer after it has been running. This may be necessary because of program failure or hardware failure.

XON-XOFF protocol A standard protocol used when information is being transferred from one computer to another. This protocol usually requires a full duplex data link. When the receiving end can no longer accept data (if it has something else to do and cannot wait for data to come to it), it can send an XOFF ASCII control character that tells the sender to wait until an XON is sent.

Index